Practicing the Kingdom

Practicing the Kingdom

Essays on Hospitality, Community,
and Friendship in Honor of Christine D. Pohl

Edited by
JUSTIN BRONSON BARRINGER
and MARIA RUSSELL KENNEY

Foreword by
DAVID P. GUSHEE

CASCADE *Books* • Eugene, Oregon

PRACTICING THE KINGDOM
Essays on Hospitality, Community, and Friendship in Honor of Christine D. Pohl

Cascade Books
An Imprint of Wipf and Stock Publishers
199 W. 8th Ave., Suite 3
Eugene, OR 97401

www.wipfandstock.com

PAPERBACK ISBN: 978-1-4982-1801-6
HARDCOVER ISBN: 978-1-4982-1803-0
EBOOK ISBN: 978-1-4982-1802-3

Cataloguing-in-Publication data:

Names: Barringer, Justin Bronson, editor. | Kenney, Maria Russel, editor. | Gushee, David P., foreword.

Title: Practicing the kingdom : essays on hospitality, community, and friendship in honor of Christine D. Pohl / edited by Justin Bronson Barringer and Maria Russell Kenney ; foreword by David P. Gushee.

Description: Eugene, OR : Cascade Books, 2022 | Includes bibliographical references.

Identifiers: ISBN 978-1-4982-1801-6 (paperback) | ISBN 978-1-4982-1803-0 (hardcover) | ISBN 978-1-4982-1802-3 (ebook)

Subjects: LCSH: Pohl, Christine D. | Hospitality—Religious aspects—Christianity. | Christian life.

Classification: BV4647.H67 P73 2022 (paperback) | BV4647.H67 P73 (ebook)

01/06/22

Contents

Foreword

DAVID P. GUSHEE

Christine Pohl's distinguished career as teacher and scholar of Christian ethics is well-worthy of this festschrift that reflects on her profound intellectual contributions. Her retirement seems a fitting moment to take special notice of these contributions, both inside and outside the classroom. It is indeed a high honor to offer a few introductory words to this volume.

I have known Christine for over thirty years, the entirety of my career as a Christian ethicist. She was one of the first ethicists with whom I connected deeply at the Society of Christian Ethics, and together we co-chaired the Evangelical Ethics interest group at SCE for a number of years. We have enjoyed a great many searching conversations at those annual ethics gatherings. I enjoyed her kind hospitality during a delightful visit to her Asbury Seminary campus, and was impressed with her way of relating to her students. She has been a reviewer and sometimes an endorser of my work, and I of hers. I have enormous respect for her as a human being, as a scholar, and as a Christian.

Christine Pohl's scholarship in Christian ethics has been fully congruent with her life—both in the issues she has addressed and in the way she has addressed them. Her issues—Christian hospitality, community, character, practices, and friendship—perfectly reflect a Christian woman deeply rooted in several concentric communities (church, school, town), embedded in profound friendships, and routinely offering hospitality to friends and strangers as part of her characteristic practice of the Christian life.

Christine has never seemed to me to be in a hurry, and her scholarship has reflected her patience and the measured pace with which she conducts her life. Her four full-length books are spaced in this way—1999, 2005, 2010, and 2012. Each, it seems to me, builds on the one before. All reflect research on and with real people and often have been undertaken collaboratively. All are rooted in explorations of real practices of Christian community, biblical research, engagement with Christian tradition, and realistic social analysis.

- *Making Room* (1999) is about recovering the biblical mandate and historic Christian practice of hospitality. It is a deep, searching, comprehensive exploration that put hospitality back on the map as a central Christian practice and has inspired considerable further research by other scholars.

- *Living on the Boundaries* (2005, with Nicola Hoggard Creegan) is a gentle but still challenging work related to the difficult journeys of evangelical women navigating conservative evangelicalism, theological education, church life, and the broader academic world. Not an angry book, but an honest one, *Boundaries* helped to consolidate and hold the ground for pioneering female scholars in a large number of evangelical traditions and institutions that once excluded them officially and still find it very difficult to integrate them fully.

- *Friendship at the Margins* (2010, with Christopher Heuertz) in one sense parallels Christine's work on hospitality by recovering yet another crucial, neglected Christian practice: friendship. The book develops into a work on missiology, healing, and reconciliation, as the authors focus on unlikely friendships with real human beings "at the margins" and their missional impact, rather than more "likely" friendships based on homogeneity and affinity, and the objectification of targets of our grandiose missionary efforts.

- *Living into Community* (2012) is another work in Christian practice, this time covering the practices that Christine Pohl says are central to sustaining Christian community: gratitude, promise-making and -keeping, and truthfulness, tied together under the theme of hospitality. The book, like all of Christine's work, exhibits her characteristic biblical seriousness, realism about the difficulties of sustaining normative Christian practices, and consistent call for the church to be a community that overcomes these difficulties in fidelity to Christ.

This brief review of Pohl's four major published works is not intended to suggest that her various lectures, book chapters, and addresses in other venues should be overlooked. But I do intend to suggest that we see a remarkably coherent scholarly program unfolding in her primary body of work over two decades. I would summarize it this way: Christine Pohl, a Wesleyan evangelical scholar, has throughout her career offered a rich character-focused and practice-based ethics, rooted in Christian Scripture, informed by Christian tradition, intended to serve robust Christian community, and relevant to individual Christians but also carrying fruitful social ethical dimensions.

While not labeling her work as "feminist" or using what might be described as feminist methodology, Christine Pohl—in her person and by her sustained presence as an authoritative female scholar in a major evangelical school—has also crucially advanced evangelical feminism. This is a major contribution that will matter to generations of evangelical women in particular, but also, of course, to the entire evangelical world as it benefits from the gifts of more women as doors are more fully opened to them.

The essays included in this volume explore various important dimensions of these major themes in, or arising from, Christine's work: hospitality, community, friendship, evangelism and discipleship, feminism, and love. Each essay can be seen as inspired by or related to Christine's work without simply being a restatement.

This collection is a gift to the whole church, even as Christine Pohl has been such a gift. I hope you will enjoy these essays, and that they will send you back to a reading of the works of Dr. Christine Pohl—Christian ethicist, honored friend.

Dr. David P. Gushee
Distinguished University Professor of Christian Ethics, Mercer University
President, Society of Christian Ethics, 2017–2018

Contributors

Jamie Arpin-Ricci is a pastoral leader at Little Flowers Community in Winnipeg, Manitoba, Canada. His books include *Vulnerable Faith: Missional Living in the Radical Way of St. Patrick* and *Living Christ Together: Reflections on the Missional Life.*

Justin Bronson Barringer is a pastor, writer, consultant, and recent PhD graduate from Southern Methodist University. He is co-editor of several works, including *A Faith Not Worth Fighting For: Addressing Commonly Asked Questions About Christian Nonviolence*, and the series "The Business of Modern Life", with volumes on such topics as war, incarceration, and agribusiness. He also teaches incarcerated students and cofounded North Texas' biggest diaper and hygiene pantry.

Nicola Hoggard Creegan lives in Auckland, New Zealand, and is co-director of New Zealand Christians in Science. She is author of *Animal Suffering and the Problem of Evil* (OUP, 2012) and co-editor with Andrew Shepherd of *Creation and Hope* (Wipf & Stock, 2013) and co-author, with Christine Pohl, of *Living on the Boundaries: Evangelical Women, Feminism and the Theological Academy.*

Mary Fisher was a pastor with the Sydney Chinese Alliance Church in Sydney, Australia. For over a decade, she was Assistant Professor of Biblical Theology at Asbury Theological Seminary. Prior to her academic work, she served as the Associate Director of Missions & Urbana and Associate Director of International Relations for InterVarsity Christian Fellowship.

Peter R. Gathje is Professor of Christian Ethics and Vice President of Academic Affairs/Academic Dean at Memphis Theological Seminary. He has written and edited numerous works, including *Christ Comes in the*

Stranger's Guise, Sharing the Bread of Life: Hospitality and Resistance at the Open Door Community (2006), *Doing Right and Being Good: Catholic and Protestant Readings in Christian Ethics* and *A Work of Hospitality: The Open Door Reader.* He is also a founder and co-director of Manna House, a place of hospitality in Memphis.

Chris Heuertz is the co-founder of Gravity: A Center for Contemplative Activism. Prior to this, he and his wife Phileena founded and worked for 20 years with Word Made Flesh, an international organization dedicating to living Jesus among the most vulnerable of the world's poor. His books include *Friendship at the Margins: Discovering Mutuality in Service and Mission*, which he co-authored with Christine Pohl, and *Unexpected Gifts: Discovering the Way of Community.*

Maria Russell Kenney is assistant professor of Christian ethics at Asbury Theological Seminary. She has contributed to the *Dictionary of Scripture and Ethics* and *School(s) for Conversion: 12 Marks of a New Monasticism.* She attends Open Door Church, a neighborhood parish in Lexington, KY. Prior to this, she was a founding member of Communality, an intentional Christian community in downtown Lexington.

Richard Mouw is a philosopher, scholar, professor, and the former president of Fuller Theological Seminary. He is also the author of nineteen books in areas ranging from theology and ethics to philosophy and interfaith dialogue including a new revised and expanded edition of *Uncommon Decency: Christian Civility in an Uncivil World.*

Tim Otto is one of the pastors at the Church of the Sojourners, a live-together church community in San Francisco, CA. He is co-author of *Inhabiting the Church: Biblical Wisdom for the New Monasticism* and author of *Oriented to Faith: Transforming the Conflict Over Gay Relationships.*

Wyndy Corbin Reuschling is Global Director of Higher Education Services at TeachBeyond, and professor emerita of ethics and theology at Ashland Theological Seminary in Ohio. She is author of three books: *Reviving Evangelical Ethics: The Promises and Pitfalls of Classic Models of Morality; Becoming Whole and Holy: An Integrative Conversation About Christian Formation* (with Jeannine Brown and Carla Dahl); and *Desire for God and the Things of God: The Relationships Between Christian Spirituality and Morality.*

James R. Thobaben is Dean of the School of Theology and Formation, Assistant Provost for Institutional Effectiveness, and Professor of Bioethics and Social Ethics at Asbury Theological Seminary. His publications include *Healthcare Ethics: A Comprehensive Christian Resource*, and several articles in the *Dictionary of Scripture and Ethics*.

Miroslav Volf is the Henry B. Wright Professor of Systematic Theology at Yale Divinity School and Founding Director of the Yale Center for Faith & Culture. His many books include the award-winning *Exclusion and Embrace*, which was recognized as one of the most influential books of the twentieth century.

Jessica A. Wrobleski is Vice President of Mission at Saint Joseph's Academy in Cleveland, Ohio. Prior to this position, she was Assistant Professor of Theology at Wheeling Jesuit University in Wheeling, West Virginia. Her first book, *The Limits of Hospitality*, deals with tensions that arise in the practice of Christian hospitality.

Introduction

In the autumn of 1994, I (Maria) made my first trip to Asbury Theological Seminary in Wilmore, KY. Having recently moved from West Texas to the heart of the Appalachian Mountains, I was homesick and lonely for friendship. I decided to take a weekend visit to nearby Asbury, where several friends from the Texas Tech University Wesley Foundation had begun studying. My friend Anna, with whom I was staying for the weekend, invited me to join her that afternoon for her class in social ethics. "You'll like what we're discussing today," she mentioned. "We're watching a movie about women who work in fast food in Appalachia." *A movie about social justice in Appalachia? The one day I visit? What are the odds?* I wondered.

During class that afternoon, I was impressed with both the content and the discussion, led by a professor with a gracious manner and an impressive grasp of the issues in the film. Hoping to continue the discussion, I approached her after class and introduced myself, mentioning that I was living in Appalachia and would enjoy hearing more about the class. Although she had no obligation to disrupt her schedule, she invited me back to her office, where we sat and had the first of many, *many* conversations.

I suppose it is fitting that my first encounter with Christine Pohl involved her making room for this casual visitor. Since that day, almost thirty years ago, she has grown from acquaintance, to professor, to mentor, to colleague. Most special of all, I have been privileged to call her friend, a friendship that has sustained me through celebration and sorrow, through endings and beginnings. This encounter also spotlights the core of Christine's impact on the kingdom, combining academic excellence and social awareness with her dedication to welcoming the stranger and growing in friendship. Through her academic ministry at Asbury Theological Seminary, her work with Apostles Anglican Church and other congregations, and her dedication to her family, Christine has continued to make room, in her schedule and her life, for students, visitors, friends, and countless others.

The timing of the completion of this book is serendipitous, as its publication follows closely upon the heels of Christine's retirement from Asbury Seminary. However, the book was begun before she announced her retirement, as we felt that discussion of these issues is always relevant. They are what Jean Porter would call "both perennial and timely."[1] Although they are timely in the sense that conversations on hospitality, community, and friendship are "hot topics" at present, they are "perennial" in that the practices themselves are enduring, rooted in Scripture, the Christian tradition, and human society itself. Thus, there is not really an inopportune moment to discuss them.

The essays build upon particularly fruitful aspects of her work, through expansion, clarification, and occasional disagreement. They contain biblical, systematic, and moral theology; they are scriptural and liturgical; they are multidisciplinary and missional. Several of them could be described as offering essays of "lived theology," writing and reflecting from within years of action and reflection. The contributors are a mix of scholars and practitioners, colleagues (both within Asbury and in the larger academy), former students, friends, and many others who are fortunate enough to inhabit several categories. They are people who, like Christine, have dedicated their lives to seeking and finding the goodness of God in the world. Whether scholar or activist, pastor or student—each person in this volume has been impacted by the fruit of Christine's labors. Perhaps most telling was the universal affirmation of the importance of participating. "I am absolutely swamped," one contributor replied to the initial invitation, "but I'll make time for this." Each person said something along these lines, and the strength and quality of the essays bears witness to their commitment and respect.

The title of this volume, *Practicing the Kingdom*, both highlights and honors Christine's commitment to two fundamental positions. First is her dedication to exploring, teaching, and living an ethic of applied, practical faith. Most of her publications contain an active verb in their title: *Making Room, Living into the Kingdom, Living on the Boundaries*. Even *Friendship at the Margins* has an active verb in its subtitle—*Discovering Mutuality in Service and Mission*. Academic reflection is intended to be applied, and Christine's focus resides clearly at the intersection of theology and praxis. Moreover, it stands at the intersection of various social, moral, and ecclesiological concerns; her choice to work with practices both reflects and informs her commitments to the margins, the church, and the world. As one contributor notes, "She takes as her first sources the messy world of human

---

1. Porter, "Perennial and Timely Virtues."

interactions across cultural, racial, gender, and class boundaries—whether these occur in the Bible, in texts, or in her own or others' experience."[2]

However, Christine's emphasis upon the importance of the practices does not degrade into idolatry or a mistaken understanding of their significance. She is quick to remind us that the practices, like other spiritual disciplines, are not salvific in themselves: "Undoubtedly," she states, "paying attention to practices is a poor substitute for a relationship with the living God."[3] Thus, this volume is titled in recognition of her faithfulness in orienting this practical, applied ethic toward its true and authentic *telos*—the Kingdom of God as revealed in Scripture, made accessible through the saving work of Jesus the Christ, and made possible by the sanctifying power of the Spirit. "The goal in all of this is not to try harder to build community or to get the practices right," she reminds us. "It is about living and loving well in response to Christ."[4] And responding to Christ, for Christine, is communal as well as individual; it is aimed at how believers "can live into the kingdom together."[5] If this book contributes to that biblical vision, then it has achieved its purpose.

Practicing Hospitality: Engaging the Fragilities

Christine Pohl is probably best known for her recovery and exploration of the practice of Christian hospitality, a theology of welcome. Because this is arguably the core of her academic work, it is a natural opening to this volume. And the aspect of Pohl's work on hospitality that generates the most discussion, both inside and outside the classroom, is her acknowledgment of the "fragility of hospitality," with its consideration of the practice's "limits, boundaries, and temptations." As she notes in *Making Room*, "We cannot separate the goodness and the beauty of hospitality from its difficulty."[6] Thus, the first three essays in this section consider some of the boundaries and limits encountered within the practice of hospitality.

Setting a tone of welcome, Richard Mouw considers the importance of making room for the ideas of others, even—or perhaps especially—those who stand outside our faith tradition. Examining the ways in which we intellectually engage the thoughts and ideas of others, Mouw argues for the inherent value of "wrestling with different realities, a making room in our

---

2. See Hoggard Creegan below.

3. Pohl, *Living into Community*, 175.

4. Pohl, *Living into Community*, 175.

5. Heuertz and Pohl, *Friendship at the Margins*, 33.

6. Pohl, *Making Room*, 127.

hearts and minds for new ideas and experiences." By pursuing and nurturing the spiritual dispositions that assist us in our intellectual hospitality—a
posture of humility, empathy, and a genuine desire to be led into the Truth
of the living God—we can counter the anti-intellectualism often lurking
behind our "commitment to truth" and open ourselves to the Spirit of Truth
that is ever-present in the larger world.

However, Mouw acknowledges that a posture of hospitality is not ab-
solute—it requires an appropriate sense of boundaries. Moreover, there may
be some tasks which hospitality is not suited to accomplish, as Pohl herself
notes: "We need a constant, complex interaction between identity-defining,
bounded communities and a larger community with minimal boundaries
that offers basic protection of individuals."[7] To this end, James Thobaben
undertakes an explicit examination of the functions of hospitality *vis-à-vis*
two other forms of "welcome": civility and market exchange. He carefully
delineates the differences between the welcome of Christian hospitality, the
welcome one can legitimately expect from the state (civility), and the welcome one may purchase from restaurants and hotels ("market exchange").
Christian hospitality, he argues, is not cheapened by its limits and boundaries; rather, these characteristics highlight the special nature—the "generosity and graciousness"—of Christian welcome.

Thobaben stresses that the distinctions between hospitality and other
forms of "welcome" are not inherently moral; that is, all are acceptable
choices in their respective spheres. However, not every construction of the
"Christian life" is equally legitimate; not all of them reflect the kingdom into
which we are invited. As believers, we may be called out of oppressive structures and into something different. In his essay, Peter Gathje addresses what
he views as a lacuna in Pohl's work on hospitality—namely, its relationship
to biblical holiness. Working from within his years of offering hospitality to
the marginalized, Gathje considers separation as a characteristic of holiness
that "invites and inspires hospitality." While separation and hospitality may
seem fundamentally antithetical to each other, this "transforming holiness"
calls the believer to separate themselves *from* what was and *for* what will
be, *from* the world and *for* the living God. This "holy separation" reflects
the upside-down Kingdom of Jesus, contrasting the "religion of creation"
with the "religion of empire." Such a separation, Gathje maintains, makes
hospitality both possible and prophetic.

As Gathje's essay so clearly illustrates, hospitality "is not so much a task
as a way of living our lives and of sharing ourselves . . .both a disposition

7. Pohl, *Making Room*, 83.

and a habit."[8] But despite the habitual, ongoing nature of the work—or indeed, because of it—it should not be surprising that the practice becomes, as Pohl says, fragile. "Because hospitality is so demanding," she maintains, "we must find a renewing rhythm of work, rest, and worship."[9] To conclude the section on hospitality, Jessica Wrobleski offers a model for this "renewing rhythm" by locating the practice of hospitality within the framework of the Liturgical Year. Wrobleski guides the reader through the liturgical season of "ordinary time," calling our attention to the resources it can provide as we negotiate the boundaries and temptations of practicing hospitality. By "recognizing the ways that life presents us with constant movement as well as discernible patterns," we encounter patterns and opportunities for cycles of work and rest, celebration and labor and respite. And by reminding us that "our time is God's time" and that our story is God's story, we place our efforts within the larger context of God's work in the world.

Practicing Community: Negotiating the Imperfections

Within her work on hospitality came fruitful new areas of inquiry. "In twenty years of studying hospitality," she notes, "I discovered that truthfulness, promise-keeping, and gratitude appeared over and over again in relation to offering welcome."[10] From these insights grew the work that became *Living into Community: Cultivating the Practices that Sustain Us*, an extended examination of four practices essential to any thriving community: promise-keeping, truth-telling, gratitude, and hospitality. This section flows naturally from the previous one, as Pohl herself notes in the introduction to *Living into Community*: "In a sense, *Making Room* provides the foundation for this book—in terms of my understanding of the practices and my interest in how they interact."[11] Alongside its reflection on these four practices, *Living into Community* also considers the damage wrought by the "deformations" of these practices: betrayal, deception, envy and presumption, and exclusion. As damaging as these distortions of healthy community can be, other deformations and dangers also lurk around the edges, undermining both the health and the preservation of community in its various forms. This section addresses three of these considerations: individuality and conformity, vulnerability, and idealism. By raising our awareness of these dangers,

---

8. Pohl, *Making Room*, 172.

9. Pohl, *Making Room*, 182.

10. Pohl, *Living into Community*, 11.

11. Pohl, *Living into Community*, 12.

the essays in this section further the conversation on the complexities of Christian community.

Tim Otto draws upon decades of experience within intentional community to examine Western culture's commitment to individuality and how it works to enslave us more deeply to the God of Mammon. Otto argues that individuality and community, when properly understood, are interdependent rather than antagonistic, and that participation in healthy community serves to accentuate our differences in positive, life-giving ways. True individuality, as opposed to *individualism*, has the potential to create true diversity, which—when supported by truth-telling, promise-keeping, gratitude, and welcome—highlights and strengthens our particular gifts and graces and, ultimately, the community around us.

One main reason for our commitment to, and our reliance upon, both individualism and conformity is the safety and shelter they can provide from the opinions and judgments of others. In a powerful example of lived theology, Jamie Arpin-Ricci explores the importance and the hazards of the practice of vulnerability, both the awareness of one's inherent vulnerability and the willingness to live within—and into—this reality. Arpin-Ricci explores how *living* vulnerably and *expressing* vulnerability can strengthen the bonds that make such communities both possible and healthy. The extent to which such vulnerability is both acknowledged and embraced directly affects the health and holiness of our communities. Rather than shielding ourselves behind a "pretense of righteousness" or the need to "pull ourselves together," he celebrates the "strength" found in acknowledging our vulnerability.

However, such vulnerability and other "weaknesses" are not always welcome in Christian community. Instead, they can be perceived as flaws, deficiencies that are unacceptable in the paradise of Christian community. To conclude the section, Maria Russell Kenney considers something that is generally unacknowledged as a danger to community—the relationship between community and the idealism that often accompanies it. Kenney explores how our "ideals"—our personal and/or particular highest guiding convictions and principles—can become idols, "gods" that we worship in place of the living God. Rather than allowing our ideals to serve us as we journey together, we allow ourselves to be mastered by them, "sacrificing each other on the altar of their preservation." She then describes how attention to the four practices of healthy community can assist us in avoiding enslavement to our idealism.

Practicing Friendship: Reorienting the Relationships

Alongside her work on hospitality and community runs Pohl's interest in friendship. Addressed most fully in *Friendship at the Margins: Discovering Mutuality in Service and Mission* (co-authored with contributor Chris Heuertz), Pohl's work on friendship has significant overlap with her other interests, as noted in her conviction that hospitality requires respect and friendship as much as food and shelter.[12] In her chapter, "Hospitality, Dignity, and the Power of Recognition," Pohl recalls the centrality of friendship to the success of the Salvation Army, as observed by its founder, William Booth: "One of the secrets of the Salvation Army is that the friendless of the world find friends in it."[13] True hospitality, she maintains, is only present when some measure of friendship is extended to its recipients and is welcomed by its hosts. These practices are mutually reinforcing—offering hospitality can lead to (often unlikely) friendships, and friendships can often lead to (often surprising) offers of hospitality. And community is where they all intersect, because community is ideally comprised of a network of friendships and is where we best offer hospitality.

Like the section on hospitality, the essays on friendship are concerned with crossing borders and contesting traditional categories. They explore the intersection of how the practice of Christian friendship, by its definition, challenge the boundaries—social, racial, economic—that are all too often created through our fear of the "other." In "Toward a Theology of Friendship," Mary Fisher makes a case for friendship as radical welcome, moving from the category of "the other" to "one another." In a rich and thorough account, she leads the reader through an understanding of friendship that is rooted in trinitarian doctrine and revealed within God's initiation and development of his covenants with his people. She explores the connections between the divine friendship offered to humanity in the Old and New Testaments and its impact on human friendships, both within the community of faith and with the larger world.

Upon this foundation, Chris Heuertz surveys the poverty of most contemporary friendships, calling us to lament and confess our "false centers" of narrow identity and self-protection. Through his narrative of a friendship "at the margins," Heuertz poses the question, "Who is my friend?" Heuertz describes his own process of interior conversion from donor to recipient, from a focus upon programs to a commitment to persons. Through fidelity, empathy, and the prioritizing of relationship, we can redefine our ideas

12. Pohl, *Making Room*, 163.

13. Pohl, *Making Room*, 84.

of "center" and "margin" and allow ourselves to enter into friendships of mutuality and acceptance.

Building upon the theme of "friendship at the margins," Justin Bronson Barringer explores how friendships should be reimagined in the Kingdom of God. "Friendship" as traditionally (and classically) understood may be no more than a "voluntary association," reflecting and reinforcing traditional structured hierarchies. However, friendships modelled upon Jesus' friendship with humanity break down these traditional hierarchies and replace them with "fluid hierarchies," which yields a more dynamic model of power, authority, and influence. These friendships are both "subversive" and "transgressive" in nature; modelled upon Jesus' own work transgressing oppressive societal boundaries, they actively disrupt the power structures that fortify these boundaries. Through the cultivation of mutuality, durability, and a willingness to take risks, friendship is the means by which we envision and enact the subversive ethic of the kingdom of God.

Practicing in Context:
New Alliances and Good News

Finally, it is essential to note that these practices do not occur in a vacuum; they are shaped by their interactions with many other elements—theologies, worldviews, sociocultural positions, ideological commitments. Accordingly, the concluding section addresses a trio of subjects that Christine has engaged, both professionally and personally, throughout her career. In *Living on the Boundaries: Evangelicalism, Feminism, and the Theological Academy*, Christine Pohl and Nicola Hoggard Creegan explored the unlikely alliance of two seemingly incongruent movements: evangelicalism and feminism. As evidenced by the content of *Living on the Boundaries*, evangelicalism and feminism have been two of the cultures within which Pohl has written and taught and mentored and lived. Both of them, she notes, "are controversial movements that provoke complex loyalties as well as ambivalence within the church and the world at large."[14] To engage one can be daunting; to engage them both, and together, is truly a formidable task. Yet Pohl has not shied away from these difficult yet timely issues, asking the hard questions in her books and her classrooms, around the lunch table with students and the dinner table with colleagues and friends.

Thus, two of the final three essays consider the reciprocal nature of Pohl's work on the areas of evangelical and feminist scholarship. Wyndy Corbin Reuschling notes the changes within the historical journey of

14. Hoggard Creegan and Pohl, *Living on the Boundaries*, 12.

evangelical ethics, notably the move away from a socially engaged ethic and towards an emphasis upon individual purity. She examines Pohl's work on practices as an essential link between personal and social holiness, the evangelical co-commitments to "justice and vital piety," and its possibilities for encouraging a return to the socially engaged ethic of early evangelicalism. Finally, she outlines how Pohl's work on the practices might inform the processes of Christian discipleship and evangelical witness. As "concrete expressions of God's extending grace and love," practices are recognized and embraced as "an important means of reaching out to the world in mission and service."

While Pohl's identification with evangelicalism is commonly known, some may question her connection with feminism. Yet Hoggard Creegan, her long-time friend and collaborator, maintains that Pohl has always been engaged in feminist work, "even if not full-time." In her essay, Hoggard Creegan examines three unlikely "new alliances" between feminism and other worldviews—post-colonialism, eco-theology, and the renewed emphasis on pneumatology within systematic theology—utilizing the "shared themes" of feminism and hospitality: hermeneutics, language, experience, and attention to power dynamics. Like evangelicalism, these philosophies hold basic assumptions about the ways in which we both see and engage the world—how we select and prioritize sources, whom we invite into discussion, and the like. Hoggard Creegan draws from Pohl's theory and praxis of hospitality to explore these emerging partnerships and encourage those working in the "borderlands," whether ethnically, academically, or geographically.

Finally, it is essential to note that for Pohl, the ethical enterprise is similar to the *exitus-reditus* format of Aquinas's *Summa*: it begins and ends with the love of God as revealed in Christ Jesus. Hospitality, community, friendship—they are Christian only insofar as they arise from the prevenient love of the living God, and only as they strengthen and expand that love for the church and the world. "Hospitality," she states, "is a concrete expression of love—love for sisters and brothers, love extended outward to strangers, prisoners, and exiles, love that attends to physical and social needs."[15] She reminds us that "sacrificial love is at the heart of mission and reconciliation," particularly as it is intimately connected with friendship.[16] And her study of Christian community revealed a "surprisingly simple" recipe for life in

15. Pohl, *Making Room*, 31.

16. Heuertz and Pohl, *Friendship at the Margins*, 10. See also John 15 and Mary Fisher's essay in this volume.

community: "It is enough to get the love of God into your bones and to live as if you are forgiven."[17]

To this end, we conclude this volume with a reflection from Miroslav Volf on Christianity as a religion of love. Volf reminds us that all loves are not equal: "Love here is not first of all human love but God's love; in relation to humans, it is primarily love received, not love practiced—or rather, it is love practiced as love received." It is, he claims, "a modality of divine love" that far exceeds any love we attempt in our own strength. Here Volf draws together several strands that are central to Pohl's work: the primacy of God's love for humanity and for all creation, and the necessity of our practicing that which we receive from God—love, friendship, welcome—as we have received it. The prodigal love of God is both our strength and our *telos*, our motive and our model.

When I (Justin) first met her, right before I began as a student at Asbury Theological Seminary, she was "Dr. Pohl" to me. At the time, I was assessing my life's call, pondering whether I should go into ethics or some other field in theology, like homiletics. I now hold a PhD in ethics, and that decision is largely due to the influence of the lady who introduced me to a number of ethical topics—including, of course, hospitality, community, and friendship.

Although she was and is an excellent lecturer and pedagogue, it was not her "teaching" that has been most influential to me and many other students with whom I have talked. Rather, it was her presence of modeling hospitality and community: asking students to participate in preparing the weekly class meal, making herself available to students and colleagues, modelling welcome and fidelity in her church ministry alongside people with various disabilities, the way she cared for her dying mother. While not every student would be so fortunate as to eventually enter into her circle of friends, each one was no doubt shown the way of friendship with God through her life. Perhaps this sounds too much like a eulogy; but as Morrie reminds his friends on Tuesdays, it is a shame to save our best reflections on another's life after that person has died. This is why a festschrift is better published for someone who is still living and still exemplifying the way of Christ. I am fine with suggesting to folks, "Imitate Christine Pohl as she imitates Christ."

Years after our first encounter, there was a shift in our relationship when Dr. Pohl told me, nonchalantly, "You can call me Christine." Honestly, that felt as rewarding to me as receiving my degree. It was a recognition that I had not only accomplished something in my studies, but that I had proven

17. Pohl, *Living into Community*, 23.

worthy of invitation into friendship. At one time I called her Dr. Pohl; now I call her Christine. Then I called her professor; now I call her friend. Here's to my friend, my mentor; may this book honor you the way that you honor God and God's calling on your life, and may it also invite others into your community and the community of the saints.

Bibliography

Heuertz, Christopher L., and Christine D. Pohl. *Friendship at the Margins: Discovering Mutuality in Service and Mission*. Grand Rapids: InterVarsity, 2010.

Hoggard Creegan, Nicola, and Christine D. Pohl. *Living on the Boundaries: Evangelical Women, Feminism and the Theological Academy*. Grand Rapids: InterVarsity, 2005.

Pohl, Christine D. *Living into Community: Cultivating Practices That Sustain Us*. Grand Rapids: Eerdmans, 2012.

———. *Making Room: Recovering Hospitality as a Christian* Tradition. Grand Rapids: Eerdmans, 1999.

Porter, Jean. "Perennial and Timely Virtues: Practical Wisdom, Courage, and Temperance." In *Changing Values and Virtues*, edited by Dietmar Mieth and Jacques Pohier, 60–8. Edinburgh: T&T Clark, 1987.

Part One

Practicing Hospitality
Engaging the Fragilities

Intellectual Hospitality
"Making Room" for the Ideas of Others

RICHARD J. MOUW

In a presentation to a conference focusing on business practices from a Christian perspective, I touched on the subject of entrepreneurship. I told a story about asking a friend, an entrepreneur, how his work was going. He responded that he was looking for a new challenge. A few years earlier he had bought a company that was not making a profit, but now it was doing well. "So I'm bored with it," he said. "I'm looking for another loser company to work on!"

I used that anecdote to point out that entrepreneurs are typically not motivated primarily by a desire to make money. Rather, they like to exercise creativity by solving problems and they get excited about risk-taking. And then I moved in a theological direction, reporting on another conversation shortly after the one with the entrepreneur. This one was with a theologian friend, who told me he was exploring the idea of divine hospitality. The God of the Bible, he said, is the ultimate host. "Did you ever think of this?" he asked. "Creation itself was a marvelous act of hospitality. God did not need the likes of us. The triune God would have been missing nothing if we had not been created. But God made room for us, inviting us into a relationship with him."

My friend was touching upon the central feature of hospitality that Christine Pohl explores at length in her important work *Making Room: Recovering Hospitality as a Christian Tradition*. In the light of the loose use of the term these days by "the hospitality industry," she insists on recovering the basic theme of hospitality as "making room" (and in a manner that does not necessitate the use of credit cards!). And it is clear throughout her discussion that our efforts as Christians to "make room" for others should be grounded in our profound gratitude for the ways in which God has made room for us through the atoning work of Jesus Christ, as captured in the refrain of the old hymn: "There's room at the Cross for you."

In my conference address, I took that point about divine hospitality a step further than my theologian friend: I said that God—like the entrepreneur—is a risk-taker. In order to genuinely invite us into a relationship with himself, I said, God had to take the risk of our rejection of his "making room." Heads nodded in my audience when I laid that out. Afterwards, several people told me that the idea of a risk-taking God cast a new light on entrepreneurship for them. But one person—a fellow Calvinist—was upset with me. "God as risk-taker? Mouw, that's simply bad theology! God is sovereign. He knew all along what would happen. There was no risk involved." What really hurt was his going on to accuse me of subscribing to "open theism." But I kept my calm and replied that while I understood the theological concern that he was raising, I was convinced that, with a little more work on the subject, I could maintain my Calvinist orthodoxy without giving up on the notion of divine risk-taking. I am not going to do that necessary work here. But I do want to emphasize my conviction that providing hospitality is a risky business, which means that God's own exercises in hospitality require a commitment to taking risks.

However, my subject here is human risk-taking, and primarily those risks that are important for the Christian scholarly enterprise (although I think that much of what I say has application to what is experienced by Christians beyond the scholarly world, as such).[1] I want to explore one aspect of intellectual hospitality and what that means for the life of the Christian. Most of us in the Christian community—whether or not we have advanced academic degrees—regularly encounter ideas that seem incompatible with our deepest Christian convictions. Some of them, to be sure, are not worth our time getting to understand better. But there are ways of entertaining—showing hospitality to—strange ideas that can benefit us as disciples of the One who is the Truth.

This kind of hospitality does not always come easily; nor should it. We need spiritual resources for the intellectual quest because of the vulnerability, the risk-taking character of intellectual activity. When we invite "the other" into our mental space, we are never quite sure how the encounter will go. But there are strong Christian reasons for inviting the ideas that come

---

1. I wish to add a qualifier here. Not every Christian needs to be actively engaged in a robust intellectual life. We have different callings as individuals. But the Christian community as a whole has to be a healthy place intellectually, which means that some members of that community wrestle with serious ideas on behalf of the whole.

from others—even new and strange others—into our hearts and minds. In one of his helpful discussions of the Christian liberal arts education, Arthur Holmes argued that we should not concentrate primarily on what we *can do with* a liberal arts education. Instead, he urged, we should emphasize what a liberal arts education *can do to us*. And again, this applies to our intellectual life beyond the academy, as such. The kind of wisdom that is necessary for effective Christian service in today's world involves wrestling with different realities, a making room in our hearts and minds for new ideas and experiences.

The kinds of things we Christians disagree about with others fall into two general categories: our disagreements with other Christians and our disagreements with those who are not Christians. In a sense, of course, the categories themselves deserve some critical attention. Our intra-Christian disagreements can be quite heated, even when the differences do not seem so great to persons looking in from outside. Freud's handy term for this phenomenon was "the narcissism of minor differences." Indeed, this is one of those areas of disagreement where the "Christian" versus "non-Christian" borders are themselves quite fluid: what I take to be an interesting disagreement about the sacraments with my Catholic brothers and sisters in Christ is viewed by some other evangelicals as a difference between "real Christians" and persons who have embraced a very different faith.

And, of course, non-Christian thought itself divides into various subcategories: other self-identified faith communities (Muslim, Buddhist); belief-systems that claim no religious ties at all, such as a naturalistic worldview; and explicitly anti-Christian perspectives, such as an aggressive atheism or a thoroughgoing Marxism. The question of what we can learn from, say, Islamic thought raises somewhat different issues than concerns about finding positive lessons about the human condition in a university course on feminist novels or about possible insights to be culled from reading "the new atheists."

While I cannot address each of these categories here, I can emphasize the importance of a general theological disposition to taking seriously the deliverances of "the unregenerate mind." The history of theology has provided rich resources for cultivating that disposition, with John Calvin's work as a good case in point. While the great Reformer is well known for his advocacy of the doctrine of the "total depravity" of fallen humanity, he found it necessary to acknowledge the wisdom of various non-Christian writers, especially Seneca and other Greek and Roman philosophers. This led him to acknowledge, in his *Institutes*, that there is an "admirable light of truth shining" in the thoughts of pagan thinkers. Even minds that are "fallen and perverted," he noted, are still "clothed and ornamented with God's excellent gifts." And if we fail to accept the truth produced by such minds, we "dishonor the Spirit of God."[2]

This acknowledgement of the presence of truth outside the boundaries of the Christian community has relied on a number of theological themes in Christian history, among them general revelation, natural theology, conscience, and the *imago Dei*. Each of these themes provides a positive assessment of ideas that are to be found where the message of the gospel is not acknowledged. These theological resources are both important and helpful for encouraging the Christian community to be open to ideas that come from outside our borders. However, to acknowledge them as theologically correct is not sufficient to nurture the kind of intellectual hospitality that I have in mind here. To counter the resistance to intellectual hospitality in the evangelical community requires attention to a number of factors.

One key phenomenon in this regard is a widespread "warfare" mentality. I saw this mindset clearly on display when conversing with a "counter-cult" activist whose public presentation I had attended. His topic was Mormonism, and some of his content was fairly accurate. But much of what he ascribed to Mormon teachings was incompatible with what I had learned through extensive dialogue with Mormon scholars over the previous decade. I approached the speaker after his talk and gently told him that, according to my Mormon friends, they actually rejected one of the key points that he had identified as central to Mormon belief. He quickly cut me off, telling me that we "don't have time for all of your polite stuff." His job, he insisted, was to warn against "false teachers." Since during his talk he had spoken much about our Christian "battle for the truth," there was an obvious irony in his response to me. How can it be that we don't have the leisure to be accurate about what our opponents actually believe when the cause we are fighting for is "the truth"? But there is more at stake in his response. His "don't have time" expressed a sense of urgency. Something needs to be done, and it must be done quickly. Worrying about "polite stuff" can only hold us back from our task.

There is much that can be said by way of correcting this mentality. For one thing, it violates a prescription clearly set forth by the Apostle Peter in his first epistle: "Always be ready to make your defense to anyone who demands from you an accounting for the hope that is in you" (1 Pet 3:15).[3] But he immediately adds: "Yet do it with gentleness and reverence" (3:16). Surely, offering a gentle reverence to the folks with whom we disagree requires being accurate about what they themselves believe. Yet more

---

2. Calvin, *Institutes*, II.11.14.

3. All Scripture quotations are from the New Revised Standard Version.

is required, as the "don't have time" clause points to other concerns. The anti-intellectualism that has long afflicted various strains of pietism has frequently created an antipathy toward spending time in the "leisure" of matters of the mind. This often is grounded in the pragmatic/activist impulse displayed by the speaker: time spent simply *thinking* about ideas is wasted time when we have so much to do and so little time to do it. However, it can be (and often is) regularly aligned with a commitment to spiritual concerns. Devotional practices are not wasted time for those committed to working for the cause of righteousness. Prayer, self-examination, reflection on biblical teaching—these are the "leisure-time" engagements that are seen as necessary for active service. For all evangelicals, spending time alone with the Lord is crucial for godly living.

This commitment to spiritual practices is an important strength of evangelical pietism, one that we can build upon in making the case for intellectual hospitality. Indeed, it is precisely a spirituality of intellectual hospitality that is the necessary undergirding for the theological awareness of the presence of truth. It is one thing to acknowledge that, for example, a Seneca can teach us something valuable about the nature of law, but it is another thing to *want* to learn from Seneca and other pagan writers—indeed, to actively *seek out* that learning. In what follows, I will offer some thoughts about nurturing the spiritual disposition required for that seeking-out.

In a reflection written during his seven-month stay in a Trappist monastery, Fr. Henri Nouwen reflected on prayer as a means for welcoming new thoughts and concerns into his consciousness:

> [P]rayer is the only real way to clean my heart and to create new space. I am discovering how important that inner space is. When it is there it seems that I can receive many concerns of others . . . I can pray for many others and feel a very intimate relationship with them. There even seems to be room for the thousands of suffering people in prisons and in the deserts of North Africa. Sometimes I feel as if my heart expands from my parents traveling in Indonesia to my friends in Los Angeles and from the Chilean prisons to the parishes in Brooklyn. Now I know that it is not I who pray but the Spirit of God who prays in me . . . He himself prays in me and touches the whole world with his love right here and now. At those moments all questions about "the social relevance of prayer, etc." seem dull and very unintelligent . . .[4]

---

4. Nouwen, *The Genesee Diary*, 74–75.

In referring to the power of prayer as "a real way to clean my heart and to create new space," Nouwen is employing hospitality imagery. Just as inviting persons into our homes often requires house cleaning and creating appropriate spaces, so prayer can serve as an effective means for "making room" for the concerns of other persons. Similarly, Christian intellectual pursuits may require a "clearing" of our mental space in preparation for welcoming new ideas.

Simone Weil makes this connection explicit in her fascinating essay, "Reflections on the Right Use of School Studies with a View to the Love of God," where she argues that the attentiveness that is essential to the life of prayer is also at work in intellectual activity. In this, she echoes Psalm 139, where the psalmist celebrates the *coram Deo* character of our human existence:

> Where can I go from your spirit? Or where can I flee from your
> presence?
> If I ascend to heaven, you are there; if I make my bed in Sheol,
> you are there.
> If I take the wings of the morning and settle at the farthest limits
> of the sea,
> even there your hand shall lead me, and your right hand shall
> hold me fast. (Ps 139:7–10)

And then, at the end of the psalm, this request: "Search me, O God, and know my heart; test me and know my thoughts. See if there is any wicked way in me, and lead me in the way everlasting" (139:23–24). The psalmist recognizes that our thoughts—the ideas that we cultivate in our mental space—are known to God, who is the ultimate Judge of truth and falsity. This awareness is foundational to the cultivation of a genuinely Christian intellectual hospitality. This is what inspired Calvin to insist that a refusal to take seriously ideas that can assist us in the quest for truth is to offend the Holy Spirit.

I have given dozens of commencement addresses, and I often begin with this tongue-in-cheek "announcement": I tell them that the administration and faculty have asked me to assure them that it "has been their pleasure to serve you on your journey thus far. They want you to know that that appreciate your business. They know you have a choice of schools and they thank you for choosing _____. They want you to know that if your future plans call for more higher education, they hope that you will think of them here at _____." And then I warn the graduates to be careful in accessing the contents in "the overhead compartments, because those contents may have shifted during your journey."

That playful paraphrase of the flight attendant's announcement makes a serious point. Academic engagement *should* shift the contents of our minds. We certainly should be different kinds of thinkers after years in a degree program than we were when we first began. To repeat an earlier question: *What are the ideas we are learning doing to us?* And that question can be extended to the larger life of the mind, as Christian intellectual pursuits can play an important role in forming us for discipleship. I turn now to some practical recommendations. What must we cultivate in our spiritual lives in order to foster a healthy Christian intellectual hospitality?

I think John Calvin had it right when he identified humility as basic to Christian spirituality. "I have always been exceedingly delighted," the Reformer wrote,

> with the words of Chrysostom, "The foundation of our philosophy is humility"; and still more with those of Augustine, "As the orator, when asked, What is the first precept in eloquence? answered, Delivery: What is the second? Delivery: What the third? Delivery: so, if you ask me in regard to the precepts of the Christian Religion, I will answer, first, second, and third, Humility."[5]

The writer of Psalm 139 offers strong support for this insistence upon humility when he expresses his own humble awareness that because God is all-knowing, the contents of human consciousness, including our motives and cognitive assessments, are open to the correction of divine scrutiny. The persistent habit of careful self-examination requires a spirit of humility, including in our intellectual lives. Again, Simone Weil points explicitly to the link between intellectual pursuits and spirituality, specifically with reference to humility. "The virtue of humility," she writes,

> is a far more precious treasure than all academic progress. From this point of view, it is perhaps even more useful to contemplate our stupidity than our sin. Consciousness of sin gives us the feeling that we are evil, and a kind of pride sometimes finds a place in it. When we force ourselves to fix the gaze, not only of our eyes but of our souls, upon a school exercise in which we have failed through sheer stupidity, a sense of our mediocrity is borne in upon us with irresistible evidence. No knowledge is more to be desired. If we can arrive at knowing this truth with all our souls, we shall be well established on the right foundation.[6]

---

5. Calvin, *Institutes*, II.11.11.
6. Weil, "Reflections," 34.

This "sense of our mediocrity" can help us to posture ourselves as learners, open to hearing the truth from an unexpected source.

Many of us who have been active in interfaith dialogue have been helped in understanding the importance of humility by Leonard Swidler's well-known "Dialogue Decalogue," where he sets forth ten principles for constructive interfaith engagement.[7] While we cannot examine Swidler's "commandments" and his accompanying commentary on each of them here, it is instructive to reflect briefly on some of the spiritual dispositions that those principles point us to in sorting out some issues regarding intellectual hospitality. Swidler emphasizes, for example, the need to approach perspectives different from our own with a humble spirit of learning. Understandably, this does not come easily for evangelicals, especially when the topics have to do with explicit religious beliefs. We have often approached other religious perspectives—Buddhism, Islam, animism—with an exclusive emphasis on soteriological concerns. We have rightly insisted that human beings can only be reconciled to God through the atoning work of Jesus Christ, and we have resisted any moves in the direction of religious relativism or syncretism.

To be sure, that soteriological focus is important. But our clear and profound conviction that Christ alone can save does not prohibit us from asking whether we can gain insights into the truth about God and the human condition by attending to the content of non-Christian thought. In approaching that question, it is necessary to "bracket" as much as possible our overt interests in soteriology and missiology. When the main question is whether we have good reasons to believe that, say, a fully committed Muslim—someone whose understanding of reality is spelled out in consistently Muslim terms—can go to heaven, then many of us will have to answer in the negative. In this context, it is appropriate for evangelicals to say that Islam is a "false religion," in the sense that a person who wants to enter into a saving relationship with the one true God will not achieve that goal by adhering to Muslim beliefs and practices. However, if we can suspend the question of whether Muslims *qua* Muslims can be saved, then we are free to evaluate this or that particular Muslim teaching in terms of whether it illuminates reality, and we may well find many good and true elements in the Muslim worldview. Indeed, we might even find things in the Muslim understanding of spiritual reality that can enrich our own Christian understanding of religious truth, even by calling our attention to spiritual matters that we have not fully considered. It is a little easier to bracket the salvific questions when we move away from explicitly theological matters. We can engage,

---

7. Swidler, "Dialogue Principles."

for example, Freud's arguments in his *Civilization and Its Discontents*, or in Simone de Beauvoir's *The Second Sex*, without focusing primarily on whether or not either of them is going to heaven.

Finally, what is just as important as our willingness to learn is the ability to admit that we have misunderstood these perspectives in the past. As the speaker on Mormonism demonstrated, it can be difficult to accept our mistakes of understanding, even when talking to an "ally." My engagement with his talk was an attempt to bring the education I had received from my Mormon friends to bear on the truthfulness of his speech; regrettably, he was not willing to acknowledge his error. As I noted earlier, to do this while "battling for the truth" is ironic, even tragic. Christine Pohl notes the relationship between how we view the significance of our work and our willingness to accept misinterpretations in a "whatever it takes" approach to success:

> Sometimes we are persuaded that a cause or result is so important that we are willing to use deceptive means to gain a person's attention or cooperation . . .[W]e characterize our opponents unfairly and distort their views because we believe our concerns are so important. When we do this, we corrupt our own message, disrespect the persons we are trying to persuade, and undermine our own integrity.[8]

Truthfulness is a key biblical ideal, and it is a sin to bear false witness against our neighbors, whether they are Muslims, Viennese psychoanalysts, or Parisian existentialists.

Another humility-related theme that Swidler examines is *empathy*— experiencing the feelings and concerns of others as if they were your own. The ability to see things from the point of view of the persons we are engaging is crucial for better understanding. Here is how Swidler puts it:

> Each participant needs to describe her/himself. For example, only a Muslim can describe what it really means to be an authentic member of the Muslim community. At the same time, when one's partner in dialogue attempts to describe back to them what they have understood of their partner's self-description, then such a description must be recognizable to the described party.[9]

Hospitality is a fine image for understanding what this means in the life of the mind. We "make room" for the ideas of a Simone de Beauvoir by attempting to grasp the feelings and concerns that give rise to her ideas about

8. Pohl, *Living into Community*, 121.

9. Swidler, "Dialogue Principles."

gender. To be sure, attempting to understand the views of a self-professed atheist, from the "inside," as it were, can be a special challenge for a Christian. But it is an important challenge.

Indeed, it may be that we Christians have special advantages in nurturing the necessary kind of empathy. The humble awareness of our own sin can lead us, as Simone Weil put it in straightforward terms, "to contemplate our stupidity."[10] We know we are finite creatures. God is God, and we are not; and therefore we fall far short of omniscience. Furthermore, the cognitive defects that stem from finitude are even more exaggerated because of our sinful rebelliousness. This means that what might, at first glance, appear to be radical disagreement with a certain point of view might actually, upon humble reflection, require a confession of sin. A case in point: I hold to conservative views about sexuality—but I also have to confess that we traditional Christians have been inexcusably cruel toward persons who experience, for example, same-sex attractions. Or, to take another perspective, my disagreements with the Wicca perspective are very real—but I have to remind myself about the witch-burnings of the past. And so on.

But there is more at stake than repentance regarding our own misdeed and misunderstandings, as important as those matters are. As already emphasized, a spirit of genuine learning must enter into the picture. Often there is wisdom to be culled from a serious reflection upon distorted truth. And, as John Calvin rightly insisted in the case of Seneca, there is sincere and positive insight to be found outside the boundaries of the Christian community. The Spirit of God is at work in the larger world, promoting the cause of truth.

Acknowledging the wisdom that lies outside the borders of the faith is not the same thing as pretending the borders do not exist. Therefore, I will close with a reflection on mental boundaries and intellectual hospitality. One of the teachers in my undergraduate studies who most influenced me was Dr. Josephine Rickard, a godly Wesleyan professor of literature at Houghton College. In one of our seminars for English majors, we engaged in a heated discussion about graphic portrayals of sexuality in fiction. I argued that as Christians, we should see fictional portrayals of the human condition as an opportunity better to understand the reality of sin in the world. "Doc Jo"—as we called her with fondness—was not happy with my line of argument. She finally reprimanded me with these words: "*Mister Mouw*," she said in a sharp tone of voice, "we can have a perfectly adequate awareness of the reality of trash without having to go around lifting the lids of every trash can in town!"

10. Weil, "Reflections," 33.

Her point was well put—and well-taken by me. And I have often thought of it as a necessary warning about my own tendencies to celebrate what I have been discussing here as intellectual hospitality. Indeed, here is another way in which the actual physical hospitality discussed by Christine Pohl has an important lesson when extended to the practices of intellectual hospitality. To make room of others, for example, in our homes is to do so with a necessary awareness of the actual physical conditions for doing so. Our homes are physical spaces, with walls and windows and doors. As hosts, we have to plan our invitations to guests in the light of those physical limitations. Genuine hospitality is not properly practiced when we allow thieves to break in and steal. Similarly, Christian intellectual hospitality must respect appropriate boundaries. Some intellectual "intrusion" can be dangerous. Just as a human invader may corrupt the very spaces that we create in our homes for extending hospitality, so there are ideas that can corrupt our mental and spiritual "spaces."

It may seem counter to my overall purpose in this essay to make a point of this as I conclude. But the fact is that an intellectual "promiscuity" is a genuine danger in the broader Christian community, and it can become a danger when evangelicals take on the intellectual challenges that we have been able to avoid in the past largely because of the heavy dose of anti-intellectualism that we have inherited. My main task here has been to offer some thoughts that can counter that anti-intellectualism by encouraging practices of intellectual hospitality, while at the same time recognizing that the alternative to anti-intellectualism is not without dangers of its own.

A healthy evangelical intellectual life must be pursued with the cultivation of the kind of spiritual discernment that equips us to recognize dangers of many varieties. While the dangers may be real, so are the benefits of "making room" for all that the Spirit has to teach us in the quest for truth.

Bibliography

Calvin, John. *Institutes of the Christian Religion*. Edited by John T. McNeill. Translated by Ford Lewis Battles. Philadelphia: Westminster, 1960.

Nouwen, Henri J. M. *The Genesee Diary*. New York: Doubleday, 1976.

Pohl, Christine D. *Living into Community: Cultivating Practices That Sustain Us*. Grand Rapids: Eerdmans, 2012.

———. *Making Room: Recovering Hospitality as a Christian* Tradition. Grand Rapids: Eerdmans, 1999.

Swidler, Leonard. "Dialogue Principles." *Dialogue Institute*, May 5, 2018. http://institute. jesdialogue.org/resources/tools/decalogue/.

Weil, Simone. "Reflections on the Right Use of School Studies with a View to the Love of God." In *Waiting for God*, translated by Emma Crauford, 32–37. New York: Harper, 2009.

Hospitality, Civility, and Market Exchange

Societal Limits on Gift-Giving Space

James R. Thobaben

Christian hospitality is nice—at least it can be nice, even pleasant, to both give and receive. And why not? Hospitality of the faithful, if genuinely expressed and politely accepted, is a foreshadowing of the Kingdom which is to come. Certainly, that should be a pleasant experience. Yet hospitality can be more, much more, than mere "niceness." Hospitality is the lowering of boundaries for the sake of temporary community inclusion, sometimes for the truly weary and the most desperate. Hospitality takes different forms in times of deprivation and times of plenty, but the faithful are obligated to sacrificially "make room."[1] While hospitality is morally desirable in all cultural groups, it is morally *necessary* for Christians.

That said, the eschaton has not arrived. The Kingdom is amongst the believers but is not yet fulfilled; and this means intentional moral ordering may sometimes be required. In other words, the act of hospitality is not an unreserved good. While hospitality is a means of achieving desired resource reallocation, it is not the only way that the person with resource needs is met. Providing space or "making room" is not always possible, preferable, or even appropriate—and sometimes the practice of hospitality generates immoral and unnecessary danger. Christians may be obligated, in some situations, to meet the "other" in a more instrumental manner or in a less

---

1. Pohl, *Making Room.*

personal "sphere," without any intention of extending hospitality even if the capacity to do so exists.

Hospitality, as a function of gracious gift-giving, can be broadly understood as an act of unmerited beneficence. The giver (or "host") recognizes his/her mastery of the space and provisions, but chooses to allow some of those to be used by another.[2] However, this is necessarily a very limited and a very personal act. Although hospitality in the sense of "good manners" or diplomatic exchange is a function of the State, true hospitality is not. And while those in the market will occasionally have "giveaways," the only time it could be argued they are being hospitable in the truest sense is when they leave the market *per se* to conduct an act of charity. Moreover, the method for the market and political sphere is through contracts (market contracts and the social contract, respectively), while gift-giving is based on covenantal relationships. Thus, hospitality properly belongs to individuals or face-to-face communities that respectfully engage persons as particular individuals. All said, the social order needs civility, market exchange, and hospitality, as Pohl herself notes:

> The opportunities for personal, face-to-face relations that can give people a place and a social network are found within churches, families, neighborhoods, and voluntary associations. These are bounded communities to which detached strangers need connection. However, many social groups find it very difficult to accept people different from their prevailing membership. Therefore, the more anonymous care of the state is essential in that it protects basic human rights while it avoids the coercion often present in very local ties; it helps to control the impact of more parochial hospitality which chooses its guests and the needs it will meet.[3]

To understand the complementary functioning of hospitality, civility, and market engagement as limited moral goods—and, in particular, how hospitality makes a stronger call on Christians than should be expected of others—the following will be offered:

- The categories of gift-giving, civility, and respectful market exchange;

---

2. The Spanish term *hospitalero/a* (used along the Camino de Santiago in the *refugios*) fits the idea of hospitality in sense of virtue better than the English word "host/hostess."

3. Pohl, *Making Room*, 84.

- The cultural shifts that have led to an increased call (both amongst academics and in popular culture) for hospitality as a governing moral good;
- The practice of Christian hospitality;
- The limits of hospitality (on this side of the eschaton);
- Why civility and respectful market exchange are complementary and, on some occasions, morally preferable alternatives to hospitality;
- Why hospitality is, nevertheless, theologically and morally essential for Christians, including why Christians should be more hospitable than those of the World.

Hospitality, Civility, and Respectful Market Exchange

Societal interaction in the late-modern or post-modern West (depending on the label one prefers) takes place in three primary ways:

- Personal (face-to-face) interactions in which individuals know and, to some extent, understand each other; each is understood as one who carries a particular biographical narrative that both affords integration of the self within the community and allows covenantal obligation;
- Market exchanges (through market contracts) in which individuals are identified by their roles as purveyors or purchasers of goods and services;
- Citizen-to-citizen, in which, theoretically, persons interact in a manner appropriate to their political status given the social contract; in the late-modern West this is, again theoretically, as equals without substantive distinction.

Obviously, these are "ideal types" (to use Weberian language), for in the real world these forms blend to various degrees within and between societies. Still, their distinctive nature can be described.

Market exchange is trade with another to achieve utility. Persons enter into market exchange to obtain a benefit (one either that is material or facilitated by material). The other "exchanger" is a mechanism of the exchange. At its best, this exchange is an open, honest (to the extent necessary), symmetric exchange, with reciprocity.[4] Yet, at its worst, the market can be contorted

4. Reciprocity in some cultural anthropological writing refers to non-monetized exchanges, but it can also be used to refer to exchanges, especially economic exchanges,

by deceit or the desperation of participants. Put simply, when all is well, the economic pie gets bigger and all participants benefit (albeit to varying degrees). When distorted, though, some get more, and others are deprived not because they took a calculated risk and lost, but because they were intentionally cheated or mistreated by system bias.[5] Regardless of whether the system is perfect or completely warped or somewhere in between, the other person in a market exchange is only a means to an end. There are rules that require politeness, primarily to ensure that "being offended" or maliciously manipulated does not interfere with both parties being satisfied in the exchange. These include rules of commutative justice such as truth-telling, promise-keeping in contracts, limited gift-giving to prevent bribery, etc.; sometimes these are enforced by the State.

Civility is the treatment of fellow citizens (understood broadly, rather than in the technical, legal sense) as worthy of respect due to intrinsic status. In the late-modern West, this means equal in pertinent characteristics.[6] In the strictest sense, the other might be understood as an acquaintance rather than a true stranger, since there is a level, albeit small, of shared morality.[7] The "more-or-less-stranger" is met civilly, then hospitality may or may not be rendered and a shift toward acquaintanceship or even friendship can occur.

These models (along with hospitality) rely on particular concepts of "respect":

- Hospitality (and gift-giving more generally) is based on the recognition of individuals as persons with specific, ongoing narratives and

---

of rough equivalence. Thus, for this study and unlike some anthropological writings, bartering refers to a reciprocal economic exchange.

5. For purposes of this study, externalities (costs not borne by the producer or the consumer) are disregarded. An example of an externality is air pollution for which neither the energy generator nor the consumer of the electricity pays, but rather those who are "downwind" from the pollution.

6. The concept of "respect" in the US, for the purposes of the civil sphere, is initially developed in the founding documents as "created equal," which does not mean, of course, identical in skills, character, etc., but equal before the State and treated as one deserving of such. Respect as a matter of civility is very limited. Another use of the word is "honoring," and that is closer to what happens in the face-to-face gift-giving of hospitality. Respect can also, as in the economic sphere, simply mean one is treated as an "exchanger" who follows market rules.

7. In the legal sense in the US, this is by consent. In reality, there is a shared cultural agreement that is recognized as silent affirmation of the need to respect the other. While certainly "[m]oral strangers can share agreements based on consent and permission," there is a transformation that occurs upon recognized shared morality (Wildes, *Moral Acquaintances*, 159).

teloi (purpose or end) that they seek to fulfill. The giver "respects" the
other as one seeking some kind of fulfillment.

- In public civility, the individual is recognized and respected as one
  "person" of the universal type. Nothing about the particular *telos* of the
  person matters as the "respect" is simply confirming negative rights of
  the individual as an expression of justice. Citizens are not obligated to
  engage one another as distinct persons with a story, but as individuals
  who are alike in significant but limited ways. This is why retributive
  justice is "blind," so as to not "see" the particularities and narratives of
  individuals.

- Respect in market interactions is limited to acknowledging the other
  participant's role as seller or buyer with mutual fairness and honesty.
  This includes basic verification of the seller as one having surplus to
  sell and the buyer as one having money (or objects to barter), without
  either acting out of desperation.[8]

While the line between respectful obligations of the market, of civility, and
of hospitality may blur (especially in traditional nomadic cultures), they are
based on different moral claims. The principal distinction is that the recipient lacks the *right* to the space and provisions or the *ability* to buy the same
(because of lack of resources or the unwillingness of the owner to sell) when
true hospitality is given.

The hotel on an interstate may welcome "guests," but this is not gift-
giving, though it is sometimes shrouded in the imagery. An expensive hotel
will "give" chocolates, laying them on the pillow; the guest will "give" tips
to various staff members. The object of the hotel is to create the sense of
being a "pampered" and honored guest. The tipping guest, then, provides
what has the veneer of *noblesse oblige*, thus elevating their own status (perhaps through smiling condescension). The staff are quite willing to play
along because the compensation is worth the roleplaying. Or, to be more
charitable in interpretation, perhaps a different set of virtues is coming into
play—those of the commutative justice of the market.

Market exchange can be done well, with the participating parties each
gaining the highest utility possible. If the room is pleasing (a nice hotel
room is better than one full of roaches or with failing septic), is reasonably priced (given the resources of the purchaser and operational costs of
the provider), has been clearly described, and does not use resources that
should be otherwise directed, then the exchange is morally good. It is not,
however, gift-giving.

8. Thobaben, *Health-Care Ethics,* 127–34.

Similarly, the State can legitimately perform the task of providing space and food. Again, this is not gift-giving but is an expansive understanding of the obligations of civility. As with market exchange, such legally required provisions can be done in a morally commendable way. The State justly provides food and shelter for citizens who are part of the military. The government is not being hospitable in doing so; it is fulfilling an obligation to those who have, as part of the social contract, entered into military service. Other citizens are obligated to fund the State's support of military personnel. This is appropriate, but it is not hospitality.

Also in the United States (and in most social contract states), some effort is made to provide for the most vulnerable. This is not generally deemed hospitality, but rather is understood as a matter of justice. It might be understood as weak hospitality, given out of pity (a sort of corporate *noblesse oblige* to the deserving poor), though most would use entitlement or positive rights language—part of the vocabulary of civil society.

So, while they contain their own sets of moral codes, the political and market spheres display a primary emphasis upon the person as a social or economic entity. There is not a need to recognize the individual as a given self through time; indeed, that recognition of the particular human individual requires the perspective or perspectives generated in community.[9]

Cultural Shifts and the Longing for Hospitality

While existing in all cultures, in the West the idea of hospitality outside kinship networks dramatically developed both in religious communities and amongst the nobility in late antiquity. Drawing on their relatively large capacity and given the religious obligation—as outlined, for instance, in the Benedictine Rule—the needy were welcomed in monasteries and convents. Religious hospitality seems to have expanded in association with the growing number of pilgrimage centers, though the pilgrimage sites soon developed commercial inn-keeping for those who could afford the higher quality services. Less significant numerically, but as important culturally, hospitality was also a noteworthy moral obligation for nobility in this era, initially following older Roman patterns and then adopting the expectations of chivalry. Amongst the elites, hospitality was a means of accruing honor,

9. Moreover, at the end of modernity, the individual as the locus of identity is itself being deconstructed and replaced with temporarily obtained traits and personality fluidity. Part of the reason for this diminishing is the displacement of the ongoing, face-to-face community with an expanding (or intruding) marketplace and the civil society.

especially for male nobles.[10] Women tended to be viewed as direct providers of service, or—in the upper class—coordinators of such service. These religious and aristocratic activities were often complementary in establishing political and social order.

The understanding of hospitality and indeed of civil order and market functions remained fairly stable in the West through the post-Roman centuries. That began to dramatically change with the development of trade and urban centers (including increased "division of labor") and the subsequent rise of "proto-nation-states." Collectively, this meant that persons would be "met" far more often as strangers. Religious interpretations of work changed, including dividing economically productive activity from the household, at least for the males (the home had been the traditional site of hospitality). Kinship models shifted, leading to an increased emphasis on the nuclear family. The middle class—previously a very small social sector consisting of a few families of skilled tradespersons, small farm freeholders, and scattered professionals—now expanded rapidly. These shifts solidified with the Renaissance, particularly the Reformation and its new ideas about vocation.

Not unexpectedly, understandings of hospitality, civility, and marketplace activity also changed. Respect was reinterpreted. Previously, persons typically encountered one another within kinship and friendship circles, or if not then in accord with fairly clear social roles. Such individuals would have been respected according to established expectation or as friends and kin in face-to-face relationships.[11] But as the economy and social order shifted, a rising number of "mere" acquaintances and strangers had to be engaged peacefully, and so persons were "respectfully" met with civility (at least within a given nation-state). This civility was not based on one being a particular person, but on being "a" person (albeit "person" in a much thicker sense than in the late-modern West).

The "other" was most often met in the market. Persons were service and goods exchangers, viewed as means to ends. The seller and buyer were treated respectfully, relying upon market rules that protected the process and allowed "coming and going." In other words, the other was met for the moment and in terms of specific, transitory roles. Respectful behavior, such

---

10. See Heal, *Hospitality*.

11. Certainly, with the arrival of mass urbanization in the US and the movement of males into non-agricultural (and non-domestic) workplaces, what remained of the "masculine" practice of hospitality diminished (excepting that which was transferred to "clubs" and "picking up the tab"). Hospitality through mid-modernity was increasingly associated with the location of a wife or mother in a domestic setting. For a good discussion of these terms, see Wildes, *Moral Acquaintances*.

as the prohibition of cheating or lying, was enforced by both civil authorities and the market itself.

Given these shifts, from around 1600 on, hospitality became primarily a friendship activity, often limited to the family sphere. Gift-giving and *caritas* to the "deserving poor" were increasingly transferred to the civil authorities or specialized voluntary organizations. The provision of space and food for sojourners who could afford to pay was almost completely shifted to the market and the nascent "hospitality industry." (A good example of the transitional state is the English or Irish pub that has a few rooms to let and is family-owned, a model now quickly disappearing with the rise of corporate "chains.")

It is no coincidence that the development of social contract theory occurred in the era following the internal migrations associated with the rise of the cities and the nationalist-religious wars of Europe. More and more persons were unknown and unidentified. The Enlightenment theorists tried to solve the problem of "strangeness" by abandoning the idea of hospitality and using the concept of the universal person.[12] The Kantian categorical imperative and the Lockean and Rousseauian contract-maker were descriptions of the pure, abstracted, political person. These are not economic (that is better described by A. Smith) nor familial (though Rousseau tries to make it such in *Emile*). Social contract theory has proven practically useful for very large, urbanized societies; it allows strangers to safely meet and thus creates the potential for becoming acquaintances, which in turn can lead to the establishment of ongoing relationships. It provides a behavioral baseline: leave the stranger alone, and that stranger should leave you alone. Talk to the stranger, and you can assume he or she will engage you civilly, according to basic rules.

While slower, the institutionalization of hospitality penetrated the rural United States during the mid- and late-nineteenth century, with specialized institutions (such as orphanages, religious communities like the Shakers, and eventually county homes) developing to serve the displaced. The expanding presence of charity hospitals, institutions for the mentally ill, homes for the indigent, and so on meant that the concept of "charity"— originally derived from *agape*, "love"—was increasingly defined as a "handout" of money or a tax-funded service, and distinguished from "opening one's home." And just as the market uses hospitality language to sell its food and hotel rooms, civil authorities employ it to validate their extension of

12. The foundations of the basic concept are present in early Hebrew thought and are further developed in first-century Christianity. That said, the full concept of the "equal" and un-embedded contract-maker is a seventeenth- and eighteenth-century concept.

power. Increasingly, centralized governmental controls expanded their presence in daily life with declarations that "it takes a village"—by which the spokespersons meant bureaucracies. Market and governmental powers mutually reinforce their growing domination of increasingly isolated, fragmented individuals, all while using hospitality, gift-giving, and charity language whenever it proves useful.[13]

By the end of modernity, the stranger, the sojourner, and the desperate neighbor might not receive the gift of hospitality, but they could purchase it from a service provider or appeal to the State for "charity." Importantly, the moral language of virtuous *caritas* was partially displaced by the deontological language of justice (specifically "rights") and the utility language of the market. These, of course, can also be languages of respect, but of very different kinds. Thus, as a result of population growth, urbanization, and value shifts, civility and market contract became vastly more prevalent than covenantal hospitality.

All three models are needed in late modernity, but the development of the market and civil sphere have unfortunately left them out-of-balance. There is a quiet desperation in the populace generated by the loss of "fit" between covenantal community, civil society, and the marketplace. Properly, Christians (as well as some others) are asserting that what is needed is a return to balance with covenantal gift-giving—perhaps, in particular, hospitality. In other words, sometimes—not always, but sometimes—persons need to be brought into one's another presence in order to receive shelter and provision—not as those who happen to have common socio-political interests or can pay for the space and food provided, but as individuals who have distinct narratives with *teloi* worthy of the host's assistance. The practice of hospitality provides an alternative.

The Practice of Hospitality

Drawing in part from *Making Room*, the practice of hospitality can be understood as asymmetric assistance distributed in the form of food and/or shelter (including protection from threat). As with other forms of gift-giving, the giving of space, food, and time is not triggered simply by the actual or felt needs of a potential recipient (physically deprived, seeking emotional or social inclusion, wanting affection, etc.). It is an offering of the self and what the self has for the ongoing well-being of the other. Receiving through hospitality is necessarily characterized as "boundary crossing," by which the

13. Perhaps the best approach, recognizing a high degree of differentiation in late modernity, is that of blocked exchanges, nicely developed in Walzer, *Spheres of Justice.*

relational status of the guest is altered such that previously established roles are changed at least to some degree. The offering is an expression of relational opening as familial bond is acknowledged, friendship is reinforced, or the potential for ongoing community is established.

The practice of hospitality, in various forms, appears in every culture. The exact expressions depend on several variables: the capacity to provide resources, the defining of "who counts," the understanding of "just deserts" or "worthy need," traditions, and (most especially) prior relational obligations. Though particular social roles vary and the socio-cultural boundaries are drawn differently, giving hospitality always requires: (1) that food and/ or temporary shelter is provided as a gift, (2) that the recipient has a genuine need (whether physical, relational, or spiritual), (3) that the potential guest is recognized as being in the category of legitimate recipient of the gift, and (4) that the host and recipient give and receive respectfully. How these requirements are specifically expressed varies widely.

When referred to as a virtue—certainly as a Christian virtue—hospitality refers to *the practice of generously receiving guests*. Each component term of this definition warrants consideration.

- *The practice:* A practice is a regularized activity, governed by formal and/or informal behavioral rules, through which the participant (practitioner) expresses shared community values. As structured gift-giving in the form of provision, hospitality is certainly a "practice" in the traditional sense.[14]

- *Of generously:* Hospitality is a gift-giving practice. Something costly is provided to another without requiring compensatory payment or encumbrance. Generosity in the act is generated by the combination of asymmetry in a costly exchange and the determination to not seek compensation. The guest, necessarily, is understood as one who cannot properly make a legal claim or demand for such care, such that the giving act is deemed a moral good. That is, the recipient cannot demand the gift of hospitality as a right, else it is not generosity.[15]

14. The most common use of the idea of "practice" at the end of modernity is as the performance of a profession, such that the skilled person is deemed excellent. This understanding of practice harkens back to the Aristotelian meaning of virtue. While the Latin word for virtue, *virtute*, refers to an honorable, dependable "manliness," the word Aristotle used was the Greek *arête*, meaning "noble excellence."

15. Heuertz and Pohl correctly tie the notion of hospitality to that of friendship in their work *Friendship at the Margins*. Too frequently, the word "hospitality" is erroneously applied to the requirements of the nation-state to meet rights obligations. If one is obligated to render care, and to not do so is proscribed by the State, then such service is much more akin to taxation than gift-giving. This is why opening borders may be a

> While the gift of hospitality can be balanced with a "thank you" gift, this is not contractual; rather, it is a form of non-market reciprocity, relational but not economic.[16]

Along with the lack of compensation, the quality of hospitality can be judged, in part, by the degree that needs are actually met. The provided food, space, and safety must satisfy needs (if not wants) for hospitality to have been properly offered. Merely "putting in the effort" without providing for the need is not true hospitality.

The moral quality of hospitality is also determined by the respect rendered. Presumably, the giver does not provide benefits simply to degrade the social status of the recipient and, conversely, raise his/her own status. The gift-giver, rather, is generously giving respect along with resources. The respect of hospitality differs from that of civility in that the recipient is treated not simply as "any person" in need, but as "the" particular person standing before the giver.

- *Receiving*: Hospitality always involves the welcome of someone into another's space, the asymmetric provision of some tangible resource, and the consumption of the host's time. The request for hospitality (verbal or not) is always intrusive, although the granting of permission makes the intrusion acceptable. That said, the intrusion can be transformed by the giver as the guest is literally and figuratively relocated from outside to inside, and from outsider status into conditional (and often temporary) community membership.

- *Guests*: The recipient of the gift of hospitality moves from outside to inside, often literally. Without exception, the guest is identifiable as a particular person, with a specific life story that provides integral,

---

matter of justice, but it is not a matter of hospitality. A categorical error is often made, such as by Derrida, when hospitality is blurred with asylum: "Not all new arrivals are received as guests if they don't have the benefit of the right to hospitality or the right of asylum, etc.," Derrida states and then erroneously continues, "Without this right, a new arrival can only be introduced 'in my home,' in the host's 'at home,' as a parasite, a guest who is wrong, illegitimate, clandestine, libel to expulsion or arrest" (Derrida, *On Hospitality*, 59, 61). Derrida mistakenly conflates categories, but correctly notes that not all strangers will be recipients of hospitality. One receiving hospitality should be offered sanctuary, not as an entitlement, but an offered grace. Asylum is to sanctuary what civility is to hospitality.

16. The New Testament includes an interesting dual-level example. In his discourse on prayer in Luke 11, Jesus offers a parable in which an obligation to provide hospitality to one friend leads to his own request for hospitality or gift-giving from another. Note that, in using hospitality as a metaphor for prayer, Jesus is defining it as (1) asymmetric gift-giving that (2) establishes or reinforces relationships (3) through the meeting of needs.

continuous identification (even if their narrative is not known).[17] Further, it is assumed that the offering of hospitality will actually improve the trajectory of the guest's narrative. Hospitality is not merely non-maleficence; it is an act of beneficence based on the virtuosity of the gift-giver in assisting the recipient toward holistic well-being.

The first interpretive act by the giver is to understand the potential guest as having characteristics that warrant inclusion. One way or another, the guest is deemed by the host to be "deserving" (which the host has the power to do, leaving aside whether or not that evaluation is morally accurate). This may be because the potential guest is considered particularly worthy, because of other relationships, or even because of the potential to bring the person into the community permanently, thus adding to that community's greater good. For Christians, the argument may be that the outsider is an Image-bearer in need or a potential brother/sister in Christ, preferably both.

Practically, the potential giver tends to experience some degree of empathy or sympathy toward the future recipient.[18] Without such, the giving of hospitality is not really conceivable. Still, these feelings do not lead to hospitality unless the giver determines to shift the status of the outsider to one within the boundary of care. Initially, the one outside must present him/herself in such a way as to warrant consideration, including demonstrating that he/she is not a threat. This is very different than the market or civil arena in which adversarial behaviors might be expected, within reason. The guest is in some sense "vetted" and determined to be a friend or a "safe" acquaintance, or a sojourner who is likely to become a friend through this gift-giving (thereby diffusing the potential for that sojourning person becoming an enemy).

Further, even beyond formal gratitude, there is an expectation of deference. That is, the offer is also conditioned on a willingness to accept the role of "guest." This does not mean that the guest is morally passive, completely dependent on the giver. Rather, a guest is not supposed to take the gift of hospitality for granted. This establishes a relationship of mutual respect. Deference actually brings the status of the recipient up in that it establishes that they are needy, but not morally incapable.

Having now described the practice of virtuous hospitality, the final consideration is what distinguishes the practice as "Christian." When early

17. Thobaben, *Health-Care Ethics.*

18. Smith, *The Theory of Moral Sentiments.* The giver who gives hospitality out of genuine concern is exhibiting sympathy (in Smith's sense) or empathy (in Stein's sense) (Stein, *On the Problem of Empathy*, 6–7). As others have noted, the word "empathy" is not a perfect translation for *Einfühlung*. See Sawicki, "Personal Connections."

Christians placed a strong emphasis on hospitality, they did so in response to God's graciousness.[19] Jesus Christ was often viewed as the eternal host who acted in this life through his servants as they opened up the space and time that they controlled (both as a moral duty and a simple expression of gratitude). The early believers did not expect any given individual to return hospitality for hospitality as *quid pro quo*. Instead, through the gift-giving and respectfulness, they expected a "return" in the form of new relationships that would honor the church and their Lord.

True Christian hospitality, therefore, is only that which is based on the singular priority of love of God as known in Jesus Christ, and thus only such hospitality is truly virtuous.[20] The practice might look supererogatory, since the recipient cannot properly make legal claim to the gift-giving, but to the believer such virtuosity is an expression of duty—not to the guest, but to God—as expressed in service to the guest. While hospitality in the broadest sense exists in some form in all cultural groups, hospitality for Christians is more specifically understood as an expression of *agape/caritas* or self-sacrificial giving that serves both the fulfillment of one's own spiritual *telos* (through moral shaping and spiritual submission to the Way of Christ) and the well-being of the other.[21]

Yet, while hospitality is deeply rooted in self-giving love—be it love of family, fellow believer, neighbor, or even enemy—it is not the same as love. Unlike love, it does not grow with every offering. To the contrary, every time hospitality is given, the capacity to continue giving is in some way

19. Pohl notes that when the early church offered hospitality, it was "responsible for imitating God's hospitable and gracious character" (Pohl, *Making Room*, 42).

20. This follows the claims of Augustine, J. Edwards, Kierkegaard, and—arguably—Wesley. Perhaps hospitality can be understood as an expression of "comfort" given 2 Cor 1:3–7.

21. Early Christians appropriated cultural concepts of familial hospitality and fairly smoothly extended them toward their new spiritual family members. In that manner, the church giving hospitality is the validation and legitimation of a spiritual kinship affiliation. Arguably, this was more expansive than the Old Testament model. While the exact meaning of these examples of the practice is debated, it is clear that the standard of the New Testament is higher. Abram and Sarai provided hospitality to the visitors at the Oaks of Mamre (Genesis 18), presumably in a manner consistent with semi-nomadic tribal expectations. Arguably, they did so to befriend the stranger who might otherwise become an enemy, and this was an entirely appropriate manner of creating relationships though gift-giving. Lot provided shelter to the angelic visitors, even though in the process he seemed to egregiously devalue his own daughters (Genesis 19). Rahab provided hospitality to the spies of Joshua (Joshua 2), though this may have been an intentional poetical betrayal of those who had mistreated her rather than hospitality *per se*. Today, these actions might be defined less as hospitality than a form of justice. Drawing such exacting lines, though, is unnecessary to determine a Christian's behavior.

increasingly limited. It is an offering of the self *and* what the self has. Simply put, it is costly—and in more than an economic sense.

Limits in Hospitality

The effort—and it is an effort—to be hospitable is sometimes burdensome. And while finitude is not a sin, it is a restriction on the capacity to express the good.[22] Because the capacity (or power) of the host to give hospitality is limited, they must use their position of authority to determine (1) how their gifts are distributed, and (2) when the situation calls for something besides hospitality. When assessing the need for civility and market rules as alternatives to hospitality and gift-giving, several types of limit should be considered:

- *Occupiable Resource Limits:* Occupiable resources are those of space; their limit is the amount of space that can be made available over a given period of time. Thus, for one or two nights, sleeping on the living room couch (in the West) or on a pallet near the door (in some tribal societies) may be perfectly appropriate. More desperately, displaced persons "staying" in tents in an area usually occupied by a garden may be necessary following a natural disaster. Having a "guest" (e.g., a foster child or needy family member) for two or three years, though, may increase the space necessary to host well. Needless to say, there is an opportunity cost; the more used, the less in reserve for other purposes.

- *Site-Specific Limits:* Hospitality is not a gift the recipients can take with them upon departure from the host. They may be able to take the newly formed relationship and some minimal provisions, but the space and reserves of food cannot, obviously, be carried away.

- *Consumable Resource Limits:* Consumable resources are exhaustible.[23] In order to provide hospitality, sufficient food is necessary (at least enough to provide sustenance). While food can be redistributed, prepared in more efficient ways, and served more sparingly, there is a

22. Pohl notes this reality, particularly its overlap with the lack of hospitality within the larger society and the inequitable distribution of resources (Pohl, *Making Room*, 132).

23. A biblical example of a consumable limit was that set by the wise virgins in the parable in Matthew 25. The wise five recognized that to offer a gift of oil to the other five would mean none of the ten would have a sufficient amount. One might counter with a reference to the miracle of the loaves and fishes or that of the widow of Zarephath.

caloric minimum. The supply cannot grow infinitely grow, nor can it be infinitely divided, thus limiting hospitality.

- *Psycho-Social Capacity Limits:* At least as costly to the giver of hospitality as consumption and occupation can be the psycho-social cost of being hospitable. Euphemistically, it is "draining." While it is true that some people thrive on "entertaining" or providing care, even the greatest extrovert has an emotional limit. As Pohl recognizes, hospitality requires "giving a person our full attention," and this is simply impossible to do for everyone in need that one might meet in a world of strangers, a world in which the stranger is generally not met singularly but *en masse*.[24]

- *Boundary Limit by Relationship:* Proximity comes in two forms: geographic and relational. Boundary limits are restrictions upon hospitality established by relational proximity. Obligations of hospitality, obviously, increase directly with geographic proximity. Yet, not everyone who is physically close receives the gift of hospitality. Even more important is relational proximity. One has a greater duty to kin, members of one's face-to-face community (the literal "neighbor"), and to fellow Christians than one does to a casual acquaintance, stranger, or enemy.[25] This does not mean there may not be an obligation, at least for Christians, to the true outsider.

- *Boundary Limit of Reasonable Risk:* Hospitality is always limited to the degree that physical threat is probable. Hospitality is easier when extended to a friend or close acquaintance because (along with other

24. Pohl, "Hospitality."

25. For instance, John Wesley referred to Gal 6:10, 1 Tim 3:12, 1 John 3:10, and James 2: "In the meantime, let all those who are real members of the Church, see that they walk holy and unblamable in all things . . . Show them your faith by your works. Let them see, by the whole tenor of your conversation, that your hope is all laid up above! Let all your words and actions evidence the spirit whereby you are animated! Above all things, let your love abound. Let it extend to every child of man: Let it overflow to every child of God. By this let all men know whose disciples ye are, because you 'love one another'" (Wesley, "Of the Church"). For a description of how the categories of friend, stranger, etc., function, see Thobaben, "Pleased to Make Your Acquaintance": "Wildes' model is ordinal. The three categories, in ascending order of shared values, are strangers, acquaintances, and friends. The categories are not to be understood as having equal ranges or being at equal intervals. Rather, the middle category of acquaintance seems to be the largest, the one used in interactions with most people. The category of stranger is not as common simply because if one interacts often with another, eventually they find some common language (become acquaintances) or begin to avoid one another. The category of friend is small because there are comparatively few in a pluralistic society who genuinely share core beliefs" (Thobaben, "Pleased to Make Your Acquaintance," 427).

reasons) these are persons who are both known and favored. These categories combine to form "trusted." Opening space is much harder when provided for the casual acquaintance or sojourner, although it can be done cautiously. The stranger may receive hospitality only if there is some "testing" of their willingness to abide by appropriate expectations. The enemy, one who is known but unfavored, can receive true hospitality only if the threat is reasonably constrained; even so, there is a high degree of uncertainty about vulnerability.[26] Some persons may forfeit the privilege of hospitality, at least temporarily. This happens when their behavior is predictably that of an enemy (e.g., takes advantage of kindness, willingly harms others). This is the reason that some Christian homeless shelters may exclude someone who simply will not or cannot be self-controlled. An appropriate boundary is created by the likelihood of disproportionate harm.

- *Limit of Compelled Reception*: Hospitality can be limited by a paradoxical response to outside authorities. If housing and food are required by threat of force, or they are granted through taxation, then they are not given as a gift. This threat of force may or may not be just, but either way paying taxes, etc., is not virtuous (even if some opposites like lying on tax forms, hiding income, and so on are vices). Hospitality cannot be compelled and remain true hospitality. Gift-giving is not giving if required by force.

- *Limit of Sold Reception*: Sharing costs with the guest is, sometimes, legitimate, but selling them is not. A nice bed at a hotel and pleasant meal in a restaurant are not immoral, but respectful market exchange is not gift-giving. The word "guest" is used by the so-called "hospitality" industry, but the term "purchaser" is more accurate. The traditional term is being appropriated in order to access previously accumulated cultural capital.

The need (whatever that may mean) of the potential recipient is a necessary but not sufficient cause for the giving of hospitality. Rather, this form of gift-giving properly occurs following an evaluation by the giver and recipient of numerous variables. The giver decides if the "want" of the

---

26. Derrida states: "How can we distinguish between a guest and a parasite. In principle, the difference is straightforward, but for that you need a law . . ." (Derrida, *On Hospitality*, 59). Or, in the more common vernacular, a defining rule is required. A more Christ-like understanding is found in Prov 25:20–22 and Paul's quotation of that passage in Rom 12:20. Even so, while a hospitable person—especially a Christian—may have a higher threshold for tolerating risk, at some point the level of hazard and likelihood of a dangerous event occurring restricts hospitality.

recipient corresponds to a real need, and the possible value of the gift to the recipient is calculated to be positive. The giver then determines, in round terms, the economic and non-economic costs and gains (lost opportunity costs, possible gain through improved reputation, etc.). Added to the assessment for the host is a determination of what risks will be assumed. The giver assesses which relationships are possibly being established, endorsed, or threatened (especially in terms of kinship, socio-political hierarchy, and obligations generated, and/or repaid). Together, then, the needy person becomes the deserving person (with "deserving" emphatically not understood as meaning only those worthy of reward).

Some now in the late-modern West are erroneously asking hospitality to do too much. A balance in how the friend, acquaintance, stranger, and enemy are met is necessary. As stated above, need is necessary but insufficient for the extension of hospitality. What options are available should an evaluation conclude that hospitality is inappropriate, impossible, or even immoral in a given case? Consider again the categories of civility and respectful market exchange.

Civility and Market Exchange as Necessary Complements to Hospitality

No community exists simply to provide unbounded inclusion to others. No community exists that has completely porous boundaries. No community can sustain fully open, unrestricted hospitality. To even attempt such would mean a hosting community would be "bled dry." Quite clearly, not all relationships are, nor should they be, governed by asymmetric, gracious giving. There are many situations in which someone should remain a stranger, be acknowledged as an enemy, or, at best, identified as a casual acquaintance.[27]

Pohl is correct in her observation that "the centrality of hospitality to the social practices of many societies attests to its almost universal importance."[28] However, the practice is simply not sustainable in an

27. As the "other" is identified, and as the situation in which the person is met is being interpreted, that individual is categorized for response. Some in some situations should be engaged primarily in terms of the roles they hold (role identification), not at a deeper, integrative, narrative level (integral identification). The vast majority of people we meet should be identified simply as holders of basic rights (species identification). See Thobaben, *Health-Care Ethics.*

28. Pohl, "Welcoming the Stranger." This does not mean social contract theory has "solved" strangeness. To the contrary, a consequence of liberal (in the philosophical sense) political thought, made quite evident throughout the past century, is how the "other" can so easily be defined as not an equal. Rather than the "other" as a potential

"anonymous society" (such as that of the late-modern West) beyond a fairly low numerical threshold for any given host. Still, when proper hospitality cannot be rendered, the alternative is not simply ignoring the "other" (whether a stranger, or mere acquaintance, or even enemy). Rather, one can be "respectful" in other ways. This means, to the degree possible, one should be civil, or one should facilitate the market, or both.

Such distancing may seem harsh or even impolite; however, it is the exact opposite. Respect for strangers and mere acquaintances, even with minimal civility, allows all (or most) to function in the market and to exercise political and civil rights. Proper market relations formed in just exchange, civility based on equal respect, and gift-giving expressed in hospitality are mutually reinforcing. Without markets, there are very few resources for protecting rights. Without gift-giving, most especially that of hospitality, there are not the covenantal bonds that make one willing to morally value the very idea of "respect." Without civility, there are no means for initiating interactions of the market with strangers, nor boundary protections for those to whom one would offer hospitality.

Clearly, both market rules about economic exchange and political rules about civility are useful at this point in human history. Still, they alone are inevitably unsatisfying. Persons want to be respected as not only members of the species with rights and as individuals holding certain societal roles, but also as persons with life stories. Yet if the State or the market is used to "fill" this need, then inevitably it will result in paternalistic authoritarianism, market pandering, or both (the United States in the early twenty-first century seems to be mixing the two). Christianity provides an alternative.

Nonetheless: The Christian Requirement

Human beings do exist as individuals before the State and participants in civil society. They, as well, monetize exchanges for goods and services, hold jobs, and fulfill other market roles. However, they are also ongoing beings with physical, emotional, and spiritual needs for face-to-face community in which, at least for a moment, their "stories" can make existential sense. For that reason, Christians have an obligation to increasingly offer hospitality. They must do so, though, even while rejecting the grand claims sometimes being made for hospitality and "community." Until heaven, hospitality is

rights-bearer, the unwelcomed is defined as completely out of "humanness." Too often, the stranger is defined as the enemy and the enemy is understood as being a polluter and a pollutant.

and must be a bounded, limited activity. Pohl notes the differences in the models and the resulting interdependence that exists between them:

> Today hospitality, rights, and entitlements are separate, and they should be. Requiring particular commitments or beliefs in order for people to receive material help or protection is very dangerous; some boundaries are properly removed for the sake of fundamental well-being. On the other hand, entitlements and rights are necessary but not sufficient for human well-being. Although persons need provision, they also need connection to living communities; otherwise, they remain anonymous and vulnerable. We need a constant, complex interaction between identity-defining, bounded communities and a larger community with minimal boundaries that offers basic protection of individuals.[29]

Hospitality requires a moral attitude of graciousness—of generosity and even gracefulness. Such an attitude, properly understood, is lacking from both market exchanges and expressions of justice. Rendering shelter to another as "due" is either a matter of civil justice or a fulfillment of a market contract. Sometimes market exchanges of space and food are right; sometimes they are wrong. Sometimes governmental taking through taxation to provide others with food and shelter is right; and, sometimes wrong. In neither of these cases, though, are they like Jesus' offering the shelter of his Father's house or himself as heavenly food. And neither is hospitality in the true sense a market exchange or a matter of justice *per se*. Christians are called to something more, and have more to offer to those who care to accept their gift-giving.

An expanding market and relative civil equality do not mean creating covenantal community ceases to be an obligation for Christians. Believers are not to adhere to the minimal standards of late-modern society, but to exceed them. Neither should they expect the state or market to offer true hospitality. Christians are to be drawn by the divine *telos* and live in a manner consistent with the imitation of Christ. This is the Christian's and the Christian community's task—not the State's nor the unbelievers.

The obligations of Christians are clear:

- First, Christians should obey reasonable rules of civility and of the market. As Taylor notes, "There are virtue terms like 'kindness' or 'generosity' which define the qualities they do partly against the background of the social interchange characteristic of a given society and

---

29. Pohl, *Making Room*, 83.

partly in the light of a certain understanding of personal dedication."[30] Covenantal gift-giving, proper market exchange, and civility are dependent on one another for successful functioning and for the full respect of persons.

- Second, Christians should give to other Christians. The church is a covenantal community as surely as any family or friendship. Christian virtue is, unlike pure utilitarianism, selective. Love is always particular which means it must always be conditioned upon the relationship of the giver and the recipient. How love is actuated depends on whether the potential recipient is friend (or kin, as special form of friend), acquaintance, or something else. *Caritas* or *agape* is not an obligation generated by the intrinsic rights of an individual in need.[31] Hospitality may be a Christian virtue, but this does not mean that the same hospitable actions are always appropriate.

- Third, Christians should provide hospitality for strangers and even enemies, within limits established by the need to have the church sustained. Arguably, this may sometimes be at great risk. Some might assert that the Pauline instruction in Romans 12 commends "heaping hot coals" in the form of such hospitality-giving. However, to claim hospitality is always and unreservedly required—or even acceptable— disregards other commands to specifically render higher levels of concern and care to other Christians (Jas 2:14–17) and to family members (1 Tim 5:8). Further, it denies the need to provide reasonable safety for those already in one's care.

Today, the "need" experienced and subsequently satisfied with sustenance and shelter in an act of hospitality may not be due to desperate deprivation. It might simply be asymmetrically offering another an opportunity for

30. Taylor, *Sources of the Self*, 55.

31. Though certainly open to debate, Matthew 25 refers to brother and sister which in the New Testament almost invariably means those of the church—the new covenantal community. This does not diminish obligation to those of the world who may need hospitality. To the contrary, the covenantal community of the church should have increased capacity. Still, there are differences in the type and level of duty to believers and to those of the world. In other words, there is always "a particularity" in giving hospitality. On this matter, G. K. Chesterton is correct: "[I]n the rationalism of the earlier eighteenth century [exists] that impartiality which is a pompous name for indifference, which is an elegant name for ignorance." Chesterton, "Puritan and Anglican." This greater capacity generated in giving the gift is described by Pohl: "[Hospitality is] certainly a personal practice, but it is never just a personal practice. It is people located in a larger community and dependent on the resources and the insights of the larger community" (Pohl, "Grace Enters with the Stranger").

comfort. Sometimes hospitality is merely a pleasant offering of coffee and cakes. Hospitality in the ancient world, according to Pohl, "was understood as a form of mutual aid, often rigorously observed, and usually associated with caring for the needs of strangers."[32] Yet for ancient and late-modern Christians, it was and is more than good manners or even mutual aid. The hospitality of God allows hospitality to the covenant community—the church—to give to each other which then creates the capacity to render expansive hospitality to those of the world.

Bibliography

Chesterton, G. K. "Puritan and Anglican." *Jolly Journalist*, January 25, 2012. https:// chestertonwritings.blogspot.com/2012/01/puritan-and-anglican.html.

Derrida, Jacques. *On Hospitality: Cultural Memory in the Present*. Palo Alto: Stanford University Press, 2000.

Heal, Felicity. *Hospitality in Early Modern England*. Oxford: Oxford University Press, 1990.

Heuertz, Christopher L., and Christine D. Pohl. *Friendship at the Margins: Discovering Mutuality in Service and Mission*. Grand Rapids: InterVarsity, 2010.

Pohl, Christine D. "Building a Place for Hospitality." In *Christian Reflection: A Series in Faith and Ethics*. Vol. 25, *Hospitality*, edited by Robert B. Kruschwitz, 27–36. Waco: Center for Christian Ethics at Baylor University, 2007.

———. "Grace Enters with the Stranger." *Faith and Leadership*, November 22, 2010. https://www.faithandleadership.com/multimedia/christine-d-pohl-grace-enters-the-stranger.

———. "Hospitality, a Practice and a Way of Life." *Vision: A Journal for Church and Theology* 3, no. 1 (2000) 34–43.

———. *Living into Community: Cultivating Practices That Sustain Us*. Grand Rapids: Eerdmans, 2012.

———. *Making Room: Recovering Hospitality as a Christian Tradition*. Grand Rapids: Eerdmans, 1999.

———. "Welcoming the Stranger." *Sojourners* 28 (1999) 14.

Sawicki, Marianne. "Personal Connections: The Phenomenology of Edith Stein." *Yearbook of the Irish Philosophical Society* (2004) 148–69.

Smith, Adam. *The Theory of Moral Sentiments*. Fairbanks: Gutenberg, 2011.

Stein, Edith. *On the Problem of Empathy*. Vol. 3, *The Collected Works of Edith Stein, Sister Teresa Benedicta of the Cross of Discalced Carmelite*. Translated by Waltraut Stein. Washington, DC: ICS, 1989.

Taylor, Charles. *Sources of the Self*. Cambridge: Harvard University Press, 1992.

Thobaben, James R. *Health-Care Ethics: A Comprehensive Christian Resource*. Grand Rapids: InterVarsity Academic, 2009.

———. "Pleased to Make Your Acquaintance: A Review of Kevin Wm. Wildes' *Moral Acquaintances: Methodology in Bioethics*." *Christian Bioethics* 7, no. 3 (2001) 425–39.

32. Pohl, "Building a Place for Hospitality," 27.

Walzer, Michael. *Spheres of Justice: A Defense of Pluralism and Equality.* New York: Basic Books, 1983.

Wesley, John. "Of the Church." *Wesley Center Online,* 1999. http://wesley.nnu.edu/john-wesley/the-sermons-of-john-wesley-1872-edition/sermon-74-of-the-church.

Wildes, Kevin William. *Moral Acquaintances: Methodology in Bioethics.* South Bend: University of Notre Dame Press, 2000.

Holiness, Separation,
and Hospitality

PETER R. GATHJE

What characterizes the holiness to which disciples of Jesus are called within the practice of hospitality? What is the holiness that sustains the practice of Christian hospitality? In conversation with Christine Pohl's work on hospitality, I will explore a central dimension of biblical holiness in relation to hospitality, namely, separation. Separation as a characteristic of holiness may at first glance seem inimical to hospitality, as separation can be understood as a way to preserve the purity of a specific community. But drawing upon Pohl's writings, a biblical consideration of holiness, and my own experience with offering hospitality, I will argue for a type of transforming holiness that includes a separation that invites and inspires hospitality. My hope is that this discussion will contribute to developing a spirituality of hospitality that reflects the biblical call to holiness.

One might think that Pohl, standing within the Wesleyan tradition, would make explicit the connection between holiness and hospitality. But in her treatment of hospitality, *Making Room: Recovering Hospitality as a Christian Tradition*, she gives scant direct attention to holiness. She does, however, pay significant attention to a "spirituality of hospitality" including the chapter "The Spiritual Rhythms of Hospitality" that connects with holiness. Additionally, in *Friendship at the Margins*, Pohl attends to "A Spirituality Fit for the Margins." There she urges that "we desperately need a robust holiness" within the practice of "friendship on the margins" which includes hospitality.[1] She is clear that the "holiness we need for living on the margins

---

1. Heuertz and Pohl, *Friendship at the Margins*, 124.

comes only as we draw closer to Christ, as we take hold of what he loves and cherishes."[2] In *Living into Community: Cultivating Practices that Sustain Us,* Pohl affirms that being true to God's ways "include[s] both welcoming strangers and living holy lives."[3] Beyond these references, she does not give specific attention to a biblically rooted discussion of holiness in relation to hospitality. Here I hope to tease out the references to holiness that she makes in her discussions of hospitality and develop those in relation to a transforming holiness that includes separation as a key dimension of biblical holiness. I see this transforming holiness as crucial to our growing in holiness in our practice of hospitality.

In *Making Room,* Pohl reminds the reader that "we nurture hospitality as a habit and disposition by telling stories about it."[4] Thus, I will begin with a story of my own.

A Story of Holy Separation

For the past twelve years, I have helped to run Manna House, a place of hospitality in the Catholic Worker tradition in Memphis, Tennessee. I was there early one morning to start the coffee for our guests, most of whom are homeless and all of whom are poor. Four-hundred-forty cups of coffee percolated as I opened my Benedictine prayer book, hoping for some inspiration. "Hospitality," Pohl writes, "is difficult because it involves hard work."[5] The hard work is physical, emotional, and spiritual. On this hot and humid Monday morning in the late summer, the work ahead seemed not simply hard but daunting. I wished I was still in bed.

I turned first to the "Saint of the Day." Perhaps the story of a holy person from the church's tradition would lift my spirits. I was confronted by the "Feast of the Archangels." My heart sank. Archangels? What inspiration could heavenly beings possibly provide for the gritty work of hospitality? After years of graduate studies in theology and ethics, I was not even sure I believed in angels.

I skeptically plowed ahead. Archangels, I read, are messengers from God. This sparked my memory of Hebrews 13:1–2, important in the tradition of Christian hospitality. "Keep on loving each other as brothers and

---

2. Heuertz and Pohl, *Friendship at the Margins,* 125.

3. Pohl, *Living into Community,* 169.

4. Pohl, *Making Room,* 173.

5. Pohl, *Making Room,* 170.

sisters. Do not forget to entertain strangers, for by so doing some people have entertained angels without knowing it."[6]

I smiled. In about an hour, there would be a band of angels coming to Manna House. They would come for coffee, showers, and clothing. They would come for hospitality. My spirit lifted somewhat. I turned to the Psalms for the morning and waited for the coffee to finish brewing and other volunteers to arrive.

When we open Manna House each morning, we invite our guests to pray with us. It is not a requirement. It began when guests saw us praying together before opening, and they asked us to pray with them. On this morning, with angels on my mind, I led the prayer. I invited guests and volunteers alike to consider the passage from Hebrews and to turn to the person next to them and say, "Good morning, angel." This led to much laughter as we greeted each other as "angel." We ended our prayer and the morning began with its usual mixture of organized chaos.

About two hours later, I was approached by a volunteer who said that a guest wanted to see me. This usually means a guest has a special request, one which another volunteer has already denied and that I will probably have to deny, as well. I find saying "no" hard, but without limits it is difficult to sustain hospitality. So, I wasn't too happy when I approached Stephen, who had arrived just a few minutes before. He had not been present when we opened and greeted each other during prayer as "angel."

"What do you want?" I asked with some impatience in my voice.

"Nothing," he replied. This further exasperated me.

"Then why did you want to see me?"

"I have something for you," he said with a smile. He handed me a small red velvet purse, about the size of a business card. I thanked him. Stephen is a bit mentally ill, and I wanted to be kind in response to his gift.

"This is a nice purse," I said, trying not to be too patronizing.

"No, you idiot," he said. "Open it!"

So I opened the small red purse and inside I saw a thin piece of cardboard. Pinned to the cardboard was a small angel. On the cardboard were the words, "Guardian angel: Wear an angel on your shoulder, to guide you through the days and nights, and brighten your life." My knees buckled. My eyes filled with tears.

"Thank you, Stephen. Thank you. You don't know how much this means to me."

Stephen simply responded, "I do, and you're welcome," and walked away. When angels appear in the Bible, they often say "do not be afraid" and

---

6. All Scripture references use the New Revised Standard Version.

then they share amazing, life-changing news from God. I was trembling, holding the gift Stephen had given me. My narrow, intellectual, far too rationalist faith was shaken. I felt like one of those self-satisfied characters in a Flannery O'Connor story who had just been smacked upside the head with the brutal force of the Holy.

Now, several years later, I still draw from this story as I practice hospitality. I remember how within hospitality the holy presence of God is known, most often through those who come as guests. And each time I remember how I felt—like my namesake Peter, who said to Jesus after experiencing God's presence in him, "Go away from me, Lord, for I am a sinful man!" (Luke 5:8).

Biblical Holiness as Transformative

This story speaks to one kind of separation in relation to holiness, a type of separation often found in the biblical stories of encounter with the Holy God. God as Holy (or an angelic messenger of God) astounds us with an unexpected call. We may call this a "transforming holiness." In transforming holiness, God cuts us away from a previous way of life and call us to a new way of life. In the midst of the ordinary, there is the sudden extraordinary demand of God to care for the vulnerable. Transforming holiness separates us *from* what was and separates us *for* what will be in accordance with God's way of life.

Such a transforming holiness can be seen when Moses encounters God in the burning bush and receives the call to lead the Israelites out of slavery. In Exodus 3:5, as Moses approaches the burning bush, God tells him, "Come no closer! Remove the sandals from your feet, for the place on which you are standing is holy ground." God will respond to the cry of the Israelites through Moses.

This transforming holiness is also evident when the angel Gabriel appears to Mary to announce her pregnancy, even though she was a virgin. Gabriel proclaims to her, "The Holy Spirit will come upon you, and the power of the Most High will overshadow you; therefore the child to be born will be holy; he will be called Son of God" (Luke 1:35). God will bring salvation through a man born of a woman on the margins. I experienced this transforming holiness at Manna House as Stephen's angelic gift forcefully revealed God's presence, cutting through my conventionally safe faith and revealing how God truly does come through the marginalized stranger. Pohl points to this transforming holiness known in hospitality when she writes,

The holiness we need for living on the margins comes only as we draw close to Christ, as we take hold of what he loves and cherishes and as we take on more of his heart and mind. The gracious surprise is that this transformation is not burdensome but a gift of freedom and grace and an opportunity to become part of God's goodness. Our holiness then is an eruption of God's goodness and beauty in the world.[7]

The transforming holiness found in hospitality has several distinctive and defining features. First, it emphasizes that we encounter the holy God when we care for the vulnerable. Within hospitality is the biblically rooted conviction that we welcome the "Holy One" (Luke 1:35; Mark 1:24; Acts 2:27, 3:14), the Christ, as we welcome the vulnerable stranger. This presence of Christ in the stranger is a theme that Pohl engages often in her writings; and this is no surprise, given that it is a major theme in the history of Christian hospitality.[8] The classic biblical text supporting this claim is Matthew 25:31–46, wherein Jesus identifies with the hungry, the thirsty, the stranger, the naked, the sick, and the imprisoned. Pohl comments on this identification, "Those who have welcomed strangers and have met the needs of persons in distress have welcomed Jesus himself, and are themselves welcomed into the Kingdom."[9] Jesus as "the Holy One of God" brings into our lives "the shocking assault of a loving invitation to whomever."[10]

Jesus' identification with the marginalized stands within a consistent biblical theme of encountering the Holy God in the "other." God as Other reveals Godself in the stranger, the vulnerable, and the rejected. God makes our treatment of such persons the very test of faithfulness to God—and the very place of God's gracious revelation. Abraham and Sarah welcome angelic visitors (Genesis 18); Exodus, Leviticus, and Deuteronomy all command that "you shall not wrong or oppress a resident alien, for you were aliens in the land of Egypt" (cf. Exod 22:21; Lev 19:33; Deut 24:18). Within the Wisdom literature, the prophetic calls to justice for the poor are a constant reminder that God hears the call of the poor, and that how the poor are treated is how God is treated (e.g., Isaiah 58; Jer 5:26–28; Amos 2:6–8, 5:10, 12; Mic 2:1–2; 1 Kings 21; Pss 9:18, 10:14, 17, 18, 12:5, 14:6, 35:10, 41:1, 68:5,6, 82:3,4, 103:6, 113:7–9, 138:6, 140:12; Prov 14:31, 17:5, 19:17, 22:23, 28:27). These texts and others point to how, in transforming holiness, God is met in those placed outside of the usual social boundaries.

---

7. Pohl, *Making Room*, 67.

8. Pohl, *Making Room*, 16–58, 67–69.

9. Pohl, *Making Room*, 21–22.

10. Mannoia and Thorsen, *The Holiness Manifesto*, 65.

Second, this transforming holiness emphasizes personal conversion. God's holy presence in the stranger changes our lives. As Pohl notes, "The gifts of hospitality do not flow in one direction only; hospitality is a two-way street."[11] Hospitality is not dispensing charity from a position of superiority. Recognizing that God comes to us through the guest, "we welcome that person with some sense that God is already at work in his or her life . . .[and thus] we are more sensitive to what the guest is bringing to us, to what God might be saying or doing through him or her."[12] By practicing this "hospitality from the margins," we learn again and again of our own need for God's hospitality and we stand in solidarity with those whom we serve.[13] Each of us needs God's welcome because we are estranged from God and each other through our sinfulness. We only offer to others what we have received from God. In this conversion, we seek to welcome others as Christ has welcomed us (Rom 15:7).

Furthermore, Pohl recognizes that practicing hospitality "requires us to reevaluate what counts as most important in our lives."[14] As we stand in solidarity with those we welcome, we come to see the need in our own lives—our need for simplicity, for community, for acknowledging our frailties, failures, and needs, and for living with humility. All of these values involve changes in our lives, which are rooted in our experience of the holy God through our guests. They become our teachers, with hospitality as a school for transforming holiness.

This is the transformative holiness I experienced in hospitality with Stephen. I had come to serve Stephen, and yet it was Stephen who offered me the very presence of God. And this has happened on many subsequent mornings: a guest brings God's gracious presence in a word or action that cracks open my heart and brings me into a deeper relationship with God and keeps me going in the practice of hospitality. In this experience of hospitality, I come to know the joyful invitation of God into fullness of life. I am also continually leaning into the grace of God as I face the ways I need to repent of my own sins—my superficial faith, impatience, racist prejudices, facile judgments, and complicity in what Dorothy Day called "this filthy rotten system."

Third, such transforming holiness also separates us from the usual social order in which the stranger is feared, denigrated, and excluded, as "Christian hospitality has always had a subversive, countercultural

11. Pohl, *Making Room*, 72.
12. Pohl, *Making Room*, 68.
13. Pohl, *Making Room*, 104.
14. Pohl, *Making Room*, 179.

dimension."[15] Hospitality points to "a different system of valuing and an alternate model of relationships" in which those whose dignity is denied are instead treated with respect.[16] This difference in assessing value rests upon a theological claim that Matthew 25:31–46 emphasizes the presence of God in the stranger: "The conviction that all human beings [are] marked with the image of God . . . bearing God's image establishes for every person a fundamental dignity which cannot be undermined either by wrongdoing or neediness."[17]

The contrast in values between honoring the dignity of the stranger rather than denying their humanity means that the longer I practice hospitality, the more separate and alienated I become in relation to the way things are in American society. Pohl points to the way in which hospitality comes to partake of the liminality and marginality of those who are served.[18] Through the guests, I learn of the injustices they suffer that include police harassment, imprisonment, lack of medical care, neglect of those who suffer from mental illness, and exploitative landlords. I become more aware of how government programs that offer lifelines to the poor are easily cut while military spending and tax breaks for the wealthiest are maintained or expanded. I see how death comes all too often and early for those on the streets, from accidents, violence, or illness due to exposure to the elements. In one year, we lost more than ten of our guests to death; none of them died from "natural causes."

Through offering hospitality, I have learned that the streets are harsh and violent and our society is mean-spirited. As I experience God's presence in our guests, I also see the absence of God in the evils that plague their lives. In all of this, I am called away from the mainstream and put into resistance to a church and society which are at best indifferent and at worst violently hostile to the poor and homeless. When the stranger is welcomed, we encounter the holy presence of a surprising and gracious God who separates us from the usual order of things and calls us to a new order rooted in justice defined by a special concern for the most vulnerable. As someone from the Catholic Worker remarked, "Hospitality is resistance."[19]

---

15. Pohl, *Making Room*, 61.

16. Pohl, *Making Room*, 61–62.

17. Pohl, *Making Room*, 64–65.

18. Pohl, *Making Room*, 105–7, 170–71.

19. Pohl, *Making Room*, 61.

Transforming or Conforming?

This transforming holiness stands in sharp contrast with what I call a "conforming holiness" that emphasizes the presence of God in purity, rather than in persons. Pohl hints at this conforming holiness when she writes of the need to not "confuse delicacy with holiness. Our protection is not in becoming prim, prudish or obsessed with rules."[20] Conforming holiness separates for the purpose of creating a "pure" community, defined by internal conformity to purity laws, rather than a community defined by relationship with people on the margins. Conforming holiness engenders hostility towards strangers rather than hospitality.

The contrast between a transforming and a conforming holiness reflects two streams of holiness in the Christian tradition and biblical interpretation. In the Old Testament, the Hebrew word *quodesh* is most often translated into English as "holy" or "sacred." This Hebrew word carries the meaning of separate or being set apart for a special purpose. But set apart in what way and for what purpose? Is holiness as separation part of God's graciously transforming liberation, a separation from a deadly or deadening way of life, and thus a separation for a new, more deeply human way of life centered on love, shared in community and practiced in hospitality? Or is holiness as separation a call to conformity, an incarceration within a sacred order, a closed system of purity and domination, practiced in hostility toward the "impure" reinforced by divine legitimation? The Bible can be drawn upon to form a transforming holiness that leads to liberation, life, and love. But the Bible can also be drawn upon to develop a hostile conforming holiness that undergirds empire, domination, and established order.

Conforming holiness finds some biblical support when holiness as separation is emphasized as standing apart in purity, away from those who are unclean. For instance, Leviticus 10 urges the Israelites to "make a distinction between the holy and the profane, and between the unclean and the clean." In the New Testament, the concern for purity is seen around sexual matters, particularly in Paul's letters (1 Thess 4:3–5; Rom 13:13–14; 1 Cor 6:13; Eph 5:3). Such texts in both the Old and New Testaments have become the basis for a view of holiness in which being pure and being holy are seen as almost equivalent. When purity is defined primarily in matters of sexual and personal morality, separation from those who are not "pure" becomes necessary in order to maintain a closed and holy (pure) community.

In *Come Out My People*, attorney and academic Wes Howard-Brook helps to place these contending visions of holiness-as-separation as part of

---

20. Heuertz and Pohl, *Friendship at the Margins*, 124.

a larger tension in biblical interpretation, between what he calls a "religion of creation" and a "religion of empire."[21] Although his focus is not limited to holiness, these divergent accounts point to two visions of holiness and two different ways of separation. The religion of creation is about human liberation grounded in God as creator; the religion of empire is about human domination grounded in a claim to the divine blessing of the established order.

> We can understand one of the Bible's religions to be grounded in *the experience of and ongoing relationship with the Creator God,* and leading to covenantal bond between that God and God's people for the blessing and abundance of *all* people and *all* creation. The other, while sometimes *claiming* to be grounded in that same God, is actually a human invention used to justify and legitimate attitudes and behaviors that provide blessing and abundance for *some* at the *expense of others.*[22]

This distinction has deep implications for our understanding of holiness-as-separation:

The religion of creation centers holiness on relationship, on the presence of God in the people (in particular the poor, the widow, and the orphan), and in places of encounter with God in creation—that is, God as Other. Such a religious vision is open to and invites hospitality. We encounter the presence of God as we welcome others.

The religion of empire is hierarchical and centers holiness in the temple and the Torah, both of those being controlled by the king and the priestly elite. For this religion of empire, hostility rather than hospitality greets those outside the center.

In the religion of creation, holiness affirms the otherness of God met in those who are "other," and so affirms the centrality of hospitality in how God opens us up to new possibilities, to deeper community, to shared life.

In the religion of empire, holiness functions as social control and is enforced by violence. The "other" is a threat to the divine order. King, temple, and Torah, focused on purity, represent God, and obedience to them is obedience to God.

In the religion of creation, God as "Other" is outside of human control; God confronts our pretensions to completion and perfection, and thus continually undercuts self-righteousness. God is always calling us toward inclusion, justice, and peace.

21. Howard-Brook, *Come Out My People,* 6. The comparisons of creation and empire are drawn from Howard-Brook, *Come Out My People,* 3–10.

22. Howard-Brook, *Come Out My People,* 7.

In the religion of empire, God is reduced to a god, one which is controllable through proper ritual. Service to this god or gods is compatible with and endorses the aims of empire, including domination of others.

Holiness is thus contested within these rival biblical interpretations of God and religion. Howard-Brook sees Leviticus as presenting an alternative to the Ezra-Nehemiah project associated with the religion of empire.[23] Leviticus has Exodus as its starting point, the great story of "coming out of Egypt." The books of Exodus and Leviticus, Howard-Brook argues, took shape after the exile in Babylon, and thus act to counter the Ezra-Nehemiah project. For Howard-Brook, the center of Leviticus is chapter 19, which focuses on social justice as crucial to what we have called a transforming holiness. God as Holy calls us into right relationship with others. And this right relationship with others includes right relationship with God's creation. Sabbath is for people, animals, and the land (Leviticus 24). We flourish insofar as we live in right relationship with each other and God's creation (Leviticus 26). Our separation is thus not about placing ourselves above others, but rather being graciously placed in right relationship with others through right relationship with God.

Stories such as the Ruth narrative illustrate how separation and hospitality come together in the religion of creation, standing against a notion of self-righteous purity as the basis for holiness. Ruth is a foreigner who, in her vulnerability, follows God's call to separate herself from her own people to join with Naomi and her people, the Israelites. This separation in turn leads to Ruth's marriage to Boaz, an Israelite, and from this line comes David and (in New Testament genealogy) Jesus. The story of Ruth thus stands in contrast to and challenges the prohibitions against marriage of foreigners as urged by Ezra and Nehemiah. Ruth's separation reflects a transforming holiness rooted in compassionate love and hospitality. Ruth's faithful relationship with Naomi affirms their shared vulnerability; and thus compassion permeates the relationships between both Ruth and Naomi and between Ruth and Boaz. And present within the story is the practice of gleaning, itself a practice of compassionate justice set out in Leviticus (23:22).

The story of Ruth stands with other biblical stories in which separation means faithfulness to God's call into community and compassion. Seen from the perspective of a religion of creation, Israel's story involves separation *from* religion of empire and separation *into* a community of compassionate justice. Israel leaves Egypt to become a people whose holiness is distinguished by welcome of the stranger, and practices such as gleaning,

---

23. Howard-Brook, *Come Out My People*, 273–78.

Sabbath, and Jubilee. This is the vision of separation as transforming holiness joined with hospitality from which the prophets and Jesus draw.

This contest of interpretations regarding God and holiness continues into the New Testament. Howard-Brook argues that Jesus as Holy embodies and teaches the religion of creation.[24] Jesus' opponents are those who seek a holiness defined by separation that isolates and elevates "holy people" above sinners. Jesus in his questions and actions, as when he heals the man with the "withered hand," challenges a conforming holiness. Keeping the Sabbath was part of the "holiness code" in Leviticus; yet Jesus asks, "Which is lawful on the Sabbath: to do good or to do evil, to save life or to kill?" (Mark 3:4). Is the purpose of holiness as envisioned by Leviticus and the prophets to open us to hospitality, to the creation of compassionate community, or to an exclusionary self-righteousness? Is holiness intended to heal or to harm? The silence of Jesus' opponents gives their answer; Jesus' answer is to heal the man.

Jesus reflects a transforming holiness as he draws upon the prophetic tradition to take on the Temple, the Torah, and the ruling elite as defined by the religion of empire. Jesus replaces the Temple "with the gathered community of discipleship as a place of prayer and spring of divine mercy."[25] Jesus offers in the Sermon on the Mount (and elsewhere) a Torah that is defined by "transforming initiatives," which break out of a cycle of sin and violence and lead instead to wholeness, a maturity in which we grow into what God has intended us to become.[26] The ruling elite is replaced by a community of discipleship grounded in God-as-creator that gratefully shares daily bread as it also gratefully shares God's graciousness.[27]

For the Apostle Paul, the transforming holiness and separating impetus of Jesus' life and teaching continues. One place this is evident is in Paul's use of the Greek word *hagioi*, meaning "holy ones." Those who are "holy" are not defined by their own moral superiority. Instead their separateness expresses their transformation, "their experience of the risen Christ 'come out' from empire and committed, through baptism, to participate in the death and resurrection of the One who is now exalted above all else as 'Lord.'"[28] Another example is his famous wrestling with "the Law." Paul affirms a "law in Christ" defined by our relationships with others as grounded in

24. Howard-Brook, *Come Out My People*, 397.

25. Howard-Brook, *Come Out My People*, 404.

26. Howard-Brook, *Come Out My People*, 414. Also see Stassen and Gushee, *Kingdom Ethics*.

27. Howard-Brook, *Come Out My People*, 415.

28. Howard-Brook, *Come Out My People*, 456.

relationship with God. We are to welcome others as we have been welcomed in Christ (Rom 15:7). He stands against a law that is used to control others or that affirms control over God.

> Paul sees how Torah has become an instrument for collabora-
> tion between the Jerusalem temple elite and the series of empires
> that have dominated God's people since the time of Babylon . . .
> he roots his radical, anti-imperial gospel in the scriptural narra-
> tive, beginning with YHWH's first call to "come out."[29]

Paul thus reflects Jesus' vision of a transforming holiness that urges a separa-
tion from that which is exclusive and imperial and to that which is inclusive and liberating. This resistance to empire takes place as we side with those who are harmed by empire; and in doing so, we seek to create a hospitable community that affirms life organized justly for the well-being of all. As biblical scholar Kent Bower points out, Jesus' vision of holiness moves from boundary maintenance or separation-as-purity to holiness as boundary-crossing and the offering of hospitality, a separation that comes as the result of the practice of costly love.[30]

Why Do Disciples of Jesus Need a Transforming Holiness?

The tensions between transforming holiness that separates us for compas-
sion and hospitality and conforming holiness that separates us into a hostile self-righteousness continue in Christian life today. It is the tension Pohl hints at when she contrasts the prim, prudish, rule-obsessed holiness with a "robust holiness."[31] She rightly urges that a "robust holiness" is needed that takes evil seriously and that is rooted in relationship with Christ: "The holi-
ness we need is simultaneously strong and tender. It is a holiness of heart that can experience genuine horror at evil, but also see human beings for what God intended them to be. It is a holiness that trusts God for redemption and therefore can sustain hope."[32]

Why do we need such a holiness today? In *Unclean: Meditations on Purity, Hospitality, and Mortality*, Richard Beck further unravels the tension between these two types of holiness while stressing the need for holiness in Christian life today. He begins with an analysis of the psychology of disgust,

---

29. Howard-Brook, *Come Out My People*, 458.

30. Bower, *Holiness and Ecclesiology in the New Testament*, 70–75.

31. Pohl, *Friendship at the Margins*, 124–25.

32. Heuertz and Pohl, *Friendship at the Margins*, 125.

an emotion which "guard[s] the border between the holy and the profane." What he calls "sociomoral disgust" centers this revulsion on "moral and social judgments" in which we separate ourselves from those who are "unclean," who disgust us.[33] How contemporary Christians address moral issues related to the marginalized and the stranger (such as poverty, homosexuality, and immigration) is intimately tied to how poor people, homosexuals, and immigrants are viewed—either "holy" or "unclean," either acceptable or disgusting. Beck argues that in responding to those issues, liberal Christians tend to discount holiness as repressive. Holiness ceases to exist as a category even worth exploring. Meanwhile, conservative Christians restrict holiness to a purity that distinguishes between the worthy and unworthy poor, "loving the sinner but hating the sin" of homosexuality, and demanding that immigrants "follow the law" of the empire.[34]

Beck argues that without the pursuit of the holy, Christian faith becomes "flat," devoid of the transforming Otherness of God. We might say that such a "flat" Christianity has neither the resources to confront evil (both personal and institutional) nor to live out a radically transformative redemption in relation to Christ. Instead, "flat" church life is little more than a social gathering, with some attention to selected social concerns as the sacred collapses into human life. Beck sees this as typical within those liberal churches which function as "humanitarian, social action group[s]."[35]

Besides lacking attention to the holy, such churches also reject what they see as the alternative, "a stigmatizing church that carves the world into 'clean' and 'unclean.'"[36] In such a stigmatizing church, which Beck identifies with conservatives, the holy-as-separation becomes a drive to conforming purity that excludes, marginalizes, and oppresses others. Such a holiness seeks to preserve the church as the sacred, as a pure realm set apart from ordinary human life. This gets reflected socially in either calls to strategic withdrawal such as in Rod Dreher's *The Benedict Option* or attempts to make the nation also reflect such purity as a "Christian nation." Such a church and its politics embody what we have identified as a conforming holiness.

Beck's analysis suggests the need for a holiness that is neither ignored nor straightjacketed into narrow exclusion. This is the holiness I have sought to describe as transformative. Such holiness is intimately tied into hospitality, since the holy God is encountered in the stranger, in those our society defines as "unclean." It recognizes that God's "Otherness" is known

33. Beck, *Unclean*, 15, 19.

34. Beck, *Unclean*, 60–62.

35. Beck, *Unclean*, 190–191.

36. Beck, *Unclean*, 191.

in those who are "other." God breaks the social judgment of the marginal-ized as God identifies with them and calls us to enter into relationship with them. And in this relationship there is personal conversion as those served are not approached as either the objects of a social welfare bureaucracy or of a "salvation" imposed by the pure and saved. Rather, those offering hospital-ity are called to a change of heart.

When Stephen gave me the guardian angel pin, he was acting as a mes-senger of God. I was evangelized by Stephen. My liberal "flat" Christianity was challenged by the holy God acting in Stephen. In the practice of hos-pitality, I am not engaging in charitable "humanitarian social action," nor am I "holier than thou" as I dispense divine (or other) favors that I possess to those who are "less fortunate." Instead, there is a transforming holiness within hospitality in which I am challenged, through those who have been marginalized, by God as Holy Other.

Transforming holiness affirms that we are "undone" in our encounter with the Holy God.[37] Pohl reflects this being "undone" as she describes how the practice of hospitality reveals our brokenness, weakness, and frailty, along with our need for God's grace.[38] The encounter with God in hospital-ity is transformative as the relationship between guests and hosts reveals that we are both vulnerable and sinners, and that we are both in need of God's saving grace. This is what I experienced that morning with Stephen. This is what happens with regularity in the practice of hospitality.

Transforming holiness is ultimately grounded and confirmed in Jesus whose holiness led him to be executed "outside the gate." Transformative holiness follows Jesus into a life in which we are separated from a life of so-cial conformity and comfort and separated for new life in him, the Kingdom of God. This is neither the liberal "flatness" nor the conservative narrowness of which Beck wrote. Rather, in writing of mission, Orlando Costas might well have been writing of this transformative holiness.

> The suffering of Jesus outside the gate implies a new place of salvation wherein the center of religious activity was moved to the periphery. Salvation lies outside the gates of cultural, ideo-logical, political, and socio-economic walls that surround our religious compounds and shape the structure of Christendom. The death of Jesus outside the gate implies also a fuller under-standing of mission. Since Jesus died outside the gate, mission has become the crossing of the walls and gates of our secured and comfortable compounds, the continuous movement toward

---

37. Sproul, *Holiness of God,* 28.

38. Pohl, *Making Room,* 117–19.

him to bear the abuse he endured for the world. Mission is crossing frontiers, geographic, political, social, economical, which lie
beyond the center of power.[39]

Jesus' transformative holiness moves us to the periphery, to those who have
been excluded and rejected; and hospitality is one important place where we
may join in this transformative holiness.

In his commentary on the rule of St. Benedict, Adalbert deVogüé
notes the relationship between the seemingly disparate categories of separation and hospitality.

Separation and hospitality are, therefore, two manifestations of
the same love: following Christ and receiving Christ. The following draws us out of the world, but there again he comes to
us under the appearances of those who are in the world, and we
receive him. Then the love which has provoked the separation is
verified in hospitality.[40]

We learn in hospitality that God-as-Holy does not call us into a life that
simply confirms a comfortable lifestyle. Separation happens as the Holy
God calls us into a transformed life in which we recognize our vulnerability, confront our own complicity in injustice, and enter in to compassionate community and the struggle for justice with the oppressed. This is
the robust holiness to which Pohl points. And as she has made clear in all
of her writings, hospitality and friendship at the margins open us to such
a transformed life. Hospitality is an invitation to what Alan Krieder calls
"holy nonconformity."[41] Thus, transforming holiness and hospitality are
intimately connected in our lives through the graciousness of the Holy God
who, as Other, comes to us through the other.

Bibliography

Beck, Richard. *Unclean: Meditations on Purity, Hospitality, and Mortality*. Eugene, OR:
    Cascade, 2011.
Brower, Kent, and Andy Johnson, eds. *Holiness and Ecclesiology in the New Testament*.
    Grand Rapids: Eerdmans, 2007.
Costas, Orlando. *Christ Outside the Gate: Mission Beyond Christendom*. Eugene, OR:
    Wipf and Stock, 2005.
Heuertz, Christopher L., and Christine D. Pohl. *Friendship at the Margins: Discovering
    Mutuality in Service and Mission*. Grand Rapids: InterVarsity, 2010.

39. Costas, *Christ Outside the Gates*, 188–94.

40. deVogüé, *The Rule of Saint Benedict*, 261–62.

41. Krieder, *Social Holiness*, 28.

Howard-Brook, Wes. *Come Out My People: God's Call Out of Empire in the Bible and Beyond*. Maryknoll: Orbis, 2010.

Kreider, Alan. *Social Holiness: A Way of Living for God's Nation*. Eugene, OR: Wipf and Stock, 2008.

Mannoia, Kevin W., and Don Thorsen. *The Holiness Manifesto*. Grand Rapids: Eerdmans, 2008.

Pohl, Christine D. *Living into Community: Cultivating Practices That Sustain Us*. Grand Rapids: Eerdmans, 2012.

———. *Making Room: Recovering Hospitality as a Christian Tradition*. Grand Rapids: Eerdmans, 1999.

Sproul, R. C. *The Holiness of God*. Carol Stream: Tyndale, 1985.

deVogüé, Adalbert. *The Rule of Saint Benedict: A Doctrinal and Spiritual Commentary*. Translated by J. B. Hasbrouck. Kalamazoo: Cistercian, 1983.

Making Hospitality Ordinary
Living into Liturgical Seasons

JESSICA A. WROBLESKI

"A life of hospitality begins in worship, with a recognition of God's grace and generosity," writes Christine Pohl in *Making Room: Recovering Hospitality as a Christian Tradition*.[1] While here she is referring more to a basic posture of gratitude and love than to a church assembly *per se*, it stands to reason that a community's liturgy—its "public work" of prayer and worship, as well as its broader engagement with the world—plays an important role in the formation of its practice of hospitality.[2] Not only the reasons for gathering as a community ("why"), but also the form that such gathering takes ("how") can shape the corporate identity of those who come together for prayer, service, and fellowship. The question of "who are *we*?"—not simply as a collection of individuals, but as a body—often can be answered by looking at what we do *together*. In a university context, for example, a way of being in the world and a sense of identity are formed through both the daily tasks of teaching and learning and through the celebration of particular traditions around sports, graduation, or events marking the beginning or end of the school year.

1. Pohl, *Making Room*, 172.

2. The term "liturgy" is taken from the Greek *leitourgia*, which can be translated "public work" or "work of the people," and can refer to any ritualized form of public gathering. Liturgy can be highly scripted and formal, or it may consist of a very simple "order of worship." For traditions that follow a lectionary, certain elements of the liturgy, such as spoken or sung responses and acclamations, will vary throughout the year in accordance with the text for a given season or celebration, but from year to year there is a standard pattern or cycle of the seasons (Advent, Christmas, Ordinary Time, Lent, Easter, etc.), much like those of the natural world.

In a similar way, as Christians, our weekly and seasonal rituals not only shape our habits, but also our way of seeing the world and of finding our place within it. A persistent theme throughout Pohl's work on Christian hospitality is the idea that the practice of offering welcome (like other practices that cultivate and sustain community) is best understood as a habit which is so thoroughly integrated into the life of a person or community that it becomes second nature—simply an outgrowth of who they are rather than a burdensome effort or even a conscious decision. Pohl explains that "[i]n general, practices are most powerful when they are not noticed, when they are simply an expression of who we are and what we do, a way of being in the world and relating to one another that seems 'natural'" as "the ordinary, taken-for-granted dynamics of good relationships."[3] Like the waning and waxing moon or the changing seasons, those whose character has been formed by the practice of hospitality can be counted on to open themselves to the needs of others in a way that appears perfectly natural throughout the seasons of their lives

And yet at the same time Pohl is also profoundly attentive to the challenges of practicing hospitality and the necessity of deliberate "spiritual rhythms" in order to sustain it.[4] Drawing upon her insights, this essay will argue that the seasons of the Liturgical Year—and in particular, the period known as Ordinary Time—offer both a communal structure and a theological symbol for living into these spiritual rhythms in ways that are deep and dynamic.[5] I'd like to suggest that recognizing the ways that life presents us with constant movement as well as discernible patterns can help to discern and navigate tensions at the limits of hospitality. Furthermore, linking these patterns to the framework of liturgical seasons can bring greater meaning to both our sacrifice and our celebration by identifying them with the life of Christ.

Scholars of liturgy are generally quick to point out that the designation of "Ordinary Time" for the periods of the Church Year between Epiphany and Ash Wednesday and from Pentecost until the first Sunday of Advent

3. Pohl, *Living into Community*, 6.

4. See particularly chapter 9, "The Spiritual Rhythms of Hospitality" in Pohl, *Making Room*, 170–87.

5. For those unfamiliar with the structure of the Liturgical Year, I refer here to the annual cycle observed by many Christian traditions which celebrates Jesus' birth, life and ministry, passion and resurrection, establishment of the church, and second coming in glory. The observance of this pattern of liturgical seasons—Advent (beginning in December), Christmas, a period of Ordinary Time, Lent, Good Friday and the Easter holidays and season, Pentecost, and a long period of Ordinary Time from early summer through November—offers the opportunity to see each year as renewed participation in the story and work of Christ.

is easily misunderstood in English due to the term's association with that which is plain, mundane, and commonplace. In the context of Ordinary Time as *Tempus per annum*—the "season of the year"—this term refers not to "ordinariness" in this sense, but to that which occurs according to a regular order or pattern; that is, an *ordo*.[6] Nonetheless, the customary (i.e., ordinary) sense of the English vernacular is also valuable to maintain as we think about the spiritual rhythms of hospitality. Indeed, the *ordo* or pattern of Ordinary Time provides an important foundation for spiritual growth through the year and a structure for thinking about the spiritual rhythms of the practice of hospitality—precisely because it invites us to welcome and receive the extraordinary within the routines of everyday life. Though there may be tempting reasons to dismiss the Ordinary/ordinary times of life or see them as incidental to the church's social ministry, the cycles of the liturgy offer a rich resource for growth in the meaning and practice of hospitality.

The Extraordinary in the Ordinary

As Ted A. Smith acknowledges in an essay on "The Fullness of Ordinary Time," many Christians tend to think of this season as "a kind of liturgical leftover" in which nothing in particular happens: there are no big events in the story of Jesus' incarnation, death, and resurrection, no Advent candles or Christmas pageants, no special Lenten observances or Easter celebrations.[7] For this reason, Smith notes, congregations are often inclined to give special attention to civic and cultural holidays (e.g., Independence Day, Mothers' Day) or church events such as Stewardship Sunday or Youth Sunday as a way to break the "monotony" of this period. "After all," writes Joyce Ann Zimmerman, "counting Sundays using ordinals as names isn't too stimulating for the religious imagination."[8] While Zimmerman's observation may hold true for human imagination in general, it is no doubt intensified in our media-saturated culture hungry for extraordinary events worthy of our scarce attention. Is there anything distinctive or worth paying attention to among those many Ordinary weeks? Does it really matter whether it's the

---

6. See, e.g., Johnson, "*Tempus per annum*," 153. There is also an association with ordinal numbers, as the Sundays of this period are counted throughout the summer and fall. In the Roman Catholic *Lectionary for Mass*, these are designated the "Sundays of the Year."

7. Smith, "The Fullness of Ordinary Time," 3.

8. Zimmerman, "Editor Notes," 191.

sixth or fourteenth or twenty-sixth Ordinary Sunday? Is this simply "vacant" time within the Church Year, as some have suggested?[9]

Quite to the contrary, Smith suggests that the view of this period as leftover or vacant time arises from forgetfulness of history and ignorance of the theology of Ordinary Time that celebrates "no *particular* aspect of the mystery of Christ" but rather "the mystery in all its fullness."[10] Pierre Jounel has written that "the thirty-four Sundays per annum . . . represent the ideal Christian Sunday, without any further specification. That is, each of them is a Lord's Day in its pure state as presented to us in the Church's tradition."[11] In fact, as a matter of historical development, the early Christian celebration of the Lord's Day on the first day of the week significantly preceded the development of other observances. Even important feasts such as Easter or Pentecost "did not displace Sunday as the first feast of Christian sacred time . . . The Sundays of Ordinary Time were rather the first rhythm of the Christian calendar, the days that oriented all others . . . not so much the leftovers of sacred time as the coals that feasts and seasons fan into flames."[12] Indeed, Mark Searle argues that Sunday is not simply the heart of the Liturgical Year, but also the foundation of how a community envisions Christian life as a whole—"as something freeing or as a burden of obligation resentfully borne"[13]—and so it is worth paying attention to how we experience and imagine these Sundays either as something to endure on the way to where the real action is, or as the primary time for the Spirit's life-giving work of transformation to occur.

Searle presents several images for understanding how the Sunday celebration functions within the Christian community: Sunday as Sabbath, Sunday as the day of resurrection, and Sunday as the "Eighth Day"—a time outside of the regular march of days and weeks, marking something special. In the first of these paradigmatic images, Searle explains that despite the tendency toward legalistic interpretations of the Sabbath as an obligation, the original texts describing this commandment (Exod 20:8–11; Deut

---

9. For example, Gregory Dix writes that the time outside the special seasons of the birth and death of Jesus "stands vacant" (Dix, *The Shape of the Liturgy,* 359).

10. United States Catholic Conference, *Roman Calendar Text and Commentary,* 10 (emphasis added).

11. Jounel, "The Sundays of Ordinary Time," quoted in Johnson, "*Tempus per annum,*" 154.

12. Smith, "The Fullness of Ordinary Time," 4. "In this way," writes Maxwell Johnson, "each Sunday is not a 'little Easter' as is often erroneously claimed, but 'Easter is a big Sunday,'" that celebrates not only Jesus' resurrection as a historical event, but also his real presence in the church today (Johnson, "*Tempus per annum,*" 154).

13. Searle, "Sunday," 59.

5:12–15) associate the rhythm of work and rest with God's merciful activity of creation and liberation. Contrary to our modern utilitarian mindset in which we tend to view rest as instrumentally valuable as an aid to further productivity, within this theological framework "[w]ork leads to rest, rather than rest being for the sake of work, and resting from labor is something which both hallows or glorifies God and sanctifies people through their imitation of God."[14] God's action in freeing Israel from slavery also serves as an image for the Sabbath: just as God freed Israel from their toil in Egypt, God's people are called to participate in God's liberating action by extending Sabbath rest to servants, animals, and even the land itself. Although the early church did not view Sunday as a Christian Sabbath (the first day of the week was a day for meeting for worship, not necessarily for abstaining from work) in a certain sense the whole Christian era participates in the twofold imagery of the Sabbath, "sharing in the 'rest' of God and enjoying, and extending to others, the freedom God has won for us."[15]

This freedom and new life are most powerfully symbolized in the resurrection of Jesus, who first appeared to his disciples on the first day of the week. Insofar as "the theology of 'Ordinary Time' is the Theology of Sunday," as Max Johnson has argued,[16] the rhythms of God's work and rest and the gifts of liberation and new life which Sunday symbolizes are the primary theological framework for this period. Such a view of the Sundays of the year reinforces the idea that conversion to new life is not a unique, once-and-for-all event, but an ongoing process of growth in freedom and depth of understanding that takes place across time and the various "spheres" of life. That is, every Sunday is resurrection Sunday, a little Easter—and so offers the grace of a fresh start amidst the flow of day-to-day realities.

Implications for Hospitality

So what might this mean for our practices of hospitality?

First, attending to hospitality as understood through the lens of Ordinary Time can help to reframe a sense of the value of our time and thus resist the temptation to use hospitality as a means to some other end—a danger that Christine Pohl has addressed in several places in her work on the topic. In *Making Room,* she directly addresses the temptation to use hospitality as an instrument for personal or corporate gain or advantage. Because we tend to be "so instrumental in our thinking, so calculating, so aware of costs and

14. Searle, "Sunday," 62.

15. Searle, "Sunday," 63.

16. Johnson, "*Tempus per annum,*" 154.

benefits," we must be on guard against turning hospitality into a form of commercial exchange, even in the name of "good stewardship." Pohl argues that "[t]o view hospitality as a means to an end, to use it instrumentally, is antithetical to seeing it as a way of life, a tangible expression of love" and a form of participation in the story of God's hospitality through Jesus.[17] She echoes this concern in *Living into Community,* calling attention to the ways that hospitality can be used as a means to ends such as building business success, enhancing our image, or growing our numbers. Our capitalist culture's emphasis on efficiency and effectiveness put the practice of Christian hospitality out of step with the ethos of contemporary society: "When we orient our lives around tasks, opportunities for hospitality often appear in the form of interruptions . . . If we are to recover the practice of hospitality, we will need to do far more than clear our schedules for one more task or activity—we will have to reconsider how we live our lives."[18]

It is instructive to look at the distinction sometime drawn between two different understandings of time, designated by the Greek terms *chronos* and *kairos*. The term *chronos,* from which we get the terms "chronic" and "chronological" designates a "space of time" or "time elapsed." *Chronos* is time that can be marked and measured by calendars and clocks, and is often contrasted with time as *kairos,* an "appointed time," an event or opportunity. *Kairos* is time as *qualitative* rather than quantitative. The *kairos* moments of our lives are, in Bonnie Thurston's words, "the defining moments of our lives, the moments of new insight, of deeper understanding—moments when everything changes. *Kairos* times are the times in our lives when we can see the hand of God at work."[19] This contrast has sometimes led writers to devalue time as *chronos,* as in Kenneth Bakken's text *The Call to Wholeness.* He writes that "*Chronos,* clock time, keeps us rushed and enslaved to our busyness. It is objective and hurried and helps fuel our fear. Clock time can be a destructive element in our model of disease, disintegration, and death. On the other hand, *kairos,* the time of fullness and wholeness, is the time lived from within, a time of grace. It is a time when I am not afraid, a time when I can hear God's promise."[20] As Thurston explains, however, "The Liturgical Year reminds us of God's intersection with human history, that God's pattern is woven through the progression of chronological time, that *chronos* and *kairos* intersect."[21]

---

17. Pohl, *Making Room,* 144.
18. Pohl, *Living into Community,* 165–66.
19. Thurston, *To Everything a Season,* 27.
20. Bakken, *The Call to Wholeness,* 60.
21. Thurston, *To Everything a Season,* 64.

By reframing our lives in terms of the new creation that God is bringing about in Christ through each successive week of the year, we are better prepared to attend to God's presence in each and every moment that offers the opportunity for welcome and sharing with others. God is not only to be found in dramatic experiences and events, but also in the everyday matters of meals together, service to one another, the taken-for-granted mechanisms of our own bodies or the natural world. The challenge for most of us is to be attentive to God in the ordinary. Though we will still live much of our lives in a cultural context where "time is money," an experience of rest and re-creation points to an alternative in which time is inherently valuable for what it contains—the laughter of friends or the play of children or a surprise encounter with a stranger—rather than for what it gets us. Such an experience of time is essential to our ability to be fully present to guests rather than seeing them as an interruption, a burden, or a means to some other end. "The most precious thing a human being has to give is time," wrote Edith Schaeffer of the L'Abri community.[22] In order to truly welcome another, to be present with and to them, we must be able to offer our time as a gift, not simply use it as a tool.

A related danger or distortion which might be remedied through the celebration of Ordinary Time is the conflation of hospitality with "entertaining." This tendency is a particular temptation in a culture that is as consumeristic, image-conscious, and entertainment-oriented as our own. We may feel like hospitality must be an "event": that is, unless we can prepare a beautiful and delicious meal and have a house that is immaculate and stylish, we cannot invite others in. But as Pohl emphasizes throughout her work, "putting on a show" for guests is actually quite contrary to a spirit of hospitality which welcomes others into the messy, imperfect, and mundane realities of our lives.[23] In a similar way, our cultural fixation with entertainment and novelty can bleed into our attitudes about worship as we look to the "special events" of Christmas or Easter or Pentecost as more important than the long stretch of Ordinary weeks. While it may seem appealing to find ways of filling that space with entertaining events or observances, as Smith argues in the essay previously cited, "something significant is lost when the whirl of special days replaces the deep, weekly rhythm of Ordinary Time."[24] Though Smith does not elaborate on what this "something" might

22. Quoted in Pohl, Making Room, 178.

23. E.g., Pohl, Making Room, 144. One interesting piece which makes a similar point about the need to let go of certain expectations for hospitality is King, "Why Scruffy Hospitality Creates Space for Friendship."

24. Smith, "The Fullness of Ordinary Time," 7. For slightly different but congruous reasons, in "Tempus per annum: Celebrating the Mystery of Christ in All its Fullness,"

be, I would suggest that it is the sense of "walking with Jesus" through the day-to-day events of his life and ministry—arguably the central meaning of the incarnation itself. Unlike the readings for Advent, Christmas, or Holy Week, which are selected to correspond with particular events, the Gospel readings for Ordinary Time are semi-continuous "in such a way that as the Lord's life and preaching unfold the teaching proper to each of these Gospels is presented."[25] While the movements may be more subtle than the dramatic events of Christmas or Holy Week, attending to them can make us more attentive to the ways that our own lives as disciples also "unfold" through the mundane-seeming patterns of everyday life.

The Liturgical Year can serve as a reminder that "our time is God's time," in Bonnie Thurston's words. "It keeps us closely in touch with the Incarnation. The seasons themselves suggest a balance for life," through the alternation of the quiet, reflective seasons of Advent and Lent, the seasons of great activity and revelation in Christmas and Easter, and the "long, slow 'ordinary' time when we are called to reflect upon our own growing life in Christ." She writes that "'Ordinary time,' time when nothing special seems to be going on, is often understood in retrospect to be time of great spiritual growth and deepening."[26] Much as the ongoing practice of hospitality creates space for the possibility of extraordinary encounters in the midst of our ordinary, commonplace lives, so also the regular sequence of counted Sundays points to the extraordinary fact of God's Spirit in the world which, in its very constancy, makes all things new.

Seasons, Symbols, and Spiritual Rhythms

In addition to the meaning of the season as it actually functions within the church and is interpreted by scholars, however, the seasons of the Liturgical Year offer a symbol of the spiritual dynamics of the practice of hospitality.

Maxwell Johnson also argues against the practice of replacing Ordinary Sundays with celebrations of solemnities and feasts. Johnson's concern in this essay is for the coherence of the lectionary and "the integrity of Sunday itself" (162) as a framework for Ordinary Time.

25. United States Catholic Conference, "Lectionary for Mass," 40. Obviously, the Gospels account for only a few episodes of Jesus' life, and the order in which these occurred as well as their validity is called into question by historical-critical scholarship. Insofar as the lectionary of Ordinary Time represents "a semicontinuous reading of the Synoptic Gospels," however, this sequence offers us a sense of how the Gospel writers saw the mission of Jesus unfolding and how the earliest communities would have experienced the proclamation of the gospel.

26. Thurston, *To Everything a Season*, 66.

That is, just as the church passes through periods of feasting and fasting as it celebrates the life of Christ throughout the year, our own lives and practices of hospitality will sometimes be celebratory, sometimes somber and sacrificial—but most often they will be "ordinary" in common actions such as welcoming neighborhood children to play, inviting neighbors, coworkers, or friends over for an impromptu meal, or making time to listen to someone who is struggling. In my longer work dealing with the limits of hospitality, I've argued that celebrating the spiritual seasons of the Liturgical Year—along with other disciplines of spiritual life—can help communities and their members to acknowledge and respect the limits of hospitality through becoming attentive to the ebbing and flowing rhythms of human life. Observing the spiritual significance of the passage of time can allow for a deeper appreciation of the truth that "for everything there is a season, and a time for every matter under heaven" (Eccl 3:1). Sometimes we are called to great sacrifice—a "Holy Week" of our practice of hospitality—while at other times hospitality will be the consolation of strangers bringing gifts to nourish and heal us, like the Magi visiting the child Jesus. "Developing sensitivity to when it is an appropriate time to weep or to laugh, to mourn or to dance, is an important part of extending and discerning hospitality,"[27] and attending to the cycles of the liturgical seasons is one way of cultivating such a sensitivity.

To reiterate my central point in this essay: the weekly and seasonal rhythms of the liturgy call us to make hospitality ordinary in just this way; that is, by attending to the small daily and weekly movements that give shape to the life and identity of a community. "Because hospitality is a way of life, it must be cultivated over a lifetime," Pohl writes; it must be regularly practiced throughout our lives or "it won't be there for the rare occasion." She continues, explaining, "We do not become good at hospitality in an instant; we learn it in small increments of daily faithfulness."[28] For these reasons, she attends to the "spiritual rhythms" of hospitality in chapter 9 of *Making Room*. In particular, Pohl describes the importance of telling stories of hospitality and nurturing its practice across generations, of celebration as well as rest and renewal, and of maintaining a sense of perspective about one's work. Each of these bears a significant connection to the celebration of the liturgy throughout the year—and perhaps a particular connection to the experience of Ordinary Time.

As noted above, the seasons of the Liturgical Year are a way of remembering and retelling the stories of Jesus. Though the specific selections of

27. Wrobleski, *The Limits of Hospitality*, 59.
28. Pohl, *Making Room*, 176.

Scripture for a given week may vary between different lectionaries or years of a cycle, the practice of following a lectionary offers a structure that attends to the entire life of Jesus (in the Gospel readings) within the context of God's revelation to humans through Israel and the church. It is interesting that in some of the more widely used lectionaries, the most notable stories of hospitality from the life of Jesus—not only Jesus' own feeding and healing of those who came to him, but also accounts of his role as a guest at the homes of others—typically occur during Ordinary Time, as if to remind us that hospitality is the "daily bread" of discipleship. "These Sundays [of Ordinary Time], year after year, repeat for us the cycles of parables and healings, teaching and preaching that make so visible for us who we are and are becoming."[29] An important part of the process of our "becoming" also involves nurturing the practice of hospitality in families and with children.[30] Though there may be particular challenges that accompany the practice of hospitality when children (small or large) are involved, these challenges themselves—scheduling, food preferences, bedtimes, and other special needs or vulnerabilities—can help to cultivate a hospitable disposition and, if embraced, allow a family to experience the practice of hospitality as something that is not just for special occasions, but a way of life. Children (and parents) are formed by the way that home life is open or closed to the presence of others. The truth that a home does not need to be perfectly clean and a meal does not have to be specially planned in order to be joyfully shared with others is something that many families know well.[31]

Pohl also addresses the link between hospitality and celebration—"not celebration as carefully planned entertainment, but celebration that reflects time set aside to rejoice in being together"—as an essential part of the practice, particularly for those whose lives have been marked by brokenness and loss.[32] I have written elsewhere about the need to acknowledge the ebbs and flows of life as they apply to hospitality as an embodied spiritual discipline which moves between practices of fasting and celebration, as well as

29. Zimmerman, "Editor Notes," 192.

30. See Pohl, *Making Room*, 175.

31. In a blog post, Jack King shares his reflections on the experience of "scruffy" hospitality, explaining that "scruffy hospitality means you're not waiting for everything in your house to be in order before you host and serve friends in your home. Scruffy hospitality means you hunger more for good conversation and serving a simple meal of what you have, not what you don't have. Scruffy hospitality means you're more interested in quality conversation than the impression your home or lawn makes. If we only share meals with friends when we're excellent, we aren't truly sharing life together." (King, "Why Scruffy Hospitality Creates Space for Friendship").

32. Pohl, *Making Room*, 180.

between service and rest.[33] Retelling the stories of Jesus' "ordinary" life, his ongoing and sustained ministry of teaching, healing, and feeding people, and acknowledging how his life passed through periods of both withdrawal and active engagement with others, we may be better able to appreciate the rhythms of our own lives and to see them within the context of a larger story. "Part of our ability to sustain hospitality in the midst of an unjust and disordered world comes from putting our small efforts into a larger context," Pohl writes. "God is at work in the world, and our little but significant moves participate in that work."[34]

On this note—that is, our participation in God's great work of creation and redemption—I want to call our attention to another way that the seasons of the year offer a rich symbol for shaping how we imagine and experience the spiritual rhythms of hospitality. Although the physical changes of the seasons may be less dramatic in some parts of the world than they are in the temperate climate of West Virginia where I live, in most places there is still a discernible difference between the seasons that correspond with the phases of the Earth's annual journey around the sun. Whether that difference is a matter of hot and cold seasons, wet and dry seasons, or simply varying amounts of daylight and darkness, such changes are entirely outside our control and yet they invite and even require our participation and response. For anyone engaged in agriculture (or even the casual gardener), such cycles are essential for the growth of crops, much as the daily and seasonal liturgies are like trellises for our spiritual growth. In a blog post entitled "The Bells of Ordinary Time," Tessa Carman offers an extended reflection on the parallels between the agricultural seasons and the rhythms of monastic life:

> On the farm, the rhythms of planting and harvesting govern the days. At the monastery, liturgical rhythms define the hours . . . But the days of the monk and the farmer are defined by more than the demands of the hour or the season. The story of death and resurrection also shapes them. Agriculture means nothing without the yearly cycle of life arising out of death. A seed must fall to the ground and die before growing into a full-grown tree. The everyday grace the farmer experiences through this cycle beautifully frames the central truth of the gospel—Christ's resurrection from the dead. The monk must die to himself daily through the discipline of the hours; the seed the farmer plants each spring must die before it blossoms into a crop.

33. Wrobleski, *The Limits of Hospitality*, particularly chapter 2.

34. Pohl, *Making Room*, 184.

This is not merely the ordinary cycle of nature; it is the cycle of the Church Year, which begins with Advent, climaxes in the death and resurrection of Christ in Holy Week, continues with Pentecost, and concludes with Ordinary Time.[35] Carman continues by reminding us once again that that Ordinary Time is the time of the eighth day, the time of God's reign, but that "even in this sanctified time, you still have to get up at 3:00 a.m. to water the crops or to pray the hours. This, too, is a gift." That is to say, God's grace does not do away with "ordinary" life, but rather transforms it into something full of meaning and possibility.

Continuing to draw on the imagery of natural-agricultural seasons, we might even come to see the green vestments[36] and of Ordinary Time as a symbol of incremental spiritual growth and the verdancy of the period from May to November in many climates. Seen in this light, Ordinary Time is not merely a time to go through the motions, waiting for the next "event" of planting or harvest, but rather affords an extended opportunity to make the small changes that lead to real growth—the daily weeding and watering and stretching toward the sun that transforms seed to fruit, or the small acts of sharing and helping and sacrifice which, while small in their own right, allow for the practice of hospitality to take deep root in our lives.

Bibliography

Bakken, Kenneth. *The Call to Wholeness: Health as a Spiritual Journey.* New York: Crossroad, 1986.

Carman, Tessa. "The Bells of Ordinary Time." *RealClearReligion,* February 27, 2015. http://farefwd.com/2015/02/the-bells-of-ordinary-time/.

Dix, Gregory Dix. *The Shape of the Liturgy.* London: Dacre, 1945.

Johnson, Maxwell. "*Tempus per Annum:* Celebrating the Mystery of Christ in All Its Fullness." *Liturgical Ministry* 17 (Fall 2008) 153–63.

King, Jack. "Why Scruffy Hospitality Creates Space for Friendship." *Knox Priest,* May 21, 2014. http://www.knoxpriest.com/scruffy-hospitality-creates-space-friendship/.

Pohl, Christine, D. *Living into Community: Cultivating Practices That Sustain Us.* Grand Rapids: Eerdmans, 2012.

———. *Making Room: Recovering Hospitality as a Christian Tradition.* Grand Rapids: Eerdmans, 1999.

35. Carman, "The Bells of Ordinary Time."

36. For those unfamiliar with this tradition, there are particular colors worn by a priest or pastor during particular seasons—purple for the penitential, reflective seasons of Advent and Lent, white for the celebrations of the Christmas and Easter seasons, red to represent the fire of Pentecost or the blood of the martyrs, and green throughout Ordinary Time.

Searle, Mark. "Sunday: The Heart of the Liturgical Year." In *Between Memory and Hope: Readings on the Liturgical Year,* edited by Maxwell Johnson, 59–76. Collegeville: Liturgical, 2000.

Smith, Ted A. "The Fullness of Ordinary Time." *Journal for Preachers* 29, no. 4 (2006) 3–9.

Thurston, Bonnie. *To Everything a Season: A Spirituality of Time.* New York: Crossroad, 1999.

United States Catholic Conference. *Roman Calendar Text and Commentary.* Washington, DC: USCC, 1976.

Wrobleski, Jessica. *The Limits of Hospitality.* Collegeville: Liturgical, 2012.

Zimmerman, Joyce Ann. "Editor Notes." *Liturgical Ministry* 17 (Fall 2008) 191.

Part Two

Practicing Community
Negotiating the Imperfections

Resisting the Borg

The Interdependence of Individuality and Community

Tim Otto

Perhaps the most frightening antagonist in the science fiction TV series *Star Trek: The Next Generation* is the Borg, a mind-hive collective that assimilates whole races in order to add the knowledge of others into itself. As they absorb their victims, they utter this simple refrain: "Resistance is futile."

Although Western society looks like a collection of radically different individuals, scratch deeper and one might wonder if the Borg hasn't devoured us. We're strikingly similar in how we express our "individuality." While our phones' ringtones shrill our uniqueness, capitalism has etched into our brains a conformist logic that makes us obedient workers and consumers in the Mammon hive. But resistance to the Borg is possible, albeit difficult. Jesus' revolutionary agenda seeks to gather a disciplined community to resist Borg-like worldly powers.

Ironically, our fear of conformity makes it difficult to join Jesus' collective. As author and activist Marty Rubin noted, "Freedom began on the day the first sheep wandered away from the herd."[1] Although we may believe we are expressing our *individuality*, we are often held captive by the law of *individualism*—an overarching commitment to self-determination, self-reliance, and not being controlled by anything or anyone but ourselves. It's as American as apple pie. We worry about giving up personal autonomy and independence, and we're aware of how communities can go wrong and

1. Rubin, *The Boiled Frog Syndrome*, 132.

do us damage. We wonder, "How can I live in community with others while retaining my individuality?"

The answer is not to give up on being part of Jesus' flock. Sheep, in general, don't do very well by themselves. Rather, we need to practice the kind of hospitality Christine Pohl advocates—hospitality that welcomes all kinds of individual difference.[2] As we do, we'll find that our differences make for a flock that is healthier because of its diversity.

In this essay, I survey how our apparent individuality masks our fundamental conformity to the god of capitalism. Then, in light of the parable of the good Samaritan, I explore how a vision for hospitality creates a community that unmasks and nourishes our unique gifts and traits. Finally, I consider how the related practices of gratitude, truth-telling, and promise-keeping help us persevere in the difficult yet rewarding traditions of hospitality and community.

How the Borg Devoured the Flower Children

The documentary *The Century of the Self* describes how the flower children—the free thinking, anti-establishment, individualist youth of the 1960s—became the fuel for the capitalist engine. Radicalized by the Civil Rights Movement and the Vietnam war, young people mobilized to defeat "the man." As one of their more extreme representatives, Linda Evans of the Weatherman Revolutionary Group, describes it:

> We want to live a life that isn't based on materialistic values, and yet the whole system of government and the economy of America is based on profit; on personal greed and selfishness so that in order to be human, in order to love each other and be equal with each other and not place each other in roles, we have to destroy the kind of government that keeps us from asserting our positive values of life.[3]

However, the fight against the government faced overwhelming military and police power. The National Guard brutally subdued thousands of protestors at the 1968 Democratic Convention, and after the killing of four students at Kent State in 1970, the movement dissipated. In its place, such activists as Stew Albert of the Yippee Party began to advocate for personal, internal transformation. Societal change apparently could not be achieved

---

2. For her complete treatment, see Pohl, *Making Room.*
3. Curtis, *The Century of the Self, Part 1.*

by fighting the too-powerful state; but if enough individuals were to change, then change would happen from within (and eventually throughout) the system.

But influenced by a psychology of personal liberation and the human potential movement, "personal transformation" lost its original objective. Instead of creating a just and good society, the focus shifted to the self and to cultivating one's own mental, emotional, and physical well-being. People's highest responsibility became, in theologian Stanley Hauerwas's telling phrase, to make one's own life a "heroic creation."[4] Meanwhile, American industry was becoming anxious as the economy cooled in the 1970s. Young people, who were disenchanted with "the system," began to resist the advertising that had enticed previous generations to buy mass-produced, consumer goods. When industry leaders turned to marketers (especially the esteemed Stanford Research Institute) for help, their research revealed a new kind of human: the expressive individualist.

As *The Century of the Self* concludes, "The world in which people felt they were rebelling against conformity was not a threat to business but its greatest opportunity."[5] Researchers discovered that goods and services could be sold not simply on the basis of their utility, but for their potential to express one's identity. For instance, trucks had previously been marketed to people who needed to haul heavy loads. Now buyers might be enticed to buy a truck in order to express their sense of being "capable," "manly," or "strong." Computers helped manufacturing diversify so that short runs of everything from pink cell phone covers to personalized soda cans became feasible.

In Western culture, the fundamental markers of identity have become what we consume and what we produce. Our social media profiles list what schools we attended (where we trained to become producers), what we do for work (what we produce), and the movies, TV shows, books, and sports teams we like (what we consume). The first question we ask each other—in order to figure out *who the other is*—tends to be, "What do you do?" (That is, "What do you produce?") We've bought the idea that one of our most sacred duties is to express ourselves, which we do by buying commodities and experiences. Although the endless variety of shirts and skirts, sodas and scooters through which we project our identities might convince us otherwise, all of this is undergirded by a remarkable conformity. The Borg has organized our thinking around Mammon and led us to believe that what we produce and consume best expresses the essence of our selves.

4. Hauerwas and Willimon, *Resident Aliens,* 55.

5. Curtis, *The Century of the Self,* Part 3.

God's Alternative Vision

God would have likely sympathized with the Weatherman Revolutionary Group. In the book of Exodus, God sees the Israelite people being exploited as economic resources by an all-powerful state—slaves to Pharaoh's building projects. God has compassion on them and frees them from oppression. But God doesn't remove their sandals, dress them with flowers, and release them to romp through fields of grass in order to express their beautiful, individual identities. God makes them a people and binds them together in a covenantal society meant to live in justice and peace, because God's vision is that *identity exists—and is revealed—through relationships.*

Before the liberation, when Moses asks about the identity of the God who proposes to free the Israelites, God discloses God's name as "I am"—the ground of existence and being. God further defines that character and identity through naming relations with specific people. "Thus you are to say to the Israelites," God tells Moses, "The LORD, the God of your ancestors, the God of Abraham, the God of Isaac, and the God of Jacob, has sent me to you" (Exod 3:15). Once freed from Egypt, God invites the Israelites to develop their identity as a just and faithful people because they are the loved children of a just and faithful God. God invites them to become God's "treasured possession out of all the people" (Exod 19:5), and gives them the Ten Commandments—the basics of what it means to live well in relation to God and others. The story of the Old Testament is of how the people of God *relate to one another and to God.*

The truth that identity exists and is revealed through relationships is grounded in the nature of God and flows into the New Testament. When Jesus claims the identity of "Good Shepherd," he bases it in how he relates to others: he lays down his life for the sheep (John 10:15). Jesus identifies "disciples of Jesus" by how they relate to others: "By this everyone will know that you are my disciples, if you have love for one another" (John 13:35). In the Gospel of John, the religious leaders want to know if Jesus is the Messiah, but rather than answer directly, Jesus proclaims, "The Father and I are one" (John 10:30). Jesus reveals his identity through his relationship with his Father. As the early church reflected on this proclamation, they concluded that God exists as one being in three persons—or, we might dare say, God exists as a *community.*

At the heart of our faith is this mystery of the Trinity—that God exists in relationship as three different persons who are nevertheless completely unified. Before going to the cross, Christ prayed that we might experience the same unity with other Christians that the Trinity enjoys between its members, "that all of them may be one, Father, just as you are in me and I am in you" (John 17:21). In spite of the Trinity's profound unity (the doctrine of divine simplicity teaches us that God is "without parts"), we can take comfort that this doesn't mean the loss or suppression of personhood. God models the possibility of entering into a radical unity with others that doesn't mean the diminishment of an individual person.

Even so, we may wonder how to preserve our individual identities in the midst of such a unity. The New Testament offers rich imagery that helps us live into a unity that respects and even promotes difference.

The Church as Body

The Apostle Paul teaches us to value difference within unity by comparing the church to the human body. He imagines the thoughts of an insecure foot: "If the foot would say, 'Because I am not a hand, I do not belong to the body,' that would not make it any less a part of the body" (1 Cor 12:15). He observes that because of Christ's work, we've been made part of the body of Christ. Thus it is absurd to say, "I'm not a part because I'm different." We're a different *part* of the body, although we are not the whole body. But just as the part needs the whole, so the whole needs the different parts. "If the whole body were an eye, where would the hearing be?" Paul asks. We need the whole body to stay alive!

As a registered nurse, the body as an image for how the whole needs the individuated parts makes great sense to me. Cancer cells are known as "undifferentiated cells." All cells start out the same, but they become distinct from others as they mature. So, a cancer might begin from a cell that is supposed to develop into a liver cell but doesn't mature into what the body needs it to be. Although immature, it begins to reproduce undifferentiated cells like itself, which grow into a bulky mass of tissue that invades the liver and surrounding organs. Eventually the cancer causes dysfunction, deforms the body, and often causes death. Ironically, by killing the whole, it also destroys itself.

Like the human body, the church needs well-differentiated members of all types. For the last thirty years, I've been part of a small, live-together, intentional church community. Through this I've learned to value the less-celebrated spiritual gifts. While gifts such as teaching and preaching are important, perseverance in community is possible because of those who have gifts of compassion, encouragement, and cheerfulness (Rom 12:8). Without them, the experience of community would become grim and unsustainable.

As a community, we've learned that difference is also important in opinions. In making decisions we try to come to consensus; and because of this, there can be peer pressure to agree. Over the years, we've learned that we need to respect the divergent voice. For example, if anyone says, "I'm not sure I'm on board, let's take more time to think about it," we put off the decision. When we come back together, sometimes we find that a better, more creative solution has occurred to someone—a solution that takes into account the concerns of the person who didn't agree. Even when the perfect solution isn't found, the willingness to wait reminds us that we need to host and encourage difference for the sake of good decision making and for the sake of communicating respect to each member.

When I first came to the community in my early twenties, I was in the process of trying to figure out who I was and how to develop my potential. When I noticed someone who had a gift that I did not, I often responded with envy and rivalry. As I've developed a greater sense of being part of a "we," those feelings have diminished. I have realized that if someone is a terrific musician or a gifted healer, I share in those gifts because we are a body together. I am enriched by her strengths, just as she is hopefully enriched by mine. Rather than thinking I need to be a heroic and "omnicompetent" person, I yearn for a more complete body—a body in which people are most themselves for the sake of us all. We need musicians and preachers, cheerleaders and naysayers, followers and leaders, both INFPs and ESTJs.[6] The body is most healthy when each person is enthusiastically functioning in his or her unique role.

During those early years in community, I had a sense of dread in my stomach that by joining community I was betraying myself. I had read Chaim Potok's *My Name Is Asher Lev*, in which Asher develops the art of his personal "scream" in the face of his community's pressure to conform. My guts churned with the fear that by aligning my life so deeply with others, I was neglecting my duty to express myself. Happily, books such as Robert Bellah's *Habits of the Heart* helped me to see that joining a community does not require a mindless conformity. In fact, it can be an act of resistance to the Borg-like culture that uses us to fuel the capitalist machine—all in the name of helping us to be inimitable individuals. Ironically, embedding ourselves within a local community can help us develop our differences as we respond to specific needs, while being radically "individualistic" as part of the global economy can make us strangely similar.

This is not to deny that there are dangers in community. Our egos can assume that "the way we do it" is the right way, and thus we insist that those who wish to do things differently submit to the group-think. Dreams can be stifled "for the good of the community." In response to the suggestions of a

---

6. Two opposite types in the Myers Briggs personality typology.

new person, we might reflexively quash innovation by questioning the person's commitment or credibility, all based on the stellar logic: "We've never done it that way before." How can we resist such instincts? The best way to receive the gift of the "other" is a passionate commitment to hospitality. Jesus' mind-bomb of a story—the story of the good Samaritan—helps us toward that commitment.

The Good Samaritan: A Framework for Hospitality

"In the parable of the Good Samaritan," Pohl observes, "Jesus redefines neighbor and love of neighbor."[7] The story begins with a crucial question, posed by an expert in Jewish law: "What must I do to inherit eternal life?" Jesus turns the question back to the lawyer and asks him what he thinks. The lawyer responds, "You shall love the Lord your God with all your heart, and with all your soul, and with all your strength, and with all your mind; and your neighbor as yourself." "Yup," Jesus basically says, "You got it." But "wanting to justify himself," the lawyer then shrewdly asks: "And who is my neighbor?"[8]

With this loaded question, the lawyer acknowledges his duty under the law to love (that is, show hospitality toward) his fellow Jews. However, he is looking for a boundary. He is hoping to exclude people who are different, like his neighbors the Samaritans. Although they shared the Israelite lineage, Samaritans differed from Jews on doctrinal and cultural issues, and the Jews considered them "the lowest of the low." At the end of the parable, Jesus asks: *Who was the neighbor* to the man who was beaten? His answer: "the one who showed mercy"—that is, the Samaritan. Jesus clearly *includes* neighbors who are different. (It is tempting to think the neighbor to the lawyer is the man who was beaten up. Hold on. We'll get to that.)

If the Samaritans are the lawyer's neighbors, why are they neighbors? Is it because the Samaritan in the parable is unexpectedly good and compassionate? Is Jesus saying that Samaritans are much nicer folk than widely thought, and therefore Jews ought to consider them as neighbors? Unlikely. As theologian Arthur C. McGill points out, parables were stories about the in-breaking Kingdom and its Messiah. McGill suggests that the good Samaritan represents Jesus. He points out that Christ, like the Samaritan, is a persecuted man. Christ loves others even while he is persecuted by them. Like the Samaritan, Christ has the power to bind up wounds and heal. Christ accepts responsibility for the man's future and promises to "come

7. Pohl, *Making Room*, 75.

8. The full parable is found in Luke 10:25–37.

again." And Christ, like the Good Samaritan, is the New Testament example for us to follow.[9]

"This intermingling of guest and host roles in the person of Jesus is part of what makes the story of hospitality so compelling for Christians," states Pohl. "Jesus needs and provides welcome; Jesus requires that followers depend on and provide hospitality."[10] If we accept McGill's logic, the parable presents Christ as the neighbor. He is an outsider coming to a Jew, who is beaten, bleeding and broken. Beyond answering the question of "Who is my neighbor?" Jesus is asking the lawyer to consider the more basic question of "Who am I?" The lawyer is most likely to see himself as the priest or Levite, but since they are the villains in the story, the lawyer won't identify with them. When Jesus asks, "Which of these . . . *was a neighbor to the man who fell into the hands of robbers?*" Jesus is inviting the lawyer to see himself as the broken, half-dead man on the side of the road (Luke 10:36). Why would Jesus do this?

Scripture tells us that the lawyer asks his question because he wants to "justify himself." The lawyer seems to think that if he can get it "right," he is better than those who are getting it "wrong," and therefore he deserves God's "eternal life." But if one must get it right, then one must shield oneself from those getting it wrong—like the Samaritans—especially in the area of religious belief. Thus the religious person who tries to "justify himself" is most unable to welcome difference. If the lawyer must protect himself from those getting it "wrong," he will resist the hospitality of those who are different. And if he never *receives* such hospitality, he is unlikely to *give* it to others who are different. But if the lawyer learns to see himself as stuck in a ditch and unable to justify himself, then he has no need to protect himself from the difference of others. He welcomes the help of whoever gives it, no matter how different—in this case the Samaritan.

Presumably, as Christians, we've all come to the point in which we've realized, "I'm stuck. I can't save myself. I need help beyond myself." We come together because we know ourselves to need God and each other's help, not because we are part of an "us" that is better than "them." With this attitude, we'll sustain a resolutely hospitable stance toward difference and form communities in which individuality flourishes.

Up to this point I've contended that (a) although Westerners highly value individuality, consumerism has made us profoundly conformist, (b) one way to resist such uniformity is to join the community of Jesus followers, and (c) this community can't be a typically "religious" group seeking to

9. McGill, *Suffering*, 109–10.

10. Pohl, *Making Room*, 17.

justify itself (which quashes difference), but rather a people radically committed to the practice of hospitality in order to welcome others who are different. Pohl observes that "the twin moves of universalizing the neighbor and personalizing the stranger are at the core of hospitality."[11] And as anyone knows who has ever tried to live hospitably, it is hard—*really* hard. This is why the practices Pohl recommends of gratitude, truth-telling, and promise-keeping are so crucial. In these next sections, I'll continue to explore the parable of the good Samaritan to show how these disciplines preserve the practice of hospitality towards difference.

Love of the Other: The Ethics of Gratitude

At the end of the parable, the lawyer responds to Jesus' question "Who was the neighbor to the man who fell into the hands of the robbers?" by saying "the one who showed him mercy." "Go and do likewise," Jesus responds. He isn't simply adding another "to-do" to the list of things the lawyer needs to accomplish to "justify himself." Rather, by helping the lawyer see himself as the one in the ditch, he has given him a different motivation for showing mercy: gratitude. If the lawyer knows himself as someone who was rescued by someone he despised, as shown mercy by someone who had every reason to pass him by, then out of gratitude, he might start picking up others on the road. What was a duty becomes a joyful response to grace.

As we feel gratitude in relation to the Merciful Other, our relationship to all others will change. If our identity is that of the "righteous," then association with people unlike us may contaminate us. But if we see ourselves as inn-dwellers in recovery, then others, even in their need, may be received with gratitude. As recipients of mercy—full of the humble and holy gratitude which comes from receiving grace—the need of others becomes an opportunity to bless others and enact our thanks to Christ.

If the need of others is an occasion for gratitude, then certainly the different abilities of others ought to call forth our gratitude, as well. A former pastor of mine, John Alexander, noticed that in Ephesians 4—a passage about how Christ went through the difficulty of the incarnation to give us gifts—the gifts we receive are not talents or abilities, but *people*. Christ doesn't give the gifts of apostleship, evangelism, teaching, and so on; he gives us apostles, prophets, evangelists, pastors, and teachers (Eph 4:11). Paul explains that as we connect our lives with others and allow them to use their gifts for our benefit, we grow up into "the unity of the faith and of the knowledge of the Son of God, to maturity, to the measure of the full stature

11. Pohl, *Making Room*, 75.

of Christ" (Eph 4:13). In this passage, growing into Christ isn't through difficult disciplines. Rather, the whole wondrous process is one of receiving gifts!

While this vision of receiving others with gratitude is essential to the practice of hospitality, we must also admit that sometimes others rob us, beat us, and leave us lying on the side of the road. So how do we guard against the sin of others? Here we turn to a second practice advocated by Pohl—truth-telling.

Truth Preserves Unity

After Paul's admonition to "grow up in every way into him who is the head, into Christ," he issues a stern warning against living in sin, as those who live "in the futility of their minds . . . greedy to practice every kind of impurity" (Eph 4:15, 18–19). Paul's prescription for this is to be "renewed in the spirit of your minds," which primarily seems to be a commitment to truth. "So then, putting away falsehood, let all of us speak the truth to our neighbors, for we are members of one another" (4:25). How might the practice of truth-telling enable us to receive difference as gift? How might we minimize—rather than escalate—the threat of others as we commit to telling the truth?

In the parable of the good Samaritan, Jesus reveals to the lawyer a difficult truth: he is not a good man on the verge of mastering the law and thus justifying himself, but rather a half-dead man lying on the side of the road. Jesus confronts him with this truth because "good" religious people are likely to abandon their neighbors on the side of the road—or even crucify the Messiah. As Miroslav Volf notes:

> Nietzsche underscored the connection between the self-perceived "goodness" of Jesus' enemies and their pursuit of his death; crucifixion was a deed of "the good and just," not of the wicked, as we might have thought. "The good and just" could not understand Jesus because their spirit was "imprisoned in their good conscience" and they crucified him because they construed as evil his rejection of their notions of good. "The good and just," insists Nietzsche, have to crucify the one who devises an alternative virtue because they already possess the knowledge of the good; they have to be hypocrites because, seeing themselves as good, they must impersonate the absence

of evil. Like poisonous flies, "they sting" and they do so "in all innocence."[12]

To play a little with the images from the parable, we might imagine the inn as the church and the church community, not as "the good religious people," but as the wounded ones who have been picked up by the Merciful Other. As Pohl writes, "We offer hospitality within the context of knowing Jesus as both our greater host and our potential guest."[13] Brought together by that common experience, we try to form a place of healing and health for all those brought in from the side of the road.

But the mission and purpose of the inn (that is, the church) gets subverted when do-gooder lawyers join up in order to justify themselves. Over time, those who know they were picked up by the Merciful Other might begin to see their good works as a way of justifying themselves, creating boundary lines between "us" and "them." These boundary lines are based on a lie that threatens to make us into self-righteous, religious people who are afraid of difference. One way of dealing this danger is to form rules: "Let anyone into the inn, no matter his or her ethnicity or how dead the person looks." Another remedy might be to form doctrines: "All people deserve our compassion."

Rules and doctrines are important, but a crucial way to correct the subtle lies that alienate us from others is to keep telling each other *the truth of our salvation story*: we are people who were (and are) broken and beaten on the side of the road, and the Merciful Other picked us up. Out of gratitude, we live as an inn to welcome and extend that healing to others. Interestingly, when the Apostle Paul identifies what is of "first importance" for the unity of the church, it turns out to be the story "that Christ died for our sins in accordance with the Scriptures, and that he was buried, and that he was raised on the third day in accordance with the Scriptures" (1 Cor 15:3–4). Paul was careful to rehearse his own story of realizing that he was a sinner and of being met on the road by a Savior (Acts 22:6–14; 26:9–18).

When we focus on the story as primary to the unity of the church, we can be less defensive and judgmental. But when we depend mostly on rules, our communities will be characterized by the coercion needed to enforce them. And if we rely principally on doctrines, then we'll inevitably fight about who should be excluded. A story, however, reminds us of what has happened. We don't expect everyone to share our story; indeed, our stories are precious because they are unique to us. We might tell a story and invite others to find themselves in it, but because it is a particular story, we don't

12. Volf, *Exclusion and Embrace*, 61.

13. Pohl, *Making Room*, 105.

expect everyone to claim it as their own. When people hear our story and then decide to live a different story, we can respect—and even bless—their difference.

By telling the truth of our salvation story, we remember that so much of truth-telling has to do with saying the good. As Pohl reminds us, "People who love truth build others up with it rather than using it to tear them down; much of our truth-telling should involve affirming what is right and good."[14] Few things lift the spirits of innkeepers more than honest testimonies of how the Merciful Other continues to work and heal.

Beyond that, we must also tell the truth about sin (while carefully distinguishing it from variations in personality, culture, and belief). Those of us picked up from the side of the road will be robbers ourselves or, if not robbers, then gossips and complainers and idolaters. Sins against one another hurt others and threaten the unity of the inn. When we find ourselves "robbed" by others in the community, we've got to have courage to tell that story. And at times, we've got to have the humility to hear from others how we have "robbed" them. As Paul puts it, we must "speak the truth in love" to one another (Eph 4:15). Otherwise the inn—intended to be a place of healing and recovery—will become its own ditch of wounding and victimization.

For those of us who dislike conflict, truth-telling is a demanding practice. Perhaps the only task more difficult is truth-hearing. The thing that can sustain such a difficult practice is commitment. The last practice advocated by Christine Pohl—promise-keeping—enables us to persevere through the difficulty.

Promise-Keeping

Identifying the good Samaritan with Jesus helps to illuminate a detail in the parable—that the good Samaritan pays the innkeeper two denarii and promises to return. As Christians we are to live with an eschatological hope. We believe that, at some point, we're going to get to see the guy who picked us up at the side of the road again. We'll have the chance to thank him, and tell the story of how we, too, have lived the adventure of being people who "showed mercy." The meaning of "eschatological" has to do with an "end goal." Because of the promise Christ has made to us, we know what the end will look like—a festival of gratitude celebrated by those who were picked up from the side of the road with their Savior. In the light of the coming

14. Pohl, *Living into Community,* 114.

party, we gather and welcome those who are "different" from the side of the road and try to live together in the inn as a unified community of healing.

In the parable, the lawyer focuses on his own goodness, but Jesus reveals that the most important thing for him to realize is *God's goodness toward him*. Similarly, in our own thinking about promise-keeping, we might think first about our own need to make and keep promises. But in fact, we first need to know that God has made promises to us, is working to keep them, and that they will come to pass. As Pohl reminds us, "It is only by the power of the Holy Spirit, the grace of God, and promises of Jesus that we are able to keep our promises and commitments in the hard places."[15] In light of this hope, we dare to make promises of our own.

As a young person, a pastor told me that "you grow up as you make promises and go through the difficulty of keeping them." I decided to put this into action by joining an intentional church community and by taking a vow of stability in which I promised to persevere with the community unless we discern together God's call for me to go elsewhere. I've now lived that commitment for over thirty years. The first years were a honeymoon in which I knew myself to be deeply loved and was grateful for the challenge to love others through things like our emergency housing ministry. After college, which I had experienced as a generational ghetto, I was grateful to have older mentors who had wisdom to share, and for children who gave me perspective through their playfulness. I've been grateful for community.

But the last ten years have been hard. I've been in a difficult conflict with another leader. We're extremely different people. From the outside, people say things like, "You're different from each other but your gifts are so complementary; it's obvious how you need each other!" But from the inside, the differences grate, hurt, and irritate. We are both learning to go through the difficulty of speaking the truth to one another, and the even more difficult practice of trying to hear the truth from each other. It is hard not to fantasize about an easier life elsewhere.

The thing that helps me stay in the relationship is the knowledge that because we've both committed ourselves to the community, we'll probably grow old together. We've got to make progress. We've got to find a way to receive the gift that is the other—otherwise life is gonna be hell. On our better days, the two of us can step back and acknowledge, "Yeah, we're such different people. If we can figure out how to work together, we're going to be a formidable team." In the process, we're both giving up some cherished illusions about ourselves. As we live the demanding discipleship of an intentional

---

15. Pohl, *Living into Community*, 108.

community, we're both tempted to justify ourselves. But as we observe the pain we cause the other, we realize we've both got a bit of robber in us.

Slowly, as we entrust ourselves to a God who is keeping covenant with us, we're keeping covenant with each other. Instead of inflicting wounds on each other, as we live with gratitude toward the Merciful Other, we're learning to bless and even help heal each other. We're learning to receive each other as gift and to live together in love and unity.

Unplugging from the Borg Matrix

As a villain, the Borg embody one of our fundamental fears: that by participating in the collective, our individual identities will be erased for the sake of the common good. We may think we've escaped that terror, but I believe another movie—*The Matrix*—metaphorically shows the reality of our situation. *The Matrix* portrays humans as bioelectric fuel cells for the machines. Each naked, weakened human is capsulated in a pod and fed a fantasy to keep her distracted while she is harvested for energy. In the same way, our modern consumerist culture uniformly exploits human beings for production and consumption, fodder to keep the capitalist machine working. We believe the myth that we're dramatically unique because we produce in different ways, and consume different products and services. But fundamentally, we all conform to the notion that we've got to feed the machine.

In *The Matrix,* a small group of humans manage to unplug from that false reality and form a community of resistance. They live together in a crowded, smelly ship. But they've decided that they want truth over fantasy. They participate together in a high-stakes adventure. They learn to treasure and care for each other. There is pain and danger in it, but each of them gets to offer their different gifts for the resistance in *a way that matters.*

In a similar way, Jesus offers us the chance to live as part of a rebel band that lives in reality as part of God's revolutionary force for the good and the beautiful. Because of our sin, banding together is challenging. But as we come to know that we are loved by the Merciful Other, and as we imitate that example, we find ourselves both being healed and healing others as we dwell in God's gracious inn.

Bibliography

Curtis, Adam. *The Century of the Self, Part 1: Happiness Machines.* 2002; London: BBC, March 17, 2002. TV.

———. *The Century of the Self, Part 3: The Policeman in Our Heads.* 2002; London: BBC, March 31, 2002. TV.

Hauerwas, Stanley, and William Willimon. *Resident Aliens: A Provocative Christian Assessment of Culture and Ministry for People Who Know That Something Is Wrong.* Nashville: Abingdon, 1989.

McGill, Arthur. *Suffering: A Test of Theological Method.* Eugene, OR: Wipf and Stock, 2006.

Pohl, Christine D. *Living into Community: Cultivating Practices That Sustain Us.* Grand Rapids: Eerdmans, 2012.

———. *Making Room: Recovering Hospitality as a Christian* Tradition. Grand Rapids: Eerdmans, 1999.

Rubin, Marty. *The Boiled Frog Syndrome: A Novel of Love, Sex and Politics.* New York: Alyson, 1988.

Volf, Miroslav. *Exclusion and Embrace.* Nashville: Abingdon, 1996.

The Gift of
Vulnerable Community

Jamie Arpin-Ricci

"He's dead."

I bolted upright in my bed, the unexpected finality of these dreaded words failing to cut through the fog of the sleep I was just dragged from. The phone pressed to my ear, I desperately tried to clear the cobwebs of sleep from my groggy brain.

"What?" I asked, sure that I had not heard correctly.

"He's dead. Alan's dead. The police and ambulance are on their way."

A long-time member of Little Flowers Community, our small urban church, Alan was living apart from his wife after recent marital problems. With his history of depression and suicidal impulses, my mind imagined the worst. Dressing in the dark, I prepared myself to break the news to his wife while still feeling as though none of it could be real. Thus began a long and difficult night of grief, fear, uncertainty, and anger. I finally returned home as the sun began to rise. I was shaken but otherwise all right.

Or so I thought. Weeks later, while attending a community block party in the local park, I fell apart. Irrational panic gripped me and I couldn't breathe. "Pull it together!" I berated myself internally, but to no avail. It only dawned on me later that the park sat within several feet of the house where Alan had died. Over the following days, it became clear that something was wrong. After consulting with a friend who is a therapist, I realized that I had post-traumatic stress disorder, or PTSD. While it was likely to have been rooted in an earlier trauma (seeing a friend publicly take his own life), recent events triggered it strongly.

Up until this point, my sense of identity and purpose had largely been built on my role as the pastor of our small urban church, where many of our members lived with mental illnesses of varying degrees of treatment and severity. It was a difficult role, but it was something I did well. I was known as the guy who was able to have the "difficult conversations." Yet where I once was the pastor *to* those with mental illness, I had now become the pastor *with* mental illness. No amount of "trying harder" or "pulling myself together" was enough. I needed help. With a sense of failure and even guilt, I shared my weakness and my need with the community, telling them that I would need time to pursue healing and to learn to manage my PTSD. In truth, I secretly felt shame. I was supposed to be stronger than this.

And yet, it was in that moment of acknowledging my weakness, of admitting my need, that the community came around me with such gentleness and compassion that I was left speechless (a rare situation, as anyone who knows me will confirm). Despite all that I had learned about humility and mutuality from such inspirations as St. Francis of Assisi and Dorothy Day, I was not prepared to be the recipient of such grace and support. This was not because of the nature of my community, as they had always been fully gracious and supportive, but because unconsciously I had internalized expectations about the role I played—the pastor who ministered to others—and the role they played—the recipients of my ministry. Confronted with my own arrogant assumptions, I was reminded immediately of the words of Christine Pohl:

> Persons who have never experienced need or marginality, or who are uncomfortable with their own vulnerability, often find it easier to be hosts than guests. Sometimes they insist on taking the role of hosts, even in the domain of another. Giving the appearance of generosity, they reinforce existing patterns of status and wealth and avoid questions about distributions of power and resources. They make others, especially poor people, passive recipients in their own families, churches, or communities. Recipients of such "hospitality" thus become guests in their own house.[1]

Everyone experiences need at some stage in their lives. While few people are guilty of intentionally undermining people in their own homes, most of us who come from positions of privilege (whether racial, socio-economic, gender-based, or otherwise) fall prey to this pattern to some degree. My own new experience of need and marginality presented me with this choice: either face and acknowledge my vulnerability or build walls of (seemingly)

---

1. Pohl, *Making Room,* 119.

protective pretense, a move that would continue to perpetuate the positions and biases of privilege while almost certainly leading to my own burnout, as well.

I came to recognize that when my friends were open about their mental illnesses (and the needs and limits that went with them), they were being vulnerable, not weak. Stop and consider the implication of that subversive and unintuitive truth: they were being *vulnerable*, not *weak*. We are all weak in one way or another; yet vulnerability distinguishes itself in the face of that weakness through its voluntary posture of honesty, dependency, and trust. Through our willing vulnerability to God and others, weakness is transformed into strength. This courage and honesty is strength in its truest form, the kind of subversive strength that makes sense of the upside-down logic of the kingdom that proclaims, "When I am weak, then I am strong" (2 Cor 12:10).

What I began to learn in the light of my community's loving support was that the vulnerability of those with mental illness was, in fact, a precious gift to me and to the wider community—a means of grace. While their illnesses were not a blessing, their faithfulness, humility, and mutual support in the midst of their illnesses were great gifts. Blessed are the poor in spirit, for theirs is the Kingdom of God! While it was important that they willingly acknowledged and addressed their illnesses, the reality of their struggles actually freed them from the pretense most of us work so hard to maintain for fear of rejection, alienation, and insufficiency. Yet, when we trust God and choose to embrace that same vulnerability ourselves, everything changes:

> When we try to hide from the reality of human vulnerability and weakness, whether our own or others', we shut out the people who manifest that condition most acutely. We certainly find it hard to imagine that we can receive help from the most marginalized people. Hosts who recognize the "woundedness" in themselves and their ongoing need for grace and mercy, but continue to care for others, find in God their sufficiency.[2]

As I found my sufficiency in God through willing vulnerability, both in and with my community, my eyes began to see things very differently. I began to recognize that those who embrace this voluntary vulnerability, choosing to admit and expose their insufficiency, were very often the healthiest, the most Christ-like. And often, they were the last group I would have considered to display this kind of character. One such group that my eyes (and heart) have been open to more than any other is Alcoholics Anonymous.

---

2. Pohl, *Making Room*, 118–19.

The Community of Alcoholics Anonymous

One evening, while flipping through channels on television, I began to notice how many shows—be they drama, comedy, or otherwise—portrayed
the church in a less than flattering light. Common themes included self-
righteousness, willful ignorance, superstition, even open bigotry. While not
always fair, the barbs stuck more often than not because they were rooted
in enough truth to catch. I was saddened (though not surprised) by how
consistently this portrayal was represented in pop culture, reflecting many
assumptions of the average viewer. Not long afterward, I came across several other TV programs and films in which Alcoholics Anonymous (AA)
was represented. Almost without exception, these groups were portrayed
with great respect. Rarely, if ever, were they depicted unfavorably or in a
disparagingly comedic style; instead, they were shown as places of genuine
safety and honesty, with members who clearly cared for one another. As
consistently as public perception (at least from the perspective of television
writers and producers) was critical of religion, specifically Christianity, it
was equally affirming—even reverential—towards AA. With a few exceptions, the contrast was quite telling.

Sadly, it is not difficult to understand where this negative representa-
tion of the church comes from. "We think salvation belongs to the proper
and pious," says Brennan Manning, himself an alcoholic, "to those who
stand at a safe distance from the back alleys of existence, clucking their
judgments at those who have been soiled by life."[3] At the same time, I was
fascinated by the generally positive view of AA held by most people. Reflecting on my own admiration of the group, I began to recognize within
myself a deep longing for that kind of freedom—a freedom to be honest and
broken around a group of people. I was attracted to the idea of being part of
a group of people who not only shared a common experience of brokenness,
but also were equally and mutually committed to the pursuit of wholeness.
It was a place where, no matter how many times you failed, you were always
welcomed back or even pursued and encouraged to return. Even as I write
these words, I find myself grieved that they so rarely describe many people's
experience with the church.

Beautifully, if unexpectedly, the core to this powerful expression of
grace and community is the foundational acknowledgment of our brokenness. This does not mean that we are intrinsically evil. Nor does it suggest
that our state of brokenness or our need for healing are somehow a condition we should prefer over wholeness. Rather, it is about the liberty we

3. Manning, *The Ragamuffin Gospel*, 22.

find in acknowledging our brokenness and the comfort in discovering the mutuality of that condition. It is only then that we can have any expectation of healing and wholeness. This willing vulnerability is clearly laid out in the first of AA's well-known Twelve Steps: "We admitted we were powerless over alcohol—that our lives had become unmanageable." In this critical first step, the addict admits the truth about the depth of their problem, however far-reaching the consequences. It is the first step because it requires, above all else, that a person addresses the excuses and rationalizations, the lies and the pretenses that mask the depth of their addiction—one that goes far beyond mere chemical dependency. This foundational vulnerability is essential for all that follows in the journey toward sobriety and wholeness. It is a theme that remains constant at every stage of the process.

All too often, we believe that the church's most attractive and compelling witness will be "lives transformed by the gospel," which we understand primarily as lives visibly free of sin and strife. However, this frequently becomes more about what is seen by others than what lies in our hearts. This well-intentioned commitment to putting our best foot forward almost always backfires, with people seeing through a pretense of righteousness to the hidden (and inevitable) brokenness beneath. Further, when we see others in the church seemingly without struggle, we are more likely to cover over our own weaknesses and challenges, perpetuating the process even further.

> Because we want to be good or at least appear to be good, because we compare ourselves to others and often come up short, and because we want what we want but can't always admit it, we are prone toward hypocrisy, duplicity, and deception. It's a vulnerability that many religious folks face. In the close connections of community life, the pressure can be significant to keep up appearances, enhance our spiritual image, and cover our failures or perversions.[4]

Pretense becomes the cheap substitute for disciplined faithfulness. By placing the emphasis and expectation on an idealized version of the product of sanctification, we lose sight of the hope and reality in the process of sanctification.

It is not an uncommon sentiment for people to say that they wished the church could be known for the same kind of vulnerability that characterizes AA, that we would be characterized by the humble acknowledgment of our own failings, both personal and collective. Yet, we often overlook the fact that this cannot happen if our greatest witness is that we have become

---

4. Pohl, *Living into Community*, 161.

faultless "saints" who have somehow transcended sin and already come through the process onto the other side. Instead, such an expectation can only be realized when we accept that we are (and in this life, always will be) in the midst of this process of humbly being redeemed. Vulnerability through repentance, time and again, becomes a beacon of hope for those mired in the fear and struggles of their own brokenness. And so, just as members of AA must "work the steps," so too must we learn the disciplines of intentional vulnerability—as individuals, as communities, and as larger bodies of believers.

Vulnerable Community as Mission

Coming to terms with my own insufficiency opened my eyes to these dynamics present in my own community. While I had not internalized them fully, those truths had been present for years. Looking back at what was likely the original cause of my PTSD—previously having witnessed the public suicide of a member of our church—I realized that this new tragedy demonstrated the reality of God's grace in the community. The day we mourned the senseless loss, we came together in unpretentious grief. Our willingness to allow space for what everyone was experiencing—including (and perhaps especially) doubt and anger—enabled us to be genuinely present with one another, and in so doing, to realize more deeply the presence of God with us. Their human presence did not seek to heal but instead, by just being together and sharing the grief, invited the Spirit to heal us. In fact, half of the church moved into one of our community houses where my wife and I lived, staying for over a week to simply be together. It was a broken yet healing presence, reflecting the beauty of Eucharistic unity: in brokenness, we discover Christ.

Unexpectedly, in the midst of this raw and messy time as a community, people began to join us. Just when we felt like we didn't "have it all together," people saw in our community a deep, compelling expression of honest unity and commitment, even in the midst of our evident challenges—perhaps especially because of that. More often than not, they were people who had been hurt by the church elsewhere, rejected for their failings (whether genuine or wrongly perceived). They were those with mental illness who couldn't "behave appropriately," thus being pushed out of communities, organizations, and even apartments and rooming houses. We drew people who, like everyone else, longed to belong, but for whatever reason struggled to find their home. Without question, our raw nature also repelled many, those who feared such "excessive need" or those who simply were not a fit for who we were. There were times we were tempted to change ourselves to appeal to those people. After all, with so many burdens in our community, we desperately needed those who would bring greater stability, maturity, and support. Yet, while those things would certainly have been useful, we soon learned that an attempt to meet those needs by compromising the vulnerable community was too high a price to pay. It remains, to this day, a struggle to find the support we need while maintaining these commitments.

However, while perhaps not reflective of the metric of success that is defined by large numbers of "converts," we cultivated a depth and consistency that was missing in many of our lives. We found that the mission of God—the passionate pursuit of *shalom* born of love—was strongest and most "successful" when we were our most vulnerable, and as a result, we grow as a true community. Thus, the logic into which I had been discipled— where our invitation to mission required a level of "maturity" that all too often required privilege and pretense—proved to be false. While true maturity and moral, ethical, and spiritual uprightness are to be highly valued, we discovered that, indeed, when we are weak, then we are strong. What's more, we became this kind of vulnerably missional people by allowing ourselves to learn from those among us who modeled it best. While their lessons were not often of the classroom and note-taking variety and instead were frequently of the "I'm in crisis and need you now!" variety, without them we would never have learned what it meant to be the kind of community—the kind of Christians—Jesus calls us to be.

Perhaps we need to redefine how we conceive of mission. Christine Pohl offers us an invitation that would make an important first step: "Deep sensitivity to the suffering of those in need," she states, "comes from our ability to put ourselves in their position, and from remembering our own experiences of vulnerability and dependence."[5] One way in which we can put ourselves in their position is by turning to the ancient discipline of simplicity.

The Necessity of Simplicity

Little Flowers Community has long been committed to find ways to embrace the disciplines of simplicity. Because so many of us live in low-income brackets, embracing these practices is both necessary and beneficial; it challenges our character while making it possible to sustain ourselves over the long term, avoiding the bondage of excessive debt (and, for some, staying off the street). Through shared resources, co-housing, and many

5. Pohl, *Making Room*, 65.

other approaches, we have both learned and benefited deeply from pursuing simplicity. However, the one aspect of simplicity that has always been most challenging to embrace is the simplicity of time. While we have gained much from the advancement of technology, its promise to "free us up" has proven empty. Never before have people been so completely overwhelmed by busyness, both in the form of everyday responsibilities and the countless additions of recreational and casual pursuits. No sooner are we able to make time and space in our schedules than we fill it up with another meeting, a new TV show, one more activity for kids, or a church program.

Though some of these are nothing more than empty distractions, many are genuinely good things which, on their own, have merit. Yet, taken together, they can become an overwhelming burden that keeps us needlessly busy. In our community, we have come to embrace the difficult but liberating truth that the hardest choices we face are less often between that which is good and that which is bad, but rather between that which is good and that which is best. Thus, while challenging, this discipline is all the more critical because it is central to the kind of intentional, vulnerable community we've talked about thus far. Learning to discern the difference takes time, the Holy Spirit, and a community committed to this same end. All too often, we fail to embrace intentional vulnerability for the simple reason that we have not learned to make the time.

In order to enter into genuinely deep and vulnerable relationships with one another, we will need time and patience. Trust is earned slowly and is easily broken. Many on the margins have experienced great betrayal and alienation, so they can often be understandably cautious. "It can be risky," Christine Pohl notes, "to take the lead in creating a truthful environment. When we publicly acknowledge our frailties or temptations, other people, if they choose, can take advantage of our transparency and vulnerability."[6] Those of us with great privilege who enter into such relationships will find (painfully) how often we betray our own best intentions by how we engage others. Thus, building true community through vulnerability needs to be a slow and careful process.

Yet, when we are able to embrace such disciplines, the world is opened up to us in ways our busyness never allowed us to experience. We begin to appreciate even the simplest things in life. We become grateful for each precious relationship. We are amazed by the beauty and peace around us that we too often rush past in pursuit of "getting it done." "Gratitude and wonder are squeezed out when our lives are packed full of busyness and responsibilities," Pohl states. "There is simply no room, no time to notice.

---

6. Pohl, *Living into Community*, 124.

We experience God's gifts when we pause long enough to notice them."[7] In a world that values fast and big success, such an "inefficient" approach will cause many to balk. However, the alternative is growth that is a mile wide but only an inch deep.

Further, such a path of simplicity requires that we divest ourselves of other activities, commitments, and even many "good things" to focus more intentionally on the better thing that God has for us. This is hard enough to do when they are activities we enjoy and value. Yet, there are times when such commitment requires even more costly sacrifices. In Matthew 12, when Jesus is informed that his family is looking for him, he replies: "'Who is my mother, and who are my brothers?' Pointing to his disciples, he said, 'Here are my mother and my brothers. For whoever does the will of my Father in heaven is my brother and sister and mother.'" For Jesus (and thus for us), fidelity to the community of God means a realignment of allegiance and commitment.

This can be a hard pill to swallow in a time when many Christians have elevated the family to the pinnacle of God's best for humanity, virtually fetishizing it in some cases. Jesus is not denouncing the family; after all, even from the cross he made sure that his mother was cared for. However, in so doing, he broke down the barriers of familial loyalty and declared her to be family with "the disciple whom he loved." In other words, faithfulness to Jesus means entering a new family with a connection that transcends blood. Such relationships are also part of what it means to participate in the vulnerable community of Jesus—not where we neglect expected family commitments, but where that bond of love extends beyond boundaries of blood. This requires us, at times, to set aside our own expectations and resist some cultural norms (including church culture) in order to forge this broader, more embracing sense of family. Such a commitment does not come without cost. It is a sacrifice that is not always easy to make, and yet one very often critical in the formation and sustaining of genuine community and in the engagement of authentic mission.

Making Room

Recently, while walking through the neighborhood with a friend who serves as pastor of a sister church, I listened to him reflect on his few visits to Little Flowers Community. In the midst of people with stories and experiences largely foreign to him, he became very aware of his own privilege—white, male, middle-class, and so on.

7. Pohl, *Living into Community*, 29–30.

"I know the problem is mine," he admitted, "but I can't imagine feeling like I could belong in such a group." While I appreciated his vulnerable confession, I found myself surprised at how different my own experience had been. While I share much of his privilege, my experience at Little Flowers was entirely different. In fact, as I reflected on my years of sharing and serving in the community, I realized that I had never felt a truer sense of belonging in my four decades as a Christian. In truth, beyond something outside of my control, this group of people would be an unlikely set to choose to be friends. How did this happen? It happened because we made space:

> Hospitality, therefore, means primarily the creation of free space where the stranger can enter and become a friend instead of an enemy. Hospitality is not to change people, but to offer them space where change can take place. It is not to bring men and women over to our side, but to offer freedom not disturbed by dividing lines.[8]

What makes this space truly welcoming, what makes it so conducive to the very transformation that is only possible when we refuse to force or coerce it, is that it is a space where Christ is welcomed in. It is only when we welcome the other as we would welcome Christ that our relationships manifest the potential to transform weakness into strength. And this happens when we embrace the impossible love of God—for wherever love is, Christ is.

Bibliography

Manning, Brennan. *The Ragamuffin Gospel: Good News for the Bedraggled, Beat-Up, and Burnt Out*. Colorado Springs: Multnomah, 2005.

Nouwen, Henri. *Reaching Out: The Three Movements of the Spiritual Life*. New York: Doubleday, 1966.

Pohl, Christine D. *Living into Community: Cultivating Practices That Sustain Us*. Grand Rapids: Eerdmans, 2012.

———. *Making Room: Recovering Hospitality as a Christian Tradition*. Grand Rapids: Eerdmans, 1999.

8. Nouwen, *Reaching Out*, 71.

The Idolatry of Idealism
How the Practices Ground Life in Community

MARIA RUSSELL KENNEY

"The weekly gatherings are a real letdown. The music is so flat
and uninspiring. I'm looking for a dynamic preacher,
and all we get are these boring discussions."

"I thought we'd be doing really dynamic outreach here. I left the
traditional church because all the focus was internal, but it looks like
y'all are just the same. When is the real work going to happen?"

"All we do is work, work, work and give, give, give. I come to these
gatherings to be built up and experience Sabbath, not work even
harder. I'm just not getting anything out of this."

"This community just isn't living up to our expectations.
We'd hoped for so much more when we heard about you.
It's been a real disappointment."

W e couldn't understand what was happening. We had such high hopes
for this endeavor; we had begun it with the best of intentions. We
had endless meetings to discern our direction as a community; we ministered morning, noon, and night. We were trying to embody the best of

what we believed the church could be. So why did the ground seem to be constantly shifting beneath our feet? What were we doing wrong?

We had grand plans when we began Communality, a missional congregation in Lexington, Kentucky. We were committed to living out our faith in active and relevant ministry, making worship organic and authentic, putting what we were learning at seminary to work in the lives of people we encountered on the streets. And while we were practicing incarnational, "authentic" ministry, we would also be creating genuine Christian community. Co-housing, shared meals, hosting community gatherings, offering hospitality to "the least of these"—we were going to do it all.

Yet as time progressed, unforeseen difficulties arose. Ministry was not as simple or divinely blessed as we'd anticipated. People didn't flock to receive the wisdom we'd acquired in our studies; they took advantage of our generosity or—even worse—responded with indifference. The dramatic conversions we had anticipated never occurred. We waited for people to completely redeem their broken lives based upon their encounter with us, but they continued to struggle. Our ministry seemed so inferior to those inspiring vignettes in our seminary textbooks. And as upsetting as the ministry disappointments were, we somehow found ourselves even more demoralized by the internal struggles. Our anticipated blissful journey through communal life felt more like a forced march. Joy and spontaneity gave way to exhaustion and resentment. If Christ calls us to be yokefellows, then we were chafing under an ill-fitting harness.

Hurt feelings, unmet expectations, distrust and disappointment and disillusionment. This wasn't supposed to happen to us. We worked so hard, talked and prayed and thought so much. Surely, we reasoned, if we can just discern the right way, the perfect formula for life in ministry—how can you go wrong with a plan like that?

During those formative years, our community found ourselves increasingly connected to a network of similar communities, in an informal association collectively entitled the "New Monasticism." Within this network, we participated in several conferences aimed at the intersections of Christian community, ministry, and activism, hosting conversations on such topics as community formation and sustainability. During one such gathering, I co-hosted a session on community formation and nurture with David Janzen, author of *The Intentional Community Handbook* and a founding member of Reba Place Fellowship in Evanston, Illinois. When a participant asked about the "fun" of living in community, I jokingly replied, "One of the most difficult parts of Christian community is that there are too many idealists per square inch." David chuckled in agreement. While I meant it in jest, my remark contained more than a grain of truth. It was not until much later that I understood its depth and significance.

The problem we faced at Communality was not a lack of knowledge of the "hows" and "whats" of community. Nor was it a lack of ideals. Instead, it felt to me like an *excess* of them. Reflecting back on my spontaneous observation, I eventually recognized my central point: idealists are drawn to intentional communities in significant numbers, and for some reason, this isn't always a good thing.

The Complicated Nature of Idealism

One of the unexpected contradictions in Christian community is its relationship to idealism. Idealism may appear an unlikely focus for critique; after all, ideals are often viewed as some of the best things people possess. Alongside its alternatives—cynicism, fatalism, even realism—idealism appears virtuous, not vicious. And there are many benefits to the possession of ideals. First, ideals can provide *purpose* to human activity. Novelist James Baldwin once described the role of his writing as making a difference in how people see the world:

> The bottom line is this: You write in order to change the world, knowing perfectly well that you probably can't, but also knowing that literature is indispensable to the world. In some way, your aspirations and concern for a single man in fact do begin to change the world.[1]

Such noble ambitions give weight and meaning to lives both individual and collective. A shared dedication to fighting homelessness or living among "the least of these" can unite a community in powerful ways, providing focus and objectives that anchor the group and create a sense of internal identity.

Second, they can provide *direction* to our endeavors. German-American statesman Carl Schurz described his ideals as the stars by which sailors chart their courses: "But like the seafaring man on the desert of waters, you choose them as your guides, and following them you reach your destiny."[2] Within the field of virtue ethics, character traits are cultivated when they steer us in the direction of our truest purposes and highest ambitions. Viewing decisions through the lens of our ideals can help us discern and refine such foundations as theological orthodoxy and praxis. When Jesus declares, "Be perfect, even as our Father in heaven is perfect," we acknowledge and

1. Quoted in Romano, "James Baldwin Writing and Talking."
2. Schurz, *Speeches*, 54.

incorporate our ideals as they arise from our relationship with the living God.

Finally, ideals can provide *motivation* and *inspiration* for our tasks and our purpose in community. They embolden us in both the ordinary and the exceptional moments, keeping our feet moving while our eyes are fixed upon the ideals that guide us. In his weekly journal *Young India*, Mahatma Gandhi once wrote: "I am but a poor struggling soul yearning to be wholly good, wholly truthful and wholly non-violent in thought, word and deed, but ever failing to reach the ideal which I know to be true. It is a painful climb, but each step upwards makes me feel stronger and fit for the next."[3] He recognized that even while he struggled to reach the ideals that compelled him, their presence ahead of him strengthened both his ability and his resolve to continue his life's work.

Yet idealism may be more problematic than it first appears. Part of the issue relates to the two primary understandings of *ideals*—"a standard of perfection" and "a principle at which to aim."[4] These definitions, while holding some common ground, are in fact quite different: one emphasizes a yardstick against which we are measured, the other a goal towards which we are progressing. In them, we hear echoes of the debate on the meaning of Jesus' instruction from the Sermon on the Mount: "Be perfect, therefore, as your heavenly Father is perfect" (Matt 5:48). Read one way, these words command us to live faultlessly; through another lens, they direct us towards the goal of maturity in Christ. The word for "perfect" is *teleioi* in the original Greek; and *telos* (the root of *teleioi*) is defined as "an ultimate object or aim." But is this an end towards which we strive, or a standard to which we are accountable? This divergence of emphasis can also be seen in the two primary definitions of *idealism*—"the cherishing or pursuit of principles and goals" and "the separation of an idea from its action/reality."[5] Idealism can signify the pursuit of our values and creeds; it can also find expression in the separation of an idea from its living and lived reality.

This difference has significance for Christian faith and practice. For Christians, understandings of perfection and holiness—the "right" and the "good" thing to do—can be fraught with multiple layers of meaning. This is perhaps especially true of evangelicals, a faith tradition born from both social justice and vital piety. Idealism's complex relationship with Christian faith is intensified within Christian community. Our overlapping passions for the individual, the church, and the world can lead us to seek community

3. Gandhi, *Harijan*.

4. *Merriam-Webster English Dictionary*, s.v. "ideals."

5. *Merriam-Webster English Dictionary*, s.v. "idealism."

as a remedy for the deficiencies we perceive in our present reality, a solution for "all that is wrong with society, the church, and the people we have
lived with so far."[6] Speaking from over fifty years of lived experience, David
Janzen acknowledges how the visionary energy of intentional community
appeals to the young and passionate, noting that idealists tend to be drawn
to the prophetic flavor of intentional community. Moreover, he affirms their
passion and "heroic impulses," refusing to reduce it to immaturity or youthful naiveté.[7]

Yet despite our energy and our bravery, community rarely proves to be
the elixir we expect. Promises are broken; people prove unreliable, or duplic-
itous, or just plain annoying. Theologian and practitioner Chris Rice lived
for many years with his family at Antioch House, an intentional community
in Mississippi dedicated to social justice and racial reconciliation. Founded
by Spencer Perkins, son of civil rights activist and Christian Community
Development Association (CCDA) founder John Perkins, Chris spent many
years working and living alongside Spencer, his family, and several others
in a multifaceted journey of reconciliation and pursuit of biblical jubilee.
While their public witness emphasized unity and redemption, their private
story was more complicated. Years later, Chris reflected on the combination
of passion and inexperience that permeated their endeavor: "We had dived
into community as raw beginners. But we doled out opinions, challenged
each other, and churned out decisions like we had already won the gold
medal of community living."[8] When the vagaries and annoyances of human
relationships become overwhelming, when the imperfections of human
fallibility get in the way of achieving our lofty ambitions, it is tempting to
retreat to the safety of ideals. Ideals, after all, are crisp and clean, perfect and
unbending and unchanging. We feel secure (both spiritually and emotionally) when we discuss them; we feel righteous; we feel justified. However,
this is precisely the problem with retreating into our ideals. In *Life Together*,
Dietrich Bonhoeffer articulates the inherent danger of idealizing one's faith
community: "He who loves his dream of a community more than the Christian community itself becomes a destroyer of the latter, even though his
personal intentions may be ever so honest and earnest and sacrificial."[9] This
statement echoes the understanding of idealism as a separation of an idea
from its reality, and the tragic consequences this can have for community.

---

6. Janzen, *Community Handbook*, 3–4.

7. Janzen, *Community Handbook*, 276–77.

8. Rice, *Grace Matters*, 97.

9. Bonhoeffer, *Life Together*, 27.

Perhaps, then, it is not so counterintuitive that idealism is both a blessing and a curse to Christian community. Yet the precise ways that idealism damages community may not be readily apparent. David Janzen pinpoints the issue at hand: an ideal is problematic, he states, because "it is abstract, it is disembodied, it is left-brain, and in the biblical sense, it tends to become an idol."[10] What does he mean by "tends to become an idol"?

The Idolatry of Idealism

Idolatry, in the biblical sense, is a matter of tremendous import; it is one of the most serious accusations in Scripture.[11] Encompassing two of the Ten Commandments, idolatry is defined both as worshiping graven images and worshiping other gods. Scriptural descriptions of idols are often located outside our contexts and customs—dancing around the golden calf, worshiping foreign gods, meat sacrificed to fertility statues. Because we associate idolatry with such dated concepts, we can easily overlook the idols in our own lives and cultures. And when we do acknowledge the idols in our midst, we often choose the more obvious targets—compulsive shopping, sporting events, technology, financial achievement. We might even consider more "traditional" values as possibilities for idolatry—the nuclear family, our country, the Constitution. Idealism, however, is often considered an unqualified moral good, guiding us towards the best in ourselves. Ironically, this often contributes to the problem. "Until the last three years with Spencer and what they revealed about myself," noted Chris Rice, "I never would have imagined that perfectionists like me, who are so obsessive about goodness, could be as lost as rebellious prodigal sons who ran with the pigs."[12] Through the lens of idealism, perfectionism equals perfection, and obsessing over goodness equals goodness.

Recognizing idolatry in our own culture is easier when we understand its basic characteristics and consequences. At its core, idolatry is confusing the eternal and the temporary, the perfect and the imperfect; it forgets what is creation and what is creator.[13] Perhaps most relevant to the connection with idealism, idolatry is giving love, attention, and devotion to something other than our one true God. We turn away from the living God towards the lifeless idol.[14] "Even good ideals that we sometimes call 'values,'" says

10. Janzen, *Community Handbook*, 277.

11. Rosner, "Idolatry," 392.

12. Rice, *Grace Matters*, 206.

13. Rosner, "Idolatry," 392.

14. Rosner, "Idolatry," 394.

Janzen, "which we might get from reading the Gospels, can become idols when we separate them from Jesus, who is a living spirit embodied in the concrete lives of humans who suffer."[15] Whereas our God is alive, enfleshed, and relational, the idols we pursue are just the opposite.

There are several reasons that community can drift towards the idolatry of idealism. First, community can be *complicated*. The compromises needed to negotiate even everyday life are challenging in themselves; add in the assortment of ideals pursued in community and the complications increase by a factor of ten. A common but often overlooked problem in Christian community is the reality of competing ideals. Some of these are practical—simplicity versus hospitality, for example. We can trade in cars for bicycles in the pursuit of a smaller carbon footprint; or we can retain vehicles so we can serve people in the community who have transportation needs. We can purchase the smallest, most basic home; or we apportion some additional space for the practice of hospitality. We can fill our schedules with good works; or we can leave space and time for the unexpected crisis, the unexpected blessing. Which of these is the more virtuous?

These dichotomies are not questions of identifying the "right" and "wrong" answers, the "faithful" and "sinful" approaches. Each of these principles is significant and relevant and biblical. Yet when we seize upon one or two particular virtues or values and promote them to the exclusion of all others, we may feel as though we are being especially virtuous, sacrificial, *holy*—when in fact we are only being extreme. A failure to understand and acknowledge these tensions can lead to community members pitting their vision of the best way to live against each other, entrenching themselves in their positions and locating "faithfulness" and "authentic Christianity" solely within their own priorities—or mere preferences.

Second, like other forms of relationship, community can be *difficult*. A common misconception is that creating community will be easy to do if we are sincere, authentic, and faithful. While these qualities are essential to genuine community, they are not sufficient, in themselves, to sustain it. "Many people seem to believe that creating a community is a matter of simply gathering together under the same roof a few people who get on reasonably well together or who are committed to the same ideal," observes Janzen, noting that "the result can be disastrous!" Important and enduring goods rarely come easily, and community is no exception. We chafe as we wait on the word of God; we grumble when asked to do the hard work of the Kingdom; we resist submitting our will to God's will. Instead of patience, we opt for progress. Instead of slow, challenging work, we prefer efficiency and

15. Janzen, *Community Handbook*, 277.

results. In short, we do not want to be bothered with the messy, uncertain, frightening, relational, self-ruling, *living* God. Yet when we forsake the path upon which God has placed us, with all its uncertainties and messes, and seek instead to follow a god that promises clarity and precision, not only do we seek our own faith weakened as a result—we also miss out on the unexpected blessings and joys that the journey can provide.

Third, community can be *disappointing*. It is tough enough to take on a difficult task when you know you will be successful. But when the task is difficult *and* disappointing, the emotional weight can be hard to bear. While our initial experiences of community may be blissful and idyllic, this honeymoon period must inevitably end. We experience a "period of let-down . . . everything becomes dark; people now see only the faults of theirs and the community; everything gets on their nerves."[16] The "saints and heroes" with whom we live now appear hypocritical, tyrannical, or incompetent.[17] We fall from the mountain of idealistic ecstasy into the valley of disenchantment. This depth of this valley is usually in direct proportion to the level of idealism we directed towards the community.[18]

Fourth, community can be *vulnerable*, which is often a synonym for *frightening* and *embarrassing*. In community, like in marriage or in parenting, we inevitably come up against the worst parts of ourselves—rough edges, insecurities, shameful secrets. When faced with our vulnerabilities, rather than drawing close to God and one another in the pursuit of sanctification and genuine growth, it is tempting to reach for an easy answer, a tidy solution. This can be difficult to negotiate, particularly in something that we have invested with a great deal of moral value. This relates directly to the nature of community as disappointing, particularly when the disappointing element is oneself.

> The man who fashions a visionary ideal of community demands that it be realized by God, by others, and by himself. He enters the community of Christians with his demands, sets up his own law, and judges the brethren and God himself accordingly. He stands adamant, a living reproach to all others in the circle of brethren. He acts as if he is the creator of the Christian community, as if his dream binds men together. When things do not go his way, he calls the effort a failure. When his ideal picture is destroyed, he sees the community going to smash. So he becomes,

16. Vanier, *Community and Growth*, 78.

17. Vanier, *Community and Growth*, 78–9.

18. Vanier, *Community and Growth*, 79.

first an accuser of his brethren, then an accuser of God, and finally the despairing accuser of himself.[19]

Expressions of idealism are often thinly veiled expressions of pride, conveniently baptized and pressed into service so we can avoid the difficult work of revealing our own imperfections. Yet expressions of pride are themselves often manifestations of insecurity and inadequacy, which can surface when we feel attacked or critiqued or exposed. "I think an idol can be whatever we turn to when we're in pain," writes Sean Gladding, long-time friend and former member of Communality. "Or when we feel powerless. When we're afraid. When we're lonely. When we feel 'less than.' An idol is whatever we turn to when we're looking for security, for identity, for meaning in life."[20] Retreating behind our ideals allows us to feel protected and sheltered when we experience the uncertainties of real life with real people.

Finally, community can be *mundane, monotonous*, and just plain *aggravating*. Much like the unfortunate romantics who dream incessantly about the nature of love yet cannot tolerate the monotony of monogamy, community members can succumb to the temptation of preferring fantasy to reality. In our search for the magic and meaning of "intentional community," idealists can overlook the very people who constitute that community; what is worse, they can begin to hold them in contempt. This tendency is often voiced by the sentiment, "I love humanity; it's people that I don't like." In the classic novel *The Brothers Karamazov*, a religious elder reflects on his own preference for holding persons at arm's length: "In my dreams, I often make plans for the service of humanity, and perhaps I might actually face crucifixion if it were suddenly necessary. Yet I am incapable of living in the same room with anyone for two days together."[21] Humanity seems worthy of great sacrifice, until they slurp their soup or talk too much.

And when we distance ourselves from the people with whom God has placed us, we inevitably distance ourselves from God, as well. Be they sacred or profane, idols lead us away from the One to whom we owe our deepest allegiance. When we lose sight of the living God who is at the center of our lives and our communities, we can fall from love into legalism. When Jesus was chastised for healing on the Sabbath, he reminded the religious authorities that the Sabbath was made for man, not man for the Sabbath (Mark 2:27). This exposed the idolatry of the religious leaders and the Law they upheld, which placed more value upon the abstract yet technical understanding of Sabbath than it accorded to either the God who created Sabbath

---

19. Bonhoeffer, *Life Together*, 27–28.

20. Gladding, *Ten*, 216.

21. Dostoevsky, *Brothers Karamazov*, 71–72.

or the people for whom he created it. The Sabbath was created to glorify God and bless humanity; yet the Jewish people were now its servants.[22]

Idealism, then, is both helpful and problematic. It is unlikely to disappear from the equation of community, nor will the dilemma simply resolve itself. Perhaps the practices that support community can be of assistance in negotiating our idealism.

The Practices as Moderators of Idealism

In *Living into Community: Cultivating Practices That Sustain Us*, Christine Pohl outlines four practices that "are basic to human life."[23] They are, in fact, so basic that they are present in virtually every form of human relationships, although they usually exist in an "ordinary, taken-for-granted" fashion.[24] These practices—gratitude, truth-telling, promise-keeping, and hospitality—strengthen the fabric of communal life, weaving people together through the bonds of commitment and honesty and welcome. Moreover, they serve as a lens for considering the ways in which community often fails to meet our expectations. "It is tempting to talk and write about community in abstract and idealized terms," she notes, "but when we focus on actual congregations and communities, we often notice the failures—the betrayals, the hypocrisy, the grumbling, the closed doors."[25] Because the practices provide ways to consider community life in a grounded manner, they may prove helpful in navigating the complex relationship between idealism and community.

The Practice of Gratitude

Perhaps more than any of the other practices, gratitude can undercut the insidious idolatry of idealism. Christians in community (and perhaps Christians in general) often make the mistake of confusing the subjects and objects of our gratitude. In general, people hold high expectations about being thanked for our service to others, particularly to those outside the community. In *The Brothers Karamazov*, a wealthy woman from the upper classes was reflecting on her lack of faith and her fear of the eternal

22. Gladding, *Ten*, 216. He continues: "An idol is whatever we turn to that is not the God who freed those people from slavery in Egypt . . .And because it is not God, it always fails to do what we want it to do. What we *need* it to do. Even if our idol seems to serve us well for a while, eventually we end up serving *it*."

23. Pohl, *Living into Community*, 5.

24. Pohl, *Living into Community*, 6.

25. Pohl, *Living into Community*, 7.

unknown. The religious elder to whom is she confessing advises her that her faith could be strengthened by the "experience of active love." She replies that she loves humanity so much that she could undergo all manner of altruistic service to the downtrodden: "No wounds, no festering sores could at that moment frighten me. I would bind them up and wash them with my own hands. I would nurse the afflicted. I would be ready to kiss such wounds." The elder commends her for this selflessness; even if it is only a hypothetical "ideal" at present, it could blossom into actual good deeds. Yet her continued reflection highlights the connection between the service we render to others and the expected responses of gratitude.

> "But could I endure such a life for long?" the lady went on fervently, almost frantically. "That's the chief question—that's my most agonizing question. I shut my eyes and ask myself, 'Would you persevere long on that path? And if the patient whose wounds you are washing did not meet you with gratitude, but worried you with his whims, without valuing or remarking your charitable services, began abusing you and rudely commanding you, and complaining to the superior authorities of you (which often happens when people are in great suffering)—what then? Would you persevere in your love, or not?' And do you know, I came with horror to the conclusion that, if anything could dissipate my love to humanity, it would be ingratitude. In short, I am a hired servant, I expect my payment at once—that is, praise, and the repayment of love with love. Otherwise I am incapable of loving any one."[26]

The woman recognizes that even in her charitable work, in her heart she is merely someone who provides a service and expects her due reward. Any proffering of active love must be met with active gratitude, or her service is exposed as a purely contractual arrangement. Such an orientation fundamentally undercuts the *agape* nature of the active love we are called to embody. When we demand gratitude for our service of active love, we can fall prey to its deformations of presumption and grumbling.[27] We see gratitude as our due, our fair recompense for the services we provide. We fail to see that our true reward comes from God.

However, the answer is not to overlook the legitimate role gratitude plays in nurturing and strengthening community. Gratitude has been shown to be essential to the faithful and authentic nature of community and service. So how do we move from an expectation of repayment into a more

---

26. Dostoevsky, *Brothers Karamazov*, 72–73.

27. See Pohl, *Living into Community*, 6, for her discussion of deformations.

holy, holistic relationship with the practice of gratitude? The answer lies in reconsidering both the objects and the recipients of our gratitude. While we demand gratitude from those we serve, we simultaneously neglect the gratitude that we should cultivate towards God. Bonhoeffer notes that gratitude fundamentally realigns the believer, allowing us to "enter into that common life not as demanders but as thankful recipients". "We thank God for what he has done for us," he states. "We thank God for giving us brethren who live by his call, by his forgiveness, and his promise. We do not complain of what God does not give us; we rather thank God for what he does give us daily."[28] Whereas presumption and entitlement condition us to overlook the small graces that sustain us, the practice of gratitude enables us to celebrate the small victories that occur, to express our thanks consistently and concretely. Through the practice of gratitude, we dethrone ourselves and our ideals, acknowledging that God is the giver of good gifts, which we would do well to recognize. Moreover, this realignment is only possible because we recognize the source of these good gifts—God himself. It is God who "has already laid the only foundation of our fellowship . . . has bound us together in one body with other Christians in Jesus Christ, long before we entered into common life with them."[29] Through gratitude, we bear one another's burdens, thus fulfilling the law of Christ.

The Practice of Promise-Keeping

Like gratitude, promise-keeping can help us negotiate between the poles of perfection and failure. Promise-keeping is essential in community, for the very nature of making a promise is an acknowledgement that we will often fail to live fully into our best intentions. Marriage vows are an explicit and public recognition of the possibility that one might want to leave the marriage, whether legally or emotionally; the vows, spoken and witnessed, remind us that we remain committed to a less than ideal situation. Promise-keeping is an intentional recognition of two things: the reality that we are flawed and fallen, and our decision to remain together in spite of that reality.

> We shouldn't seek the ideal community. It is a question of loving those whom God has set beside us today. They are signs of God. We might have chosen different people, perhaps people who were more caring, cheerful, intelligent and like-minded. But these are the ones God has given us, the ones he has chosen

28. Bonhoeffer, *Life Together*, 28.
29. Bonhoeffer, *Life Together*, 28.

for us. It is with them that we are called to create unity and live in covenant.[30]

In community, especially Christian community, promise-keeping can take on a larger role, a deeper import than is initially apparent. Commitments made to one another, covenants into which we enter, tend to have a special and weighted significance, particularly our commitment to the community itself. When people value their ideals (and their vows) so highly, choosing not to stay can be experienced as a deep form of betrayal. Very often, when people choose to leave community, the words used to describe their departure are morally laden and quite negative: "quitting," "desertion," even "divorce." Instead of being a pillar of community, promise-keeping becomes a sledgehammer that knocks it down.

Even when everyone remains fully embedded in community, it is easy for people to believe—and then to assume, and then to expect—that our companions in community will always prioritize the same commitments that we hold as sacrosanct. Failing to acknowledge this can have complicated and unforeseen consequences. It can lead to homogeneity of community, falling back onto the human tendency to partner only with those whose lives most closely mirror our own. After all, it is easy to make commitments to a radical lifestyle, or certain forms of ministry, or to home schooling, if we know that the people with whom we are partnered value the same things in the same order. Problems arise, however, when people make commitments that differ from our own, thus leading to misunderstanding, disunity, and judgment. It is helpful to recognize that we live and operate within a constellation of promises, a network of commitments and vows and relationships. This does not imply weakness or compromise. Rather, it helps us to honor the varieties and locations of relationships into which God has placed us; it opens up our eyes to see the variety of ways in which God is working in our lives. Simply acknowledging that our commitments are complex and layered goes a long way in preventing idealism from undermining community.

Finally, we recognize that keeping ourselves rooted in Christ, first and foremost, is itself a kind of promise-keeping. "If we have other ideals that are higher than community in Christ, our attachment becomes conditional," says David Janzen. "But if our deepest desire is to live together as a witness to the kingdom of God, then we will find a common way."[31] Seeking first the Kingdom of God is an affirmation of our most fundamental commitment,

---

30. Vanier, *Community and Growth*, 45.

31. Janzen, *Community Handbook*, 299.

which is to God himself. Through this, all other things may be added to our fellowship (Matt 6:33).

The Practice of Truthfulness

Truthfulness is an another essential element of human relationships, and the practice of truth-telling is one of the primary ways this truthfulness is expressed. However, the complexities of life in community require some clarification on what this means and how it is done.

First, we need to be committed to a truthful way of seeing—a truthful, truth-*filled* acknowledgement of the moral complexity of our lives. Truthfulness is often a complicated business. This is not meant in a relativistic sense; we do not believe that truth is situational and subjective. Rather, it is a recognition of the fact that the reality of a given situation is rarely clean-cut or one-sided. In most situations, people genuinely intend to do the right thing. We try to love one another well; we try to deliver good sermons, or always do the dishes, or be faithful and trustworthy friends. The reality, however, is that we cannot always fully embody our good intentions. We are a mix of inconvenient adjectives—people are imperfect, finite, fallen. Circumstances arise, charge, and create conflict; promises are broken; commitments go unmet. A robust commitment to truth-telling—*and* a commitment to a robust understanding of the fullness of truth—stands against a flattened, two-dimensional, abstract understanding of "truth" that makes no allowances for human frailty, unforeseen circumstances, or tragic occurrences. The ability to assess a situation, to discern the factors at work and the relationships between them, are skills that are essential for truth-telling. Employing these skills, and bearing witness to the reality of a situation, can take communities far beyond the entrapment of ideals.

> One of the foundations of community is knowing that you will sin and be sinned against. It needs to be our daily expectation. But there also needs to be an expectation of forgiving others their sins and being forgiven. For some of us, "being forgiven" is harder, because we want not to sin . . . we need to create a culture that expects people to sin, and also expects them to be forgiven.[32]

When ideals are not met—and this will often be the case—the ability to perceive and bear witness to the whole of the truth reminds us that shortcomings need not be catastrophic. Failure need not be final, nor fatal.

Second, we must embody a commitment to speaking the entirety of the truth about a person or situation—the good as well as the bad. The

32. Rice, *Grace Matters*, 203.

common understanding of "telling someone the truth" usually means "telling them something they need to hear but probably won't want to hear." Its undertones are largely negative, and this reflects the relative importance we tend to place upon what we find to be "necessary criticism." This is certainly something that Christians require, both in community and in other relationships. "A Christian needs another Christian who speaks God's Word to him," Bonhoeffer reminds us. "He needs him again and again when he becomes uncertain and discouraged, for by himself he cannot help himself without belying the truth."[33] However, we are inclined to stop after the negative portions. Instead, Christians need to cultivate the practice of seeing and articulating the entirety of "the truth" about someone—recognizing the positive as well as the negative, acknowledging the daily struggles *and* the daily victories. Christine Pohl observed that practitioners of hospitality seemed to have learned this skill, and could be "startlingly honest about their own frailties and failures."[34] This is likely connected to their sustained engagement with the grittier realities of human life, as a robust commitment to lovingly speaking the whole of the truth reminds us of the realities within which we operate as people. We recognize our fallen nature; we remember that finitude is natural, not inherently sinful. We remind one another that our commitments are not to abstract principles, but to the living God and to the ones whom he has entrusted to us.

Third, when difficult words need to be spoken, we must speak them lovingly and within the context of committed relationship. This is not the same thing as the popular approach of conveying criticism by "speaking the truth in love." Truth-telling need not always be brash, confrontational, or negative. When we are frustrated by someone's inadequacies (or insecure about our own), it is easy to baptize our desire to lash out behind the phrase "speaking the truth in love." One friend described such an incident in his own life as "being a victim of a drive-by truth-telling!" We seem to think that adding that phrase to our words gives us license to speak any matter of criticism, no matter how wounding the words might be. In our words and deeds, "truth" should be as inextricably joined with love and compassion as they are in the character of God. Only then are we being truthful, in the fullest sense, to who God is calling us to be.

The Practice of Hospitality
Hospitality, the "making room" within ourselves for others, can be difficult to practice when caught in the web of idealism. Idealism is often paired with

33. Bonhoeffer, *Life Together,* 23.
34. Pohl, *Making Room,* 12.

productivity, efficiency, and outcomes. Hospitality, with its risky vulnerability and inherent "fragility," turns all this sideways. The very nature of hospitality can lead to both problematic idealism and to its disgruntled cousin, cynicism. Hospitality, especially when practiced in a counter-cultural way, may appear as an exciting adventure. It also presents an opportunity to "save the world," fixing all the problems we encounter. Yet hospitality is a difficult and demanding practice. Offered in the midst of scarcity, struggling to keep both doors and hearts open, it is easy to slip into pessimism and fatigue. "Charitable impulses can fade," notes Pohl, "as hosts grow wary or overwhelmed."[35] How do we avoid a problematic idealism that sets the stage for cynicism?

One of the most significant ways hospitality grounds Christian community is by the constant awareness of its "fragility," the honest recognition of the "difficulties, frailties, and failures" that accompany it.[36] Hospitality is a lived reminder that perfection is not possible in any sustained sense. Whereas idealism seeks to dominate and direct, hospitality necessarily "makes room" for the unexpected. Hospitality is about openness to the unknown, to the "other," a move that is inherently destabilizing. Christian hospitality is about recognizing that the locus of control lies outside ourselves, and that goodness can still occur when we don't always "get it right." While our attempts at hospitality may not "save the world" in the grandest sense, they can offer "a living demonstration of what is possible when people care."[37]

And this is how hospitality can, paradoxically, be one of the places where the best of our idealism is embodied. "The contemporary church hungers for models of a more authentic Christian life in which glimpses of the Kingdom can be seen and the promise of the Kingdom is embodied," Pohl states. "More than words or ideas, the world needs living pictures of what a life of hospitality could look like."[38] This emphasis upon the living nature of goodness as displayed in hospitality reclaims our idealism from the realm of the abstract, planting it firmly in the daily, embodied reality of Christian life. Peter Maurin, co-founder of the Catholic Worker Movement, stated it even more explicitly: "We need Houses of Hospitality to show what idealism looks like when it is practiced."[39] This practice of idealism will inevitably be messy and flawed; but it will be real, and alive, and good.

---

35. Pohl, *Making Room*, 133.

36. See Pohl, *Making Room*, 9, 12, 118, 171.

37. Pohl, *Making Room*, 132.

38. Pohl, *Making Room*, 10.

39. Peter Maurin quoted in Pohl, *Making Room*, 10, n. 9.

Finally, it is important to recognize that the practices themselves can become idols. "We are not saved by practices or by doing them well," Pohl reminds us. "We can make an idol out of a practice, imagining that through it we can define our identity or become good."[40] In turning to these practices to mediate our idealism, we should not substitute one rigid system for another. Like ideals, practices are good servants but bad masters. The good news is that we already have a master, the risen Christ. His yoke is easy and his burden is light.

Beyond Idealism

The statement by Peter Maurin points to a significant clarification in the discussion. It is important for communities to avoid the idolatry of idealism. However, this does not mean that we abandon any concept of values or standards. Nor do we want to devolve into cynicism, which was referred to earlier as idealism's "disgruntled cousin." In actuality, cynicism is a distortion of idealism, rather than its opposite. In the same way that grumbling, deception, and betrayal are deformations of gratitude, truthfulness, and promise-keeping, cynicism is a deformation of idealism, the same material but misshapen and corrupted. Comedian George Carlin once joked, "Inside every cynical person, there is a disappointed idealist," and the humor highlights the insight. The path from idealism to cynicism runs through disappointment; and because disappointment and disillusionment are so common in human relationships, cynicism can be difficult to avoid. However, while this may feel like a sign that we have made a mistake in pursuing community, it is actually an opportunity for sanctification. Disillusionment, when it does not lead to cynicism, can be a powerful tool in our spiritual maturity and growth in community, guiding us towards "a knowledge of genuine Christian fellowship."[41]

Communities should always strive to discern and embody "a life worthy of the calling which we have received" (Eph 4:1). And our ideals can play a significant role in this discernment. In many ways, they are the signposts on the journey of community, helping us navigate the journey and reminding us of our ultimate destination. They are also a natural manifestation of the commitment of youth and passion:

> Prophetic communities attract idealists, and it is not fair to
> dismiss their heroic impulses. Ideals are sometimes all that the

40. Pohl, *Living into Community*, 175.
41. Bonhoeffer, *Life Together*, 26–27.

young have for vision and motivation, lacking the experience
of suffering, of trying many things some of which fail, and of
finding renewal in God over a long-term struggle for justice.[42]

Yet the concept of idealism remains fairly problematic. Might there be other, more fruitful alternatives? Two possibilities are *vision* and *excellence*.

In *Resurrecting Excellence: Shaping Faithful Christian Ministry*, Gregory Jones and Kevin Armstrong speak of the need to pursue "excellent ministry." Yet the concept of excellence can easily fall prey to the very problems discussed above. But by tying it to resurrection, Jones reminds us that the excellence we seek is inextricably bound to the resurrection of the crucified Christ, who was broken and bloodied; it arises directly from it. This has clear implications for our understanding of excellence, and thus on our ideas for how to achieve it. Rather than looking to the predictable mechanisms of productivity and power, a faithful Christian approach to excellence makes space for the realities of our failings and weaknesses.[43] Excellence is cognizant and accepting of our frailties in ways that idealism is not. Indeed, this is partially the point, as Paul notes when discussing the spreading of the word of God: "Who is sufficient for these things?" (2 Cor 2:16). The answer, of course, is nobody. Our strength and striving will never be sufficient to accomplish the tasks he has set for us; we cannot complete them by living better or being smarter or working harder. Instead, the Kingdom will be declared through the creative activity of God and humanity and through communities of commitment and faithfulness.[44]

They then relate a story from Christine's visit to their colloquium on excellence. In the midst of a discussion on the "beauty, history, and mystery" of church liturgy, a graduate student in this field related to Christine that "she could not bear to participate in the liturgy of the church when it wasn't done well." Excellence, for her, could only be found in "a flawless and beautiful performance." Reflecting on that conversation, Pohl contemplated the "mysterious connections" between our fallenness and our blessedness:

> Somehow, there have to be congregations willing to acknowl-
> edge the mysterious connections between the cross and their

42. Janzen, *Community Handbook*, 276–77.

43. Jones and Armstrong, *Resurrecting Excellence*, 40.

44. Jones and Armstrong, *Resurrecting Excellence*, 40–41. They go on to remind the reader that this "is necessarily communal in nature, as Paul knew when he developed the image of the body of Christ. . .[this] communal understanding of excellence requires the cultivation of friendship instead of competition. It focuses on the life of the community instead of individual achievement alone. It reflects the willingness to share in the burdens and joys of others instead of measuring them by their skills and productivity" (Jones and Armstrong, *Resurrecting Excellence*, 41).

healing, between brokenness and the goodness of their life together. Excellent ministry must ultimately draw us nearer to the
brokenness of the cross as it simultaneously draws us to holiness
and wholeness.[45]

If our understanding of excellence moves us away from the cross and the
tomb, it will lead us away from the risen Christ as well.

Another valuable paradigm to consider is *vision*. Vision, as the people
of Antioch community so often noted, was often a gift from the Lord, and
without it "the people perish" (Prov 29:18). Vision was what empowered
Gandhi and Martin Luther King Jr. to stand in the face of formidable odds,
bearing witness to the reality of social injustice and the need for change.
"The power of vision was sacred," noted Chris Rice in his reflections on his
time at Antioch. "With vision, the ill-advised became everyday reality; and
foreboding obstacles and sacrifices became like mirages in the light of further great destinations."[46] Ideals can become ossified, fossilized. But vision
sees a path, a way forward, a promised land; and like pillars of cloud and
flame, a vision from the Lord leads us down the path towards the promised
land. With vision, you could begin the journey whenever the Lord called
you—"all the questions did not have to be answered before you undertook
the quest."[47] Vision, like excellence, makes room for both the problems and
the promise of Christian community.

Conclusion

*"This community just isn't living up to our expectations. We'd
hoped for so much more when we heard about you. It's been a real
disappointment."*

Years after this conversation took place, with all parties now invested in
new cities and new communities, the people in this conversation gathered
for dinner after a conference. With the hindsight of continued and varied
experience, and the additions of marriage and family, we reflected on our
years together at Communality. It was tempting to mourn the loss of our
"youthful idealism" and consign those years to the folly of youth. However,
the blessing of remaining connected—both to each other and to enduring
forms of vital ministry—pushed us to a deeper, more nuanced remembrance

45. Pohl, "Reflections," 4–5.

46. Rice, *Grace Matters*, 82.

47. Rice, *Grace Matters*, 206.

of our shared history. We were able to make allowances for our missteps that had previously angered us; we recalled our imperfections with laughter instead of embarrassment. The years had granted us wisdom and maturity, and with it a living awareness of the genius of Bonhoeffer's description of life together—"not an ideal which we must realize, but a reality created by God in Christ in which we may participate."[48] To participate in this gracious reality is a blessing and a privilege, and we recognized this, and rejoiced in it.

Bibliography

Bonhoeffer, Dietrich. *Life Together: The Classic Exploration of Christian Community.* New York: HarperCollins, 1954.

Dostoevsky, Fyodor. *The Brothers Karamazov.* New York: Bantam Classics, 1970.

Gandhi, Mahatma. *Harijan,* July 12, 1942.

Gladding, Sean. *Ten: Words of Life for an Addicted, Compulsive, Cynical, Divided and Worn Out Culture.* Downers Grove: InterVarsity, 2013.

Janzen, David. *The Intentional Christian Community Handbook: For Idealists, Hypocrites, and Wannabe Disciples of Jesus.* Brewster: Paraclete, 2013.

Jones, L. Gregory, and Kevin R. Armstrong. *Resurrecting Excellence: Shaping Faithful Christian Ministry.* Grand Rapids: Eerdmans, 2006.

Pohl, Christine. *Living into Community: Cultivating Practices That Sustain Us.* Grand Rapids: Eerdmans, 2011.

———. *Making Room: Recovering Hospitality as a Christian Tradition.* Grand Rapids: Eerdmans, 1999.

———. "Reflections on Excellent Ministry." Colloquium on Excellence in Ministry, Duke Divinity School, Durham, NC, September 27–28, 2001.

Rice, Chris. *Grace Matters: A True Story of Race, Friendship, and Faith in the Heart of the South.* San Francisco: Jossey-Bass, 2002.

Romano, John. "James Baldwin Writing and Talking." *New York Times,* September 23, 1979. https://www.nytimes.com/1979/09/23/archives/james-baldwin-writing-and-talking-baldwin-baldwin-authors-query.html.

Rosner, Brian. "Idolatry." In *Dictionary of Scripture and Ethics,* edited by Joel B. Green, 392–94. Grand Rapids: Baker Academic, 2011.

Schurz, Carl. *Speeches of Carl Schurz.* Philadelphia: J. B. Lippinctt & Co., 1865.

Vanier, Jean. *Community and Growth.* Rev. ed. Mahwah: Paulist, 1989.

48. Bonhoeffer, *Life Together,* 30.

Part Three

Practicing Friendship
Reorienting the Relationships

Toward a Theology of Friendship

Mary Fisher

As an adult, I have lived in four nations—Australia (twenty-two years), the United States (seventeen years), the People's Republic of China (eight years), and the United Kingdom (four years). Each sojourn has granted the extraordinary gift of friends—friendships with women and men from many races, economic and national backgrounds, religions, secular worldviews, and political ideologies. After committing to following Jesus of Nazareth as a young university graduate, years of study in Beijing in the late-1970s and early 1980s placed me among the first Chinese University students to enter university after Mao's disastrous Great Cultural Revolution. My fellow students also included hundreds of foreign students from scores of nations, including Palestine Liberation Organization personnel; the then-Khmer Rouge, extremely regimented North Korean students, wonderful young persons from the Philippines who were fleeing President Marcos, and two Coptic Christians from Egypt.

Fellow students challenged and consoled each other as they were affected by political trauma around the globe. Growing friendships led to my being questioned about life and I, too, was asking questions. Together, we suffered individual culture shock in many ways—the foreigner learning about China, the Chinese transitioning into new realities in their own nation. Some Chinese friends became the closest friends I have ever had. These friendships and later gifts of the "other" easily continue to be one of the two richest aspects of my life, including the gift of friends who do not journey in my faith path.

Over the past decades, each of these four nations has undergone extensive change. Australia has had four prime ministers between 2013 to 2015, and it has experienced economic change as China cut down on mineral imports. Domestic violence is on the increase, with governments seeking policy solutions. Debate on many issues is often hostile: immigration, refugees, treatment of indigenous persons, issues of racial cohesion, concepts of marriage, climate change, environmental degradation, religion, education policy, medical care, and international security. Sadly, a large percentage of persons ignore such issues, entertained instead by the illusions of celebrity in popular media ranging from YouTube to radio and television.

Similar debates have been heard in the United States and the United Kingdom. In a pessimistic 2016 column about the seemingly definite selection of Donald Trump as the Republican presidential candidate, conservative op-ed columnist David Brooks stated:

> This election—not only the Trump phenomenon but the rise of Bernie Sanders, also—has reminded us how much pain there is in this country. According to a Pew Research poll, 75 percent of Trump voters say that life has gotten worse for people like them over the last half century.[1]

He continued, citing fellow *New York Times* columnist Sabrina Tavernise: "This declinism intertwines with other horrible social statistics. The suicide rate has surged to a 30-year high—a sure sign of rampant social isolation. A record number of Americans believe the American dream is out of reach. And for millennials, social trust is at historic lows."[2]

In the United Kingdom, issues similar to those in the United States and Australia are amplified by referendums on membership of the European Union. The Conservative Party candidate attempted to link the Lord Mayor of London, a Muslim Labor politician, to Muslim extremists. Syrian and North African chaos has created refugees fleeing the aftermath of war, while the tragic aborting of the "Arab Spring" movements has further splintered the discussions of race, refugees, and indigenous peoples in the three Western nations. Disagreements on college campuses in these countries is increasingly perceived by some students and authorities as discrimination, with possible alternative discriminatory legal responses. Social media heightens such tension. Thus, it is clear that tolerance at a societal and personal level is no longer sufficient for cohesive civic stability.

In China, repression is reaching its highest levels since the Tiananmen Square protests of 1989. A tightening of political control has seen over a hundred-thousand persons removed from Communist Party membership

1. Brooks, "If Not Trump, What?"

2. Brooks, "If Not Trump, What?" In the USA 42,773 people died from suicide in 2014, compared with 29,199 in 1999 (found in Tavernise, "US Suicide Rate Surges").

in a mere eighteen months.[3] Political crackdowns in early 2016 resulted in the disappearance of Chinese nationals, if their emigrant relations (now Western nations' citizens) criticize the Communist government.[4]

All four of these nations are witnessing a significant and growing disparity between the wealthiest and poorest citizens. Each one increasingly displays an isolation of the wealthy, some in gated communities; housing developments where poorer citizens lose their rooted and placed community due to "gentrification"; ongoing drug use as a virulent social problem; and escalating rates of incarceration, particularly of poorer citizens. Single-occupant vehicles—often in extremely slow-moving commuter traffic during peak traffic of major cities—symbolize the increasing isolation of citizens. Even on "public" transport, citizens' isolation is marked by the dominance of individual smartphone addiction. Change clearly needs to occur for community cohesion, but life seems stalled in journeys divorced from fellow travelers whose lives seem to have no healthy destination.

In this environment of contending ideas and sociological forces, Charles Taylor's books *Sources of the Self, A Secular Age,* and *The Language Animal* give a philosophical history of different aspects of our journey into today's societal structures. Over three-hundred years of sweeping urbanization—through industrialization with consequent transport changes, the mechanization of production, and the passing of the guild-dominated industry and commerce technology—is largely responsible for the modern, Western model of the isolated, two-income-earning nuclear families (or, increasingly, single parent families). While this development has raised (for the majority of people) the standard of living from its pre-industrial level, globalization's moving economic forces have led to uncertainty amid the increasing sense, for many, of a loss of community at any level. This urbanization and globalization has been marked by a secularization of cultures, which is not necessarily a decline in religion, but rather a pluralization of the spiritual and religious components of society. He argues, furthermore, that this secularization has been marked by religion being used in political identity in ways that both reflect and result in conflict and violence.

Professor Taylor helps us understand how we ended up where we are, but we may still be unsure how to move towards change. I would like to consider friendship—both divine and human—as foundational for the Christian church, the eschatological, Spirit-filled community discipled to Jesus of Nazareth. Through friendship, we practice what it means to be human—to be embraced in the holy love of God. I believe the narrative

---

3. "Robber Barons, Beware."

4. E.g., Ramzy, "China's Cultural Revolution, Explained."

shaping of canonical trinitarian unveiling is crucial to our forming ecclesial practices of friendship. Such practices are essential to forge communal life empowered of the Spirit of resurrection, shaping us in the cruciform ways to be the new covenant community. Through and within this community, we follow the incarnate Son who invites us as family and friends into the presence of the Father.

As I observe the contemporary political, economic, social, and personal health fabric of those nations where I have lived, I am desperately aware of the need to reconsider the divine gifting and virtues foundational to sustaining practices of friendship. This particularly is true as friendships sustain the civic life of our communities, much like the salt and light of Matt 5:13-16. Today, I choose to live in a suburb of Sydney that contains over seventy nationalities among its one-hundred-thousand residents. Of the children in the local primary school, 89 percent do not speak English in their homes. In this environment, developing friendships has been my major daily emphasis as a citizen of the Kingdom of God, a sister within an eschatological community of predominantly Chinese persons. We are a community of the Kingdom, inaugurated in and through Jesus of Nazareth in the incarnation of the Son, who was sent of the Father anointed and empowered by the Spirit of God.

During my second season in the United States, I was gifted with the friendship of Christine Pohl. From the first day we met, in the chapel of Asbury Seminary, she encouraged me. She sought to guide me, a young academic, through the complex responsibilities of faculty life. She was quick to affirm where she heard positive student response to my teaching and was able to advise when faculty responsibilities appeared overwhelming. Years later, in a moment of serious illness, she was to ferry me to hospital after my doctor told her I could not wait for an ambulance. That first day in the hospital was September 10, 2001; and she sat with me the whole day. (The next day was her birthday—September 11, 2001.) Over the next two years, she cared for me for several months in her home as I dealt with major medical issues. She lived as the people who in 1972 welcomed me into journeying with Jesus. Her faithful presence in my life shaped my thinking on the practice of friendship as central to discipleship to the trinitarian creator covenant God of Israel, Father, Son, and Holy Spirit. Likewise, her practice of friendship shaped my understanding of the church as the eschatological Spirit-enlivened community of cruciform character, following after Jesus of Nazareth to serve others in the trinitarian-empowering of our heavenly Father's love. Her life, as much as her theology, challenged me to consider intellectually how hospitality was central to Israel's covenant narrative, unveiling the creator God as One desiring friendship with his covenant community for the *shalom* of all creation.

Her life also directed me to understand two things about ecclesiology. First, ecclesiology is about a worshipping community, shaped by Jesus' unveiling of the creator covenant God of Israel as Father, Son, and Spirit. Second, ecclesiology is about the divine gift of a God-indwelt community of people to the world. Through the divine-human friendship climaxing in the first-century, trinitarian, Jesus of Nazareth event, the creator's holy hospitality exploded forth in new life into human history. I more deeply understood that when God in Christ called human creatures his "friends" and gifted them with the divine Spirit, friendship between persons—divine and human—came to reflect a new way, a way of being human that was conformed to the way of the last Adam, Jesus Christ the life-giving Spirit (1 Cor 15:45).

In friendship with the creator, and through friendship with other persons, we are called to manifest divine hospitality to the world. Rather than seeing the "other" as enemies, we are to extend friendship to enemies through divinely empowered hospitality. And so, shaped by Christine's life of hospitable friendship, I reflect on initial fragments of a theology of friendship as foundational to the covenant hospitality of Israel's creator covenant God, who calls us into participation in the hospitality of divine friendship.[5]

Covenant Initiation as a Journey into Friendship: Abraham as the Friend of God

In his compendium of essays *The Weight of Glory*, C. S. Lewis speaks of the wonder of engaging daily with other persons.

> It is a serious thing to live in a society of possible gods and goddesses, to remember that the dullest and most uninteresting person you can talk to may one day be a creature which, if you saw it now, you would be strongly tempted to worship, or else

5. The other persons who have shaped my understanding of a canonical theology of friendship are Prof. Dennis Kinlaw and Prof. Joel Green. Dr. Kinlaw is the former President of Asbury College and my Professor in Old Testament and Christology at Asbury Seminary in 1983. Conversations for hours with him over decades since meeting him in Hong Kong in 1982 while on a break from China cause me to wonder if any thoughts I have are not simply Kinlaw echoes. Dr. Green since 1999 has encouraged me to continue in my struggle to understand the importance of trinitarian theological hermeneutics. Such consideration is essential if we are to read the canon not as modernist historians but through a trinitarian lens unveiled in the climax of Israel's covenant history in the first-century Jesus of Nazareth event and the eschatological outpouring of the Spirit birthing of the New Covenant cruciform community in the holy love of the Father.

a horror and a corruption such as you now meet, if at all, only in a nightmare. All day long we are, in some degree, helping each other to one or other of these destinations. It is in the light of these overwhelming possibilities, it is with the awe and the circumspection proper to them, that we should conduct all our dealings with one another, all friendships, all loves, all play, all politics. There are no ordinary people. You have never talked to a mere mortal. Nations, cultures, arts, civilizations—these are mortal, and their life is to ours as the life of a gnat. But it is immortals whom we joke with, work with, marry, snub, and exploit—immortal horrors or everlasting splendors.[6]

The wonder expressed by Lewis in encountering another person—a fellow immortal—must be considered in light of the early chapters of the Hebrew Scriptures. In the Genesis narrative, Abram encounters a god who is referred to by name—*El Shaddai*, the personal name of the God of Israel. The narrative God, revealed as creator, now initiates the covenant calling of Abram.

> Now the LORD said to Abram, "Go from your country and your kindred and your father's house to the land that I will show you. And I will make of you a great nation, and I will bless you, and make your name great, so that you will be a blessing. I will bless those who bless you, and him who curses you I will curse; and by you all the families of the earth shall bless themselves." (Gen 12:1–3)

It might be expected that this spectacular promise would guarantee that Abram's journey moves smoothly forward, characterized by obedience and trust. However, Genesis tells a somewhat different story, one of doubt and uncertainty, vacillation and maneuvering. After his initial calling, Abram moves through the land and worships at Shechem and Bethel in remembrance of the promise of God—which God himself repeats at Shechem (Gen 12:7–8). Yet as he goes into the land of Egypt, he risks the offspring God had promised him by allowing Sarai (masquerading as Abram's sister) to be taken into the Pharaoh's house (Gen 12:10–16). When plagues descend upon the land and the Pharaoh discovers the deception, he is outraged and orders Abram to leave Egypt (Gen 12:17–20).

From here, Abram is given the vision of the smoking pots of flame, as God himself—again initiating the covenant promise with Abram and his as-yet-theoretical descendants—solemnly confirms the covenant between them with the ritual of the animals divided in two (Genesis 15). But again, Abram acts from uncertainty instead of trust, turning to Hagar for

6. Lewis, *The Weight of Glory*, 46.

the inheritance he anticipates. The Lord then returns for the third time to Abram, this time establishing circumcision as the physical sign of the covenant between them and explicitly promising a son with his wife Sarai (Genesis 17). Yet even after this miraculous promise has been given, Abram—now renamed as Abraham—repeats his mistake of presenting Sarai—now renamed as Sarah—as his sister to ensure their safety in the land of Abimelech, King of Gerar (Genesis 20). God must again work through the person whom Abraham has deceived to restore Abraham and Sarah to the journey of covenant (Gen 20:3–8). Thus, Abraham's own narrative is a chronicle of calling, warring agony, mystery, wonder, stumbling questioning, and ongoing conversation—a dialogue of command and response between the creator God YHWH and Abram, who becomes in this journey Abraham.

This narrative reveals numerous important things about God. First, God is *personal*, named as One who can be addressed within an intimate, I-Thou relationship. Second, God is *narratival*, calling Abraham into a story that will be unfolding through him and yet beyond him. Finally, God is *faithful*, his faithfulness revealed in establishing both friendship and covenant with Abraham. This repeated divine, self-revealing faithfulness is exhibited in Genesis 12, then again in Genesis 15, and then again in Genesis 17 and 18 and 20. However, this faithfulness is inviting Abraham into a particular kind of relationship with God: Abraham is to be called the "friend of God." In Isaiah, the creator covenant God declares that "you, Israel, my servant, Jacob, whom I have chosen" is "the offspring of Abraham, my friend" (41:8). In remembering Israel's earliest covenant calling, both the Old and New Testaments refer to the patriarch Abraham's relationship with the creator God as defined in terms of being the friend of that God (2 Chr 20:7; Jas 2:23).

The wonder of such naming of the relationship is startling. Abraham is portrayed as afraid before the Pharaoh and King Abimelech. He is doubtful and uncertain about the manner in which the Lord will fulfil his promises, asking him outright: "O Lord YHWH, how am I to know that I shall possess it?" Abraham's calling, his journeying marked in remembering in worship, his presence with others in all the extreme complexities of life—from sexual intimacy as lover and husband to claiming territory to war—his strange blessing by a mysterious King Melchizedek, his covenant questioning, his conflicted fathering of Ishmael and Isaac, his patriarchal relationship with Sarai and Hagar, his being in both uncertain and occasional faithfulness, Abraham's contending with this creator covenant God—all these realities are grounded and intertwined in the creator covenant God calling Abraham and upheld by his continuous, divine, self-revealing faithfulness.

The narrative intertwines with C. S. Lewis's challenge: although Abraham's life is messy, the creator God calls him friend. This divine-human friendship is cradled amid displacement, and the confusing narration of a haphazard life reveals above all the faithfulness of this divine friend. Certainly, the creator covenant God encounters Abraham where he is, where Abraham resides and walks and continues to journey. And this creator God reveals Abraham's character to him (and to others around him) through a friendship that is rooted in covenant commitment. The startling ceremony in Genesis 15, wherein the creator humbles himself in a one-sided covenant commitment as Abraham's friend, reveals their relationship to be totally dependent upon the faithfulness of the creator. This friendship in all its complexity is purposeful, as it starts to unveil the creator to a broken creation. The covenant calling of Abraham in Genesis 12 is a response to the schism between YHWH and his creation so evident in Genesis 1–11; no friendship can be considered apart from this preliminary unveiling.

Furthermore, the creator God's friendship with Abraham has a teleological purpose that is uniquely unveiled within the Christian canon. In Abram-become-Abraham and Sarai-become-Sarah, all the families of the earth are to be blessed. This divine calling of Abraham as an initiation in friendship—with the express intention and purpose of blessing others—is a provocative notion in today's age, where the relationships are so transitory and where the language of "unfriending" another has arisen. That the creator's friendship with the covenantal patriarch is such a friendship should be a challenge to how we understand our choosing to be friends with all kinds of persons around us. This other-centered vision of friendship can be seen in Abraham's intercessory efforts on behalf of Sodom, as he repeatedly urges God to spare their lives (Gen 18:22–33).

Friendships of all kinds are unveiled in the Hebrew Scriptures, with the story of Job's friends on the one hand and the narrative of Jonathan and David on the other. Psalms, Proverbs, and the Song of Songs further contrast the wise practices of friendships with the folly of foolish friendships (Prov 13:20, 18:24). The prophets and the intertestamental writings all herald motifs of friendship which bring wisdom or folly. But the climax of Israel's story, narrated in the Gospels and other New Testament texts through theological narrative and practice, heralds the shaping of the eschatological, Spirit-led community following the Jesus way. As Stanley Hauerwas describes in *A Community of Character*, we are shaped by a particular theological narrative as a community of particular practices, and these practices sustain the vision of divine-human friendship that enables human friendship to reflect the inbreaking Kingdom to the world. Such a theology is foundational to our understanding the purposeful nature of the mystery of friendship, both divine-human friendship and human-human friendship.[7] And it cannot be understood without recognizing the Abrahamic covenant, which initiates divine-human friendship within the creator's covenantal commitment to all humanity.

But how do we participate, through friendship, in the creator's purposes for the world? For the answer, we now focus on new covenant friendship. This theology of friendship, grounded in the divine friendship of the creator covenant God of Israel towards men and women created in the divine image, is progressively unveiled in the Father sending the Son, both incarnate through the Spirit *and* anointed by the Spirit as the Messiah, Jesus of Nazareth.

Unveiled through Friendship: Jesus Inaugurating the Divine New Covenant

The narratives of friendship in the Gospels result in a transforming of our imaginations, as Jesus redefines friendship in what he reveals, critiques, and establishes. These new covenant friendships, arising as they do from the divine friendship extended to us by a gracious covenant God, invariably change how we see ourselves and how we see others. In the fifth chapter of Luke, we find the story of the paralytic who is unable to be transported through the crowd surrounding Jesus, and is then carried by his friends and lowered through the roof tiles into the middle of the crowd. Here an astounding story of co-inhering relatedness is unveiled. The wonder of friendship within the covenant community is emphasized. Their commitment to placing their friend literally at Jesus' feet reveals the deep reality of their faith, which results in Jesus pronouncing forgiveness to the paralyzed man (Luke 5:17–26). The willingness of these friends to act on behalf of another contains echoes of the intercessory friendship of Abraham pleading his case over the fate of Sodom with the creator. Paul reaffirms this understanding of covenantal, other-focused, divine-human friendship lived for the sake of others in Gal 6:2: "Bear ye one another's burden, and so fulfil the law of Christ." As we are friends with others, we reflect something of the teleological emphasis of friendship, in that our friendships—when rightly lived—point to our eternal friendship with God, who carries and even removes our burdens.

---

7. Recent work in trinitarian pneumatological Christology by persons such as Ralph Del Colle and Myk Habets is an important pathway into further understanding a theology of friendship. But such extensive work is beyond the province of this essay.

This story of the paralytic so early in Luke's narrative frames Israel's friendship with the creator covenant God in a new light, moving away from self-preoccupation into inhabiting a divine-human friendship for the sake of others. Luke further expands this by acknowledging that Jesus-friendship is not to determine the parceling out of possessions among family but rather inculcates a generosity of spirit toward the extended Kingdom purposes. In cultures where gifts of possession are often related to advancement, the community is being challenged to move beyond self-preoccupation toward a sacrificial care for the "other." Luke also highlights this other-oriented friendship in Jesus' command to select banqueting guests from the company of the lowliest—those who are unknown (Luke 14:7–14). Neither friends, nor relatives, nor the rich—but rather the poor, the crippled, the lame, and the blind are to be preferred with relationships of friendship. The host chooses to exalt such a Kingdom-shaped guest as "friend" and worthy of honor; and the upside-down nature of Kingdom friendship, always focusing beyond ourselves toward others, is firmly reinforced.

Furthermore, earlier in the text, Luke has exposed our often-judgmental assumptions, as Jesus characterizes those "friendships" that primarily involving critiquing one's neighbor as the action of hypocrites, who seek a speck in their neighbor's eye while ignoring the log in their own (Luke 5:13–34). Such critique heralds a transformation of how to see those around us, a sobering thought for Israel's covenant community (particularly as rendered in the Gentile author's Gospel). One notable example is Jesus' rather notorious designation as a "friend of tax collectors" (Matt 11:19; Luke 7:34). In first-century Israel, tax collectors were essential fund raisers for the occupying Roman garrison, which was housed in the Antonia Fortress overlooking the Second Temple. The garrison represented the authority and might of Rome's Emperor and Rome's imperial gods, looming above the Temple both figuratively and literally. How could the Messiah be the friend of such persons? Within these friendships, Jesus is redefining what Israel's distinctive relationship with the creator God is about. This is not a covenant relationship seeking national recognition and power for the covenant community. A challenge of Israel's understanding of covenant membership is underway. Acknowledging Jesus, who has identified the disciples as friends, is to be the standard of being included as friends in the covenantal community. As Jesus confounds much Jewish expectation of his day, the call to friendship with him is a call which is fraught with trials.

Perhaps one of the most startling reflections on friendship found in the Synoptic Gospels is Jesus' betrayal at the hands of Judas (Matt 26:47–56). Although Judas is designated in the text as "one or the twelve," he does not arrive with the other disciples; instead, he is "with a large crowd with swords and clubs, sent from the chief priests and the elders of the people" (26:47). At this crucial moment, Judas has left the friendship group to which he has belonged for three years and aligned himself with strangers. Even more poignant is that Judas chooses a kiss as his sign of betrayal: "'the one I will kiss is the man; arrest him.' At once he came up to Jesus and said, 'Hail, Master!' and kissed him" (26:48–49). Jesus responds in Matthew's account: "Friend, do what you are here to do" (26:50).

Thus, the narrative draws us in to consider that even in the greatest betrayal, the betrayer, the one for whom "it would have been better not to be born," is still potentially a recipient of Jesus' friendship. The least, the enemy, even the betrayer—do we comprehend the space that the grace of friendship with Jesus offers, how it "makes room" for those whom we would never view through the lens of such a relationship? What are the consequences of our comprehending this radical, reckless welcome?

Jesus maintaining his offer of friendship—even within a narrative of betrayal and desertion—reminds us of two realities. First, it is the Father's gift of the Son, in the power of the Spirit, that best exhibits what friendship is about. Our human understanding of friendship is too often reflected in the actions of the disciples, in treachery and abandonment. What's more, the poverty of how we humans view friendship when compared with Jesus' view of friendship is recorded in the Lukan account of the trial of Jesus. It is said that "politics makes strange bedfellows," and this is certainly the case in Luke's narrative: "That same day Herod and Pilate became friends with each other; before this they had been enemies" (Luke 23:12). Israel's dehumanizing political authority (represented by Herod) colludes with Rome's authority (depicted in Pilate); and those persons representing the cosmic opposition to Israel's creator covenant God are now described as "becoming friends."

Yet this should not be surprising, because the other reality to which the narrative points is that the disciples' ability to imitate the friendship Jesus offers is not yet possible. The life-giving Spirit has not been poured out; without it, human beings are not able to follow the gracious faithfulness of Jesus friendship. The feebleness of how we respond, in our own strength, to the grace of friendship is revealed in the failures of friendship that punctuate this narrative. As Jesus waits in sorrowful prayer for his betrayer to arrive, the friends whom he has brought with him to the garden repeatedly fall asleep (John 22:36–46); after his arrest, all the disciples desert him and flee (John 22:56); and in the midst of his trial, Peter denies Jesus three times (John 22:69–75). Only with the eschatological outpouring of the Spirit is the Spirit-empowered friendship of Jesus made possible; only then can we truly become imitators of Jesus' friendship.

Perhaps there is no better place to transition to the Johannine empha-sis on Jesus' naming his disciples as friends. After Jesus has prophesied his betrayal during the Passover meal in John 13, he continues to speak with his disciples in what is often known as the "high priestly" discourse. The in-terweaving of Jesus' co-inherence with the Father is repeated and repeated: "If you know me, you will know my Father also. From now on you do know him and have seen him" (John 14:7). He continues: "Whoever has seen me has seen the Father. How can you say, 'show us the Father'? Do you not believe that I am in the Father and the Father is in me? The words that I say to you I do not speak on my own; but the Father who dwells in me does his works" (John 14:9–10).

Here Jesus unveils what is referred to as the "perichoretic" or co-in-hering relationship between the Father and the Son. Trinitarian theologians in the last fifty years have spoken at length of this. For example, Dennis Kinlaw defines our inclusion in the co-inherence between the Father, Son, and Spirit in terms of perichoresis as explained by John of Damascus:

> The inner life of the triune Godhead is thus a life of commu-nion in which the three divine persons live from, for, and in one another. This concept implied a completely new perspective on what it means to be a human person. In Jesus, we confront both the eternal Son of God and Mary's Son. Jesus was not only divine; he was, and is, human. In showing us what an original divine person is, he also revealed what a human person was meant to be and—through Christ's atoning sacrifice—can be. As Paul would say, he is the second Adam, the last Adam, the true Adam.[8]

The explanation continues on of this co-inherence between the Father and Jesus and includes the giving of the Spirit by the Father in Jesus' name. It is in this ongoing exhortation by Jesus that the discussion of Jesus friendship receives its full meaning.

> This is my commandment, that you love one another as I have loved you. No one has greater love than this, to lay down one's life for one's friends. You are my friends if you do what I com-mand you. I do not call you servants any longer, because the ser-vant does not know what the master is doing; but I have called you friends, because I have made known to you everything that I have heard from my Father. (John 15:12–15)

---

8. Kinlaw, *Let's Start with Jesus*, 83.

Calling us friends, unveiling the relatedness of Father, Son, and Spirit for our benefit, focusing on his giving his life for his friends, and seeking the gift of the Spirit for our lives—through these actions, we start to understand the kinds of practices that are involved in friendships between Jesus followers. We understand in part that friendship with another is always "other" oriented. We live cruciform lives as friends for the well-being of others. But in an ecclesiology shaped by a trinitarian unveiling, in the incarnation of the Son and the eschatological outpouring of the Spirit, the Johannine Gospel further engages the focus of eschatological friendship.

Eschatological friendship within the Spirit community has three interwoven threads. First, our participation in friendship in the triune life of God—through abiding in Christ and being gifted in love by the eschatological life-giving Spirit—always hears the echo of Jesus' words: "As the Father sent me, so send I you" (John 20:21). It is missional in its very conception. Second, friendship for the Christian manifests the life-giving love of the Father, Son, and Spirit for a broken creation. Its foundational mission is to be one of bringing *shalom* to the world for whom Jesus gave his life. Third, this necessary divine-human friendship, incarnational and Spirit-led, cannot be divorced from our communal participation in the eschatological Spirit community. It necessitates that we learn the practices that will shape Christian virtue in our lives, for it is only through this discipleship that the world may know the love of the Father:

> The glory that you have given me I have given them. So that they may be one, as we are one, I in them and you in me, that they may become completely one, so that the world may know that you have sent me and have loved them even as you have loved me. (John 17:22–23)

The creator, the Spirit indwelt community, and the world are constantly in an inter-penetrating process through the life of the Spirit birthing friendships. Dennis Kinlaw locates friendships between human persons within the same perichoretic reality, drawing our attention to the life-giving reciprocity they generate: "Thus, persons are always found in webs of relationships. The relationships are reciprocal, a matter of giving and receiving. Persons draw their lives from others and find their fulfilment in giving themselves to one another."[9]

---

9. Kinlaw, *Let's Start with Jesus*, 83.

Forming *Shalom* Friendships in the World: The Practices of *Allēlōn* as Essential

It is one thing to state that participating in Spirit-breathed, divinely modeled friendship generates reciprocity and the promulgation of *shalom*; but how is this actually lived out within the eschatological Spirit community? A clear understanding of this economy of the Spirit may be best reflected in the Greek word *allēlōn*, translated by the two-word phrase "one another." Found over one-hundred times in the New Testament across ninety verses, its primary, fundamental emphasis is on loving one another, as the Johannine narrative clearly shows: "A new commandment I give to you, that you love one another; even as I have loved you, that you also love one another. By this all people will know that you are my disciples, if you have love for one another" (John 13:34–35). It is the clear and concise summary of Jesus' command to his disciples, "that you love one another as I have loved you" (John 15:12). Christ followers are called to love one another "with brotherly affection" and to "outdo one another in showing honor" (Rom 12:10). Loving one another is the only thing we are to owe each other; indeed, it is the very fulfilment of the law (Rom 13:8).

Some of these exhortations give greater content to this in-cohering love. We are to live in harmony with one another (Rom 12:6); we are to be patient, kind, and compassionate with one another (Eph 4:2, 32). We should confess our sins to one another and then pray (Jas 5:16). Some are quite practical, such as waiting for one another to begin a meal (1 Cor 11:33) and washing one another's feet (John 13:14). We are to instruct and admonish one another (Rom 15:14; Col 3:16); we are to accept and encourage one another (Rom 15:7; 1 Thess 4:18; Heb 3:13); we should "spur one another on to good deeds" (Heb 10:24). We should forgive one another (Col 3:13), submit to one another (Eph 5:21), and consider each other "better than ourselves" (Phil 2:3). We are not to lie, slander, or grumble against one another (Col 3:9; Jas 4:11, 5:9). And we should greet one another with a "holy kiss" (Rom 16:16; 1 Cor 16:20; 2 Cor 13:12)!

This taxonomy of the *allēlōn* verses in the New Testament also unveils how ecclesial friendship is established so that the nations may be discipled into the friendship of Jesus. Divine-human friendship always has its purpose in the establishment of the missional-minded, eschatological Spirit-breathed community, which understands that as the Father sent the Son empowered by the Spirit for the sake of the world, so too Jesus calls and sends us. "You did not choose me, but I chose you," Jesus tells the disciples. "And I appointed you to go and bear fruit, fruit that will last, so that the Father will give you whatever you ask him in my name. I am giving you these commands so that you may love one another" (John 15:16–17). Friendship with the triune creator covenant God of Israel—Father, Son, and Spirit—is foundational to understanding our purpose in this world. And friendship with each other in the eschatological Spirit community, following the cruciform life of Jesus and fulfilling the commandment to love one another, is foundational to achieving this purpose, which is exhibiting the love of the Father for the world.

In a world marked by secularization, conflict, and violent estrangement of the "other," I maintain that further discussion of a theology of friendship and its theological and teleological purposes is essential. Such a theology would be attentive to the creative construction of meaning and oriented towards the fostering of *shalom*. A theology of friendship that welcomes the excluded, the outsider, the other, the alienated, the enemy, is foundational to understanding the Spirit-empowered, cruciform life of Christ—sent of the Father for the sake of the world, which so desperately needs to experience friendship with God. It must therefore be sustained through practices of friendship that are immersed in hospitality, both towards one another and others, whom so often we desire to name as our enemies. And as Jesus shows us in unveiling the love of the Father, such hospitality is costly and only truly occurs where the Spirit is confounding our inclination toward enmity with the creator, each other, and the world. My friend Christine reflects such hospitality, and I am profoundly grateful.

Bibliography

Brooks, Davis. "If Not Trump, What?" *New York Times*, April 29, 2016. https://www.nytimes.com/2016/04/29/opinion/if-not-trump-what.html.

Hauerwas, Stanley. *A Community of Character: Toward a Constructive Christian Social Ethic*. South Bend: University of Notre Dame Press, 1991.

Heuertz, Christopher L., and Christine D. Pohl. *Friendship at the Margins: Discovering Mutuality in Service and Mission*. Grand Rapids: InterVarsity, 2010.

Kinlaw, Dennis. *Let's Start with Jesus: A New Way of Doing Theology*. Grand Rapids: Zondervan, 2005.

Lewis, C. S. *The Weight of Glory*. New York: HarperOne, 2001.

Pohl, Christine D. *Living into Community: Cultivating Practices That Sustain Us*. Grand Rapids: Eerdmans, 2012.

———. *Making Room: Recovering Hospitality as a Christian* Tradition. Grand Rapids: Eerdmans, 1999.

Ramzy, Austin. "China's Cultural Revolution, Explained." *New York Times*, April 14, 2016.

"Robber Barons, Beware." *Economist*, October 22, 2015.

False Centers
and Shifting Margins

Lamenting the Poverty of Our Friendships

Chris Heuertz

In the mid-1990s, a few friends from college and I shared an apartment in south India. We would frequently make trips up to Kolkata to do volunteer work with Mother Teresa and the Missionaries of Charity. One rainy night, we took refuge in a restaurant for dinner. Having ordered too much food, we packed our leftovers to go. Upon leaving the little hole-in-the-wall diner, we sloshed through mud puddles down a side alley and bumped into a quiet, unassuming homeless man with big, pleading eyes. Trying to stay dry, he sat on the side of the road wrapped in a rain-soaked blanket. Though he didn't ask, we offered him what remained from our dinner and he gladly accepted it. That's my first memory of Tuna. Since meeting him, I have never been the same.

It wasn't until a few years later that I actually started to get to know him. Tuna often sleeps on the sidewalk across the street from one of Kolkata's largest outdoor markets. He usually spends his days outside the city's famous Government Art College. Tuna carries all he owns in a dirty old bag or tied up in a thin frayed blanket. He almost always has a few old notebooks or a newspaper completely filled up with sketches and drawings. Sometimes he has an extra shirt or a tiny bar of soap, and every once in a while he manages to find a toothbrush for his few remaining teeth—but that is about all. Occasionally, he makes friends with a street dog (or a pack of them) that follows him around, sleeping with him at night on the sidewalk. At a mere ninety-six pounds, Tuna is worn out and tired. Poverty has had its way with him—and you can see it on his face, which looks about twenty years older than his actual age.

Trying to get to know Tuna has never been easy. For the past twenty years, as I make short visits to the city several times a year, I've spent quite a few meals trying to get him to talk about himself. After gentle persistence, he sometimes begins to recall things from his "old life." In eruptions of surprising vulnerability, Tuna has said that he had three brothers and sisters. He has said that his real name is Dipankar Pal (a typical Bengali name). When someone is able to make a tangible connection with him, it's short-lived and easily interrupted by the slightest of distractions. The folks who live and work in the neighborhood where Tuna spends most of his time have filled in some of the mysterious gaps about his past. They say that Tuna was a very talented and successful art student until something terrible happened to his brother; another version of the story hints at a lost love. Whatever the crisis, it was so traumatic that Tuna broke under the burden of it and went to the streets. Tuna is a visibly broken man. Sadness is carved into his face, and his kind eyes reflect a deep sense of the tragic. He seemed to want to remember, but there was something that wouldn't let him. For the most part, Tuna lives in his own world, and trying to tap into it is a difficult task.

Who Is My Friend? The Poverty of Our Friendships

Friendships are undoubtedly one of life's greatest gifts. However, they take real work and require quite a bit of effort if we want them to be authentic. Intimate, personal relationships can be tricky and uncomfortable, even with folks who are significantly like us. When we try to be friends with someone as visibly scarred as Tuna, our discomfort can cause us to turn away, rejecting them instead of reaching out.

What is a "poverty of friendship"? How do we discern it? I often ask people to take out their cell phones and look over their most recent phone calls and texts. Who is on that list? What names come up? How many of our recently contacted friends are people of a different race, ethnicity, or nationality? Do any folks outside our age bracket show up? For Christians, how many people are Hindu, Muslim, Jewish, or even non-religious? What about sexual orientation? What does our circle of friends communicate to people whose sexual preferences are different than ours? Presumably a list of our closest friends, how inclusive or isolated is our call history?

Certainly one's cell phone usage is not *the* singular measure for the diversity of their relationships, but for many people, the people whose names appear in the call history staring back at us from our phones look a lot like we do. Many of us have a homogenized circle of friends who live like us, look like us, and probably even worship like us. Our call history is often a mirror of who we are. This is the poverty of our friendships.

You see, most of our friendships can be incredibly self-serving or self-affirming. Typically, we surround ourselves with friends who reflect back to us a mirror of ourselves. This is our "false center"—the over-identification of parts of our core identities that we use to keep others at a distance. For example, I know that I fortify and perpetuate my own false centers by the ways I qualify those around me. Most of us are guilty of this. We commonly tuck little qualifiers into our colloquialisms while describing our friends by saying things like, "my gay friend Danielle . . . my black friend Shariff . . . my Muslim friend Jeelan . . . my Mexican friend Cesia." As a heterosexual, white, Christian, North American male I typically don't say "my straight friend Brent," or "my Caucasian friend Gabe," or my "Christian friend Ying," or "my American friend Leroy." The more differentiated someone is from me, especially based on their race, nationality, religion, or sexuality, the more I use descriptive terms to highlight our differences. This is perpetuated by the kinds of groups within which we insulate ourselves.

In the well-known parable of the Good Samaritan, Jesus has an exchange with a lawyer who knows that he is supposed to love his neighbor, but who seems to want to avoid this demand. To this end, he cleverly puts Jesus on the spot by asking for clarification on who is actually his neighbor. Jesus responds, as Jesus often does, by telling a story about responding to a person in distress, a story that Jesus follows up with his own question. In effect, Jesus turns the interrogation back towards the lawyer, asking instead: "To whom are you being a neighbor?" We could pose the same question about friendship. Like the lawyer seeking to justify himself, we question Jesus about who our friends should be, often assuming the answer is simply those who are like us—who are in our social or economic circles, who offer us advantages or comfort or pleasure. Indeed, many commentators on friendship throughout the years have said that these sorts of friendships are most common. Few people realize that Jesus is reversing the question, asking us: "To whom are you being a friend?" Fewer people still would guess that they are called to be a friend to someone like Tuna whose very presence is demanding and discomfiting. For followers of Jesus, however, this is precisely the case. Brian Edgar, one of Christine's Asbury colleagues, reminds us that our "Christian calling" is best understood as

> a life to which we are called, rather than primarily as specific
> activities of some kind . . . Christ calls us to a relationship—a
> friendship—with him and with all his other friends. This is the

primary focus. Every person, every relationship, every friendship is unique and important. These relationships certainly include different activities, including the exercise of various gifts and ministries and other occupations, but it is a mistake to turn what is secondary into what is primary. The gifts and occupations we engage in contribute to the relationship that is building between us and Christ and other friends of Christ—but it is the relationship that is primary.[1]

Most of my interactions with Tuna happen over a meal at Khalsa's, a little Northwest Frontier restaurant run by a kind Punjabi Sikh family. Over the years, a handful of friends have tried to keep in touch with Tuna, contributing to a running account that allows him to eat a couple of meals a day there. For most of us this is not a big deal, but for someone who lives on the streets it has been an answer to his prayers.

The thing is, Tuna doesn't like to eat alone. Sadly, he often skips meals while waiting patiently on the streets, looking for a friend to join him for lunch. When Tuna does see a friend, he shouts out their name and comes running. He immediately asks to be taken to lunch (or at least for a cup of tea) or the movies, if someone will take him. Though he expects you to pay for it, he is not looking for a handout. Rather, he is looking for an opportunity to be known and accepted over a plate of fish curry or a near-boiling cup of sweet milk tea (with lots and lots of sugar). An artist, Tuna is constantly drawing. And as a form of payment for the meals provided on his behalf, he loves to draw the faces of the friends with whom he eats. Nearly every one of these precious portraits are scribbled out on a slightly used Khalsa's napkin. As he sits down with a pen, he begins to fill whatever paper he has at hand with tiny, seemingly confusing little scratches and lines. Magically, they become the portrait of whoever has joined him for the meal. And as he draws, he shares his story bit by bit.

Pursuing relationship over activity is truly a demanding calling. Yet when we make the effort, friendships take on a life of their own that is larger than the sum of their parts, more than just the individual friends themselves. What I love about my friendship with Tuna is that it isn't based on what I can give to him, or on what he offers me, but what emerges among us when we're together. Tuna seems to know this instinctually, which is one reason he might forego meals when he has no one to share them with him. We both become someone greater than ourselves when we're able to share time, space, and life. And when we're not together, I attempt to live a life

---

1. Edgar, *God Is Friendship*, 241.

that reflects respect for the way that he suffers, hoping that I continue to be a good friend to him while we're apart.

Redefining Margins and Centers

By affirming our commitment to those on the so-called "margins," we reveal our pre-judgments and assumptions about the "center." The dominant culture attempts to define the social, economic, and political "centers" and tries to dictate our values so as to direct our way of life. The voice of the dominant culture tells us how we should relate to one another, what we should own, and how we should exert ourselves on the world. These centers are accepted to such an extent that they are seldom called into question.

It is not surprising that we begin to redefine our understanding of the world's centers after becoming Christians, but this is often not radical enough. We may unwittingly find ourselves reaffirming the world's centers long after becoming Christians. Although we see the value of serving others, relinquishing our power and possessions, and living a just life, we may continue to esteem progress, pop culture, business agglomerations, and American democracy. While one could argue the benefits of these ideologies and entities, they largely remain unquestioned centers of the dominant culture.

It is only when we detach ourselves from the world's claims on us that we can find the power to criticize its values. In fact, when we call these "centers" into question, we find ourselves marginalized. Yet, by holding up "marginal" as a value, we may unwittingly validate the centers. Instead, we must subvert the centers and redefine them. Living in the world, the dominant culture acts like a gravitational force, pulling us towards its values and ways of living. The orientation towards the margins is a task not only for us as individuals but also for our communities. The church's active presence on the margins is informed by its hope and vision for the future in which Jesus returns to renew the heavens and earth, to restore his Kingdom in fullness, and to bring those on the margins into his healing hands.

Sadly, when the church became a power-wielding institution, the original hopes for the future were co-opted. The institutional church's vision came to see the future as the continuation and extension of the church's power in the present and the establishment of the Kingdom of God through the expansion of the church's reign. In contrast to the institutional church's vision, mendicant orders and monastic communities saw the future in radical discontinuity with the present reality in which the church is a sign, but not the realization, of the Kingdom.

While the institutional church's hope for the future legitimized its actions, claims, and power in the present, the monastic and mendicant communities denounced that power, its claims and its legitimacy. Today, that which equates with the institutional church believes in the continuation of the present. It seeks political, economic, social, and even military might, believing that Christians are the best candidates to wield power in the interests of humanity and, ultimately, in the interests of God. The thought is that though the future may entail great calamity and destruction, the church's power in the present will be transferred to its power in the future. Therefore, the institutional church defends its power in the status quo.

When we want to move our sets of friendships or relationships into more accountable and grounded communities, we must begin by lamenting these divisions and our own racialization. For many of us, this posture of lament (simultaneously grieving what is wrong while hoping for what can be) starts by simply asking ourselves non-judging questions: "How full are the layers of my life? How 'community' are the communities I'm a part of?" Simple awareness or recognition of these divisions in our friendships and communities produces a spirit of lament that opens us up to the courage to confess, specifically confessing the poverty of our friendships.

So what do we do with this? Lament opens us up to the possibility of confession, but where does confession lead us?

Dismantling False Centers

The movement from lament to confession inevitably leads us to a practice of dismantling our false centers. Since recognizing how I qualify others as I describe them, I've tried to listen to myself and bring balance to how I speak of others. Sure, it's possible, and likely probable in most cases, that our false centers are simply an identification with the groups to which we belong. It's usually unintentionally fortified and almost always perpetuated without negative or harmful motivations. But the challenge is to dismantle these false centers towards an inclusionary posture grounded in love—one that creates open and safe spaces for the poverty of our friendships to be addressed and corrected. When we don't recognize the false center we've created around ourselves, we perpetuate exclusive environments that over-identify people by their differences, differences in relation to us.

When we don't lament, confess, and dismantle these false centers, we are guilty of perpetuating margins and unconsciously claiming the power of defining the marginalized. Redefining the margins and the center is a confessional journey held accountable in relationships, in friendships with the so-called "other." This journey requires a dismantling of the false centers through friendships that allows for our experience of friendship to become a crucible for conversion. Apart from the gift of friendships with those who are different from me, I become my own false center.

So what is it that compels us to develop relationships with those on the so-called margins? What makes someone willing to make themselves available like this? What are the implications of a spirituality that discovers Christ among the most vulnerable of the world's poor?

Over the years, the communities I've been a part of have spent countless hours reviewing passage after passage of Scripture referring to the orphaned and widowed, the hungry and defenseless, and the vulnerable and needy. Throughout Scripture, we find a number of generative and recurring themes that challenge our isolationist mentalities regarding the needs around us.[2]

Rather than simply reading the passages out of context or merely reducing them to trite and formulaic responses of benevolence to be practiced by the non-poor, we read the Scripture and then ask the question, "What does this say about God's character or action on behalf of those on the margins?" Reading and re-reading Scripture in this way has not only opened our minds to a depth of God's essence expressed in God's love, but it has softened our hearts as we allow ourselves to be embraced by our friends who suffer.[3] Put simply, Christ makes it very clear that all in need are our neighbors.

Engaging Scripture together has also shaped our understanding of "poverty" as understood in the "kingdom of humanity" versus the Kingdom of God. Poverty in the kingdom of humanity is a lie that dehumanizes the very essence of humanity by marring identity and dignity. Poverty in the Kingdom of God releases and enables our identity and dignity to be found in the slain Lamb. Poverty in the kingdom of humanity is offensive. Poverty in the Kingdom of God is redemptive. Poverty in the kingdom of humanity is imposed; people who are poor do not choose their poverty, it is forced

2. For example, God identifies with those who are poor (Prov 14:31, 17:5, 19:17; Isa 3:14–5); God establishes reciprocal relationships for those available to the needs of friends who are poor (Deut 15:4; Ps 41:1; Prov 21:13, 22:9); God validates the authenticity of our Christian virtue in relationship with poor people (Prov 19:17, 21:13, 22:9, 28:5, 29:7; Isa 28:17, 58:6–11; Jer 22:16; Jas. 2:5; 1 John 3:16–8); God uses the poor as a standard for judgment (Matt 25:36–9).

3. I have done much work to reclaim the distance created by referring to my friends as "the poor." Though much of the world is in fact very poor, many of them are theologically our brothers and sisters, and all of them our neighbors. Our community collectively embraces a vocation that seeks to identify with the poverty of our friends as an effort and attempt to humanize all of humanity.

upon them. Poverty is embraced in the Kingdom of God; Jesus became poor that we might become rich.

As Christians, it is imperative for us to find our true dignity and identity in Christ. Part of this process will include overcoming the false identities that hinder us from knowing God, such as identities formed through our lusts for power, security, and self-importance. By denouncing our status and self-centeredness, we can embrace through Christ our true identities as frail and interdependent. Jean Vanier, who has given his life to the mentally and physically disabled through the L'Arche communities, sums it up beautifully:

> Mission, then, does not imply an attitude of superiority or domination, an attitude of: "We know, you don't, so you must listen to us if you want to be well off. Otherwise you will be miserable." Mission springs necessarily from poverty and an inner wound, but also from trust in the love of God. Mission is not elitism. It is life given and flowing from the tomb of our beings which has been transformed into a source of life. It flows from the knowledge that we have been liberated through forgiveness; it flows from weakness and vulnerability.[4]

It is through our wounds that we journey towards healing; it is through our brokenness that we find the pathway to resurrection.

On Imperfections and Betrayal

Embracing our frailties and interdependence also serves to help us live well within community, where relationships often founder on the rocks of our imperfections. Sadly, I've lost quite a few friendships throughout my years of living, serving, and working in intentional communities. In my own experience I think back on how many of these friendships could have been saved had we not put our ideals of community first, causing the depth of friendships to go under-developed or unformed.

My teacher and friend, Fr. Richard Rohr, a modern mystic and spiritual master, often reflects about this in his teachings on community, which he defines not as "a system or structure, but a network of relationships."[5] "Without connectedness and communion," Rohr maintains, "we don't exist fully as our truest selves. Becoming who we really are is a matter of learning

4. Vanier, *Community and Growth*, 99.

5. Rohr, *Essential Teachings on Love*, 106.

how to become more and more deeply connected."[6] From over fifty years of community life, Fr. Richard shares about the dangers of those who join communities for the sake of community—often apart from authentic relationships within community. Rohr describes these kinds of folks as people arriving with a script, and everything in their community is assigned a role in their contrived drama, a role that each of the unknowing and unsuspecting actors can't help but fail in. Not knowing they are being used, they are bound to disappoint. The one with this quiet script predetermines how the community will be used; they've already mentally narrated to themselves how community will meet all their unmet needs to be accepted, loved, understood, celebrated, or whatever it is they feel so compelled to take from their new community. They idealize notions of community apart from the reality of what communities are made up from: real people who bring with them the beauty and tragedy of their flaws, woundedness, and brokenness.

In *Living into Community*, Christine sets practices that sustain community against deformations of those practices in order to show that the healthy and unhealthy realities of human life together are often fundamentally connected. For instance, she reminds us that "our deepest betrayals are tied to failures in our most significant relationships and commitments."[7] It is not surprising, then, that betrayal is usually a way of loving each other poorly. Discovering new kinds of friendships, friendships that dismantle our unfair expectations and take the focus off us, help ground our other relationships. When we can explore the gift of friendship we learn that most of our betrayals aren't betrayals at all, rather a failure of friendship.

It's tragic but true more often than not that in many communities friendship gets missed entirely. Though it's common, it still surprises me when I come across groups that are formed and held together without the basic bonding factor of friendship. Groups that struggle to endure or thrive in their community life apart from friendship are clearly fighting an uphill battle.

Of course, we are sometimes drawn together by shared interests or vocations, other times merely by geographical proximity—whatever the case, quite a few communities are formed, and in fact sustained, by factors other than friendship. However, I believe that friendship is the foundation for many of the strongest communities out there. Communities built around friendships have an anchor that grounds them throughout transitions, betrayals, and all sorts of unexpected gifts or challenges. Through friendship and the gifts of forgiveness and fidelity that accompany it, we find the

6. Rohr, *Essential Teachings on Love*, 105.

7. Pohl, *Living into Community*, 93.

means to continue in community, as Rohr affirms: "Of course, we won't be vulnerable enough to connect unless we learn to trust over and over again."[8] If we miss out on the gift of friendship in weaving our lives together, then our communities may simply perpetuate experimental spaces set up to fail or lead to deep resentments—something that few of us seem to have the emotional energy to continue to work through.

Tuna's acceptance of me isn't based on the good or bad things I've done; in fact, I'm pretty sure he doesn't really care that much about my achievements and disappointments. Tuna wants to be accepted, known, and loved.

True friends are the people in your life who aren't surprised by your accomplishments and least disappointed by your tragic failures. Our true friends know us enough to manage their expectations around the sense that we're not as bad as our worst moments and often better than our best. Learning to love each other, accepting the best and worst of each other, helps us avoid the misfortunes of betrayal. Building community around friendships creates accountability, and protecting friendships in community allows us to hold in check our notions or externalized abstractions of what we try to take from community.

Conclusion

Being friends with Tuna has been transformational for everyone who has met him. It has challenged us to move from a mindset of programmed ministry to one of relationship. For so long, many of us have perpetuated a mentality that has viewed the poor as objects and recipients of compassion and charity. But Tuna has reminded us of our need to include those who are poor in our lives through intimate relationships—not to see those who are poor as people we "minister to," but those with whom we identify. When we view him as a person with intrinsic dignity that points to his proper identity, we receive tremendous gifts from him. Being in relationship with Tuna has allowed us to move from giver to receiver. In our efforts and prayers to help "liberate" Tuna from his physical, emotional, and spiritual poverty, we have found ourselves being "liberated" by his presence in the life of our community. Though we had hoped to give to Tuna, he always seems to give us more.

Though he's been offered all forms of assistance, he opts to stay on the streets and live on his terms. As strange as it might sound to others, he has his rhythm of life. This is one of the challenges of being in friendship with Tuna. But it is those who seemingly have nothing to give who will give us the most. In seeking to love God, we must follow God's children—those

---

8. Rohr, *Essential Teachings on Love*, 105.

who are weak, those who are vulnerable—with an expression of that love embodied through voices reminding us to keep our love pure.

Inspired over one of these meals with Tuna, another friend, Matt Ammerman, wrote a moving song about friendship with Tuna, called "Don't Let Me Eat Alone":

> He put his paintbrushes away for a few
> The masterpiece become a fool
> He likes painting people he will never know
> They are high and he is low
> He draws my portrait and through confusing lines
> I see my face yeah it is mine
> I go to bed; the subject is for me so light
> But for you it's very, very cold tonight
> I like crows, man, and I read Edgar Allen Poe
> 'Cause he's a poet don't you know
> He took it fast, let's take it slow
> And he said
> I never read any of Poe
> So he's a poet, I guess you'd know
> I don't think so good and I speak kinda slow
> I never did read that much, but man I'd like a bite of lunch
> Don't make me eat alone
> Do I ask of you too much?
> I guess I could put down my book for a while
> Just to enjoy your crooked smile
> The pages don't give me the same sort of effect
> 'Cause I like your face and your dialect
> And I want to know just who you are
> But your words evade like covered stars
> You don't deserve this life you live
> To be the joke of some street kid
> If I met this devil in your head
> I'd push him down till he was dead
> It's a tragedy and it's killing me
> This daily mental killing spree
> Hey, if I could help you
> I'd really love to
> Yeah if I could help you
> I'd really love to
> I never read any of Poe
> So he's a poet I guess you'd know
> But I don't think so good and I speak kinda slow
> I never did read that much, but man I'd like a bite of lunch

Don't let me eat alone
Do I ask of you too much?[9]

Although we know that we are continually the rough draft of an unfinished novel, what's unresolved in his life is painful for him and painful to many of his friends. Tuna's story is unfinished, a restless reminder of process and longing. The stories of our lives will perpetually be incomplete and unresolved. In our relationship with Tuna, we are reminded that our call is not to save them, but to join together on a journey of love.

Bibliography

Edgar, Brian. *God Is Friendship: A Theology of Spirituality, Community, and Society.* Wilmore: Seedbed, 2013.

Heuertz, Christopher L., and Christine D. Pohl. *Friendship at the Margins: Discovering Mutuality in Service and Mission.* Grand Rapids: InterVarsity, 2010.

Pohl, Christine D. *Living into Community: Cultivating Practices That Sustain Us.* Grand Rapids: Eerdmans, 2012.

Rohr, Richard. *Essential Teachings on Love.* Maryknoll: Orbis, 2018.

Vanier, Jean. *Community and Growth.* 2nd ed. Mahwah: Paulist, 1989.

9. Lyrics from Matt Ammerman's song are used with permission.

Transgressive Friendships, Subversion, and Fluid Hierarchies

Justin Bronson Barringer

"God is friendship," posited Aelred of Rievaulx.[1] This is a bold statement, as philosophers and theologians have argued for millennia over the nature, meaning, and constitution of friendship. Cicero, for example, defines friendship as "mutual harmony in affairs human and divine coupled with benevolence and charity."[2] While generally satisfied with this definition, Aelred ultimately condenses Cicero's definition down to mutual charity (understood as "love").[3] Although Aelred admits that God is never described as friendship in the Bible, he concludes that what is true of charity must also be true of friendship, "since 'he that abides in friendship, abides in God, and God in him.'"[4] Thus, the character of friendship must be modeled upon the character of God. If he is correct, then friendship cannot be mere sentimentality, the clicking of a Facebook button. Rather, friendship is the place where righteousness and justice intertwine, where charity becomes mutual, where hell is overcome and heaven comes to earth. This is an eschatological reality because, as Pohl and Heuertz write in *Friendship at the Margins*, "Jesus offers us friendship, and that fact shapes a surprisingly subversive missional paradigm . . . Offering and receiving friendship breaks down the barriers of 'us' and 'them' and opens up possibilities of healing and

1. Aelred, *Spiritual Friendship*, 47. Aelred was a twelfth-century Cistercian monk known for his writings on spirituality and history.

2. Aelred, *Spiritual Friendship*, 34.

3. Aelred, *Spiritual Friendship*, 46.

4. Aelred, *Spiritual Friendship*, 47.

reconciliation."[5] To paraphrase 1 John 4:19, we offer friendship because he first offered friendship to us.

This essay will articulate the ways in which friendships subvert oppressive structures by creating and maintaining what I refer to as *fluid hierarchies*. As opposed to static hierarchies, in which there is always a clear authority structure, fluid hierarchies allow for authorities, decision-makers, and power-holders to change based on factors including the needs of the situation, the expertise of the people involved, and sometimes just the simple choice of one party to defer to another for the sake of maintaining the relationship. Further, this essay will argue that godly friendships are the context in which the Kingdom of God is most clearly seen on earth, and thus they are the very relationships against which even the most oppressive powers, the gates of hell, cannot prevail (Matt 16:18). Three particular elements of what Aelred calls true or spiritual friendship serve to create fluid hierarchies, namely *mutual charity, durability*, and *risk-taking*.

Many of the Greek philosophers, Aristotle among them, argued that friendship of people of different socio-economic groups was impossible; and to think one could be friends with the gods was absurd. However, in recognizing that God is friendship, Aelred was articulating the truth that it is in God's very nature to invite humanity into friendship with Godself. The biblical account of Jesus' life reveals the way that God befriended not only humanity, but those considered the outcasts and the reprobates. Jesus' friendships were sometimes considered problematic, even offensive, because they defied the ancient logic of the philosophers and the religious and moral codes of the Jews. Jesus' apparent transgression was highlighted when he was called "friend of sinners," and that transgression was part of what led him to the cross where he made a spectacle of the powers and principalities by giving up his life. Thus, Jesus provides humanity with the ultimate example of "transgressive" friendship.

Breaking with Tradition

I am not a fan of karaoke, but if I was ever going to participate I would sing Garth Brooks' song "Friends in Low Places" (and not only because it somehow sounds right even when sung off key). Jesus found many of his friends in low places. Not only did Jesus make friends while sitting at the tables of tax collectors and drinking with sinners, he was happy to dignify his tablemates as hosts and make himself their servant. Therefore, it seems plausible that when the religious elites called Jesus a "friend of sinners,"

---

5. Heuertz and Pohl, *Friendship at the Margins*, 30.

they were emphasizing their disgust with him; Jesus must be one of "those" people, the sinners. In one sense, they could not have been more wrong, as Jesus was certainly no sinner. However, in another sense they were quite right, as Jesus identified so closely with these sinful friends that he became sin on their behalf, living on the margins and dying the death of a criminal.

Heuertz and Pohl likewise note the Greek philosophical tradition that says "friendship requires equality of power and status" and therefore can only happen among equals.[6] However, in his genuine and mutual friendship with the "wrong" people, Jesus provided an alternate model to the gatekeepers of the Jewish faith and the traditions of Greek philosophy. For Christians, then, it is within friendship that each person should relate to the other as an equal. It is not so much that Christianity disagreed that friendship could only happen among equals; rather, "it was much more radical in that it argued that a common faith in Jesus Christ provided the basis for the equality that is needed for genuine friendship."[7] Living the reality that "all are one in Christ Jesus" makes possible the inclusivity and mutuality of Christian friendship.

One of the qualities I have observed in Christine is that she does not just teach about the practices of friendship, hospitality, and community; she embodies them. Because of her friendship with Jesus, she lifts her students up, making room for them to grow in friendship with God. Her classes have food so students will feel welcome; her lessons are often conversational so each person can share a word; and as students complete their studies, she gestures to them, "I no longer call you students, but friends." For me personally, she made this gesture when she told me I could call her "Christine" rather than "Dr. Pohl."

Mutuality and Fluid Hierarchies

Mutuality is a central aspect of Pohl's work on friendship, as it is and should be central to the life of discipleship. In our world, relationships often contain a clear and static hierarchy, but the mutuality among friends causes this type of hierarchy to dissolve in favor of more fluid ones. It is through and within mutually charitable friendship that the fluid hierarchies of a just community become possible, which in turn restores creation to the place where equity among humans is more important than position, privilege, and prosperity.[8] The friendships necessary for these personal and social

6. Heuertz and Pohl, *Friendship at the Margins*, 102.

7. Edgar, *God Is Friendship*, 154.

8. A brief caveat may be necessary here. The beginning of a friendship may involve a clear static hierarchy. The more powerful one may have to open up to the less powerful.

transformations require the shared pursuit of virtue. For instance, Aelred says true friendship is only possible "among the good."[9] Therefore, spiritual friendship does not depend on anything except that each friend is seeking virtue with the other.[10] Concern for one's own growth in virtue, and concern for a friend's growth in virtue, set the foundations for a more equitable relationship. Virtuous friendships are, therefore, the grounds for virtuous and equitable societies.

Friends might defer to one another when they recognize that the other friend is more virtuous, knowledgeable, or adept in a given area, as this can be a catalyst for growth for the one choosing deference. Thus, mutual charity is perhaps most clearly seen through mutual deference in the pursuit of virtue. This reflects the nature of the Trinity in which each one subordinates to the others at one time or another. In fact,

> Jesus' declaration of friendship, "I no longer call you servants
> . . . [but] friends" . . . is spoken as part of a passage of teaching
> that is permeated with reference to the dynamic Trinitarian re-
> lationships of the Father, the Son, and the Spirit. Jesus draws his
> disciples into a relationship that not only involves the believer
> and Jesus . . . but also the Father . . . and the Spirit.[11]

In the trinitarian relationship, into which we are called as the circle of friendship expands, we see the Son submitting to the Father's will, and the Father in turn exalting the Son (Luke 22:42; Phil 2:9–11). Edgar even makes the bold claim that "without friendship the concept of Trinity is sterile and pointless."[12]

This is what happens when Jesus bestows upon his disciples the title of friends. St. Ambrose expounds upon this declaration of Jesus by writing,

> [Jesus] gives the formula of friendship for us to follow: namely,
> that we do the will of our friend, that we disclose to our friend
> whatever confidences we have in our hearts, and that we be not
> ignorant of his confidences. Let us lay bare to him our heart and
> let him disclose his to us. For a friend hides nothing. If he is

9. Edgar, *God Is Friendship*, 67.

10. Edgar, *God Is Friendship*, 67. This is true even if they are only doing so within the friendship. See the discussion later in this essay in which more of Aelred's explanation of the way in which virtue is sought specifically within the bounds of friendship, even if vice prevails outside those bounds.

11. Edgar, *God Is Friendship*, 126.

12. Edgar, *God Is Friendship*, 127.

true, he pours forth his soul just as the Lord Jesus poured forth the mysteries of the Father.[13]

For Ambrose, then, Jesus' words to his disciples "you are my friend if you do what I command" are not really about Jesus forcing a static hierarchy on his disciples (John 15:14). Rather, he is clarifying for them how spiritual friendship works, wherein each member must be willing to defer to—perhaps even obey—the other. "Changing our way of life because of the example of Jesus," Edgar states, "indicates that we are his friends."[14] This is the kenotic ethic of Jesus who condescends to become the friend of sinners and even gives up his life for those friends, while simultaneously making a spectacle of the powers that be. The intensity of the friendship that Jesus shared with his disciples, one which he continued by sending the Spirit, provided them with the motivation to live an alternative society where the least were actually the greatest.

However, Christian friendship is not merely an exercise in duty or self-sacrifice. On the contrary, such friendships ought to be mutually beneficial.[15] This is especially important because, *contra* many of the classical Greek philosophers, friendships can happen between people with different levels of power. It is precisely this aspect of Christian friendships that makes them transformative, because it is the difference in experiences that often causes people to evaluate their beliefs, convictions, and actions. There are times when fluid hierarchies grow out of the friendship without any particular effort on the part of the friends themselves. It is often the case that the powerless in a friendship actually have the power to change the powerful through their very presence.

> Friendship . . . puts pressure on our lifestyle choices because our possessions and consumption patterns are hard to hide from friends. That is why it is often easier to keep people who are poor at a distance . . . Close proximity makes us more conscious of both abundance and lack. Friendships can move us to choose generosity over stinginess and modesty over extravagance.[16]

When each is concerned about the well-being of the other then, almost paradoxically, the friendship benefits both people and shapes communities of trust that birth and sustain fluid hierarchies. While it often seems that people of low status have nothing to contribute to a friendship with

---

13. Aelred, *Spiritual Friendship*, 108.

14. Edgar, *God Is Friendship*, 64.

15. Aelred, *Spiritual Friendship*, 72.

16. Heuertz and Pohl, *Friendship at the Margins*, 85–86.

someone who has material resources or power, the former can offer such things as "counsel in doubt, consolation in adversity, and other benefits of like nature."[17]

In Christian friendships, we are able to realize that "mutuality does not come from everyone doing the same thing or making the same contributions. It comes from shared humility, respect and appreciation for the other person, and some sense of shared vision or purpose."[18] Like the apostles, the church is comprised of people from all parts of society, even from segments that may be otherwise opposed to one another, because it is only in this diversity that we understand the complex interconnectedness of creation and appreciate the friendship extended by our creator.[19] If we only seek certain types of friends, namely those with material resources or lofty status, then "how many most worthy of all love shall we exclude" because we feel like they cannot help us improve our position in life?[20] But the transformation of self and society is made possible by friendships across social and power boundaries. As Heuertz and Pohl observe, "Having friends who are poor at the center of a community's life, rhythms, and purpose offers glimpses into what reconciliation with the so-called other actually looks like."[21]

Spiritual Friendships Are Durable

Along with mutual charity, friendships must be lasting. Spiritual friendships last through eternity as we learn to go ever deeper into our friendships with one another and with God. Dennis Billy, a commentator on Aelred's work, writes that

> [Friendships] are a primary means through which God's love comes into the world. They have a sacred, almost sacramental, quality to them that draws people closer to each other and to God. Spiritual friendships are eternal. They last forever, because they are forged in the love of one who has laid down his life for his friends.[22]

---

17. Heuertz and Pohl, *Friendship at the Margins*, 72.

18. Heuertz and Pohl, *Friendship at the Margins*, 78.

19. This is especially remarkable because we were enemies of God in our sin.

20. Aelred, *Spiritual Friendship*, 72.

21. Heuertz and Pohl, *Friendship at the Margins*, 12–13.

22. Aelred, *Spiritual Friendship*, 21.

As evidence for his belief in the eternal nature of true friendships, St. Jerome writes, "Friendship which can end was never true friendship."[23]

Spiritual friendships develop and endure over time because they are anchored in the bedrock of love. As Aelred notes about King Solomon, a friend loves at all times, which makes true friendships eternal.[24] True godly friendships are necessarily lasting because they are part of our sanctification. Friendship may begin with mere shared interests or good feelings, but it cannot be spiritual friendship "unless reason lead it, honor temper it, and justice rule it."[25] As a friendship grows, it ought to cause the people in it grow in their contemplativeness, integrity, and equity.

The fluid hierarchies necessary for a more just society take time to construct and reconstruct; therefore, the friendships that produce them must continue to grow over time. This requires both durability and faithfulness. Genuine friendship leads to "an *ongoing* community of love," which bears witness to the larger society that justice and mutuality are possible. However, this is risky because "such a love is self-giving and vulnerable; it puts the other person first."[26] Whenever we open ourselves up to another and expose ourselves to any number of hurts, we take the risk that the other will indeed exploit us. Jesus befriends sinners and gets crucified. So, too, when we befriend others we might face similar consequences.

Friendships Require Risk-Taking

In conversation with Aelred, one of his companions comments that perhaps friendship is too demanding and thus "should be avoided."[27] Aelred responds saying that it is worth the demands because virtue cannot be "acquired or preserved without solicitude."[28] Billy summarizes this position,

---

23. Aelred, *Spiritual Friendship*, 47.

24. Aelred, *Spiritual Friendship*, 35. Later, Aelred adds that "friendship bears fruit in this life and the next," which is indicative of the fact that spiritual friendships endure even death (59).

25. Aelred, *Spiritual Friendship*, 71. It is worth noting that Aelred is writing before the Enlightenment, so he means something very different that many moderns when he uses the word "reason." For him reason is more likely to mean something like "contemplative" or "thoughtfulness."

26. Heuertz and Pohl, *Friendship at the Margins*, 42. Emphasis mine.

27. Aelred, *Spiritual Friendship*, 67.

28. Aelred, *Spiritual Friendship*, 68. I am reminded here of C. S. Lewis's depiction of hell as a place where people are separated from one another so that they can be alone without the demands of relationships.

> To many, the potential risk of failure and heartbreak that will almost surely follow [having friends] are reasons enough for avoiding any close personal ties . . . Aelred could not disagree more with such people . . . The need for companionship is so deeply rooted in our hearts that it would be impossible for us to enjoy anything without it. Our yearning for friendship says something about the very fabric of our lives and about the nature of God in whose image, as Aelred so firmly believed, we are made.[29]

Such a relational ontology—the belief that humans are necessarily and fundamentally social beings made in the image of the triune God—stems from reading the Gospels, in which we see Jesus' acknowledgement of the importance of friendships, even when betrayal by one of those that Jesus called friend ended up in Jesus' shame and death.[30] There is a sense in which all friendships are risky because in friendship we open ourselves up to intimacy and vulnerability; however, the risk is multiplied in the sort of transgressive friendships that seek to replace oppressive hierarchies with ones that are just and fluid. Jesus' choice to build boundary-transgressing friendships not only made him vulnerable to betrayal by a friend, it caused the powers that be to actively pursue his death. Their power, fixed in place by societal rules and expectations, was threatened by his willingness to defy those conventions, which empowered the lowly and disempowered the high and mighty.

Furthermore, it is notable that "friend of sinners" is not a self-designation on Jesus' part, but the recognition of Jesus' reality as one who built friendships with those unlike himself. Jesus identified so much with these sinner friends that he even became sin on their behalf in order that they might identify with him as they are made into God's righteousness (2 Cor 5:21). Thus, when we enter into friendships with people unlike ourselves, those from different social, ethnic, or economic positions, we can—through our mutual sacrifice—become sin for one another as we are together made righteous with Christ in the midst of our friendship.

Spiritual friendship also allows friends to point out each other's bullshit.[31] As Heuertz and Pohl note, "Friendships are revelatory of truth."[32] This quality is a microcosm of what is needed in the wider society, one

---

29. Aelred, *Spiritual Friendship*, 78.

30. Jesus even refers to Judas as friend in the very moment in which Judas is to betray him (Matt 26:50), and the Judas' kiss would be recognized by early readers as a particularly perverted act of betrayal because kisses were usually shared between friends.

31. For an enlightening chapter on this concept, see B. Blodgett's chapter "Bullshit" in Blodgett, *Lives Entrusted*.

32. Heuertz and Pohl, *Friendship at the Margins*, 10.

which is necessary for destroying oppressive power structures. It excels in speaking truth to power because it forces each person in a friendship to consider humility, to fight inborn hubris as together they seek to serve rather than have people "serve" them through shallow affirmations of their own nonsense. Often it is the case that people flatter a person with wealth and power, but a true friend will risk her own well-being in order to speak truth to such an individual.[33]

Aelred writes about having one friendship with an irascible man, leading others to ask how the man could be admitted into friendship when he does not meet the requirements of friendship as "one seeking virtue." Aelred responds by saying that within the bounds of their friendship, the friend's bad behavior does not surface, and that because of their friendship Aelred can say that this friend "preserves the law of friendship toward me in such a way that I can restrain an outburst at any time by a mere nod, even if it is already breaking forth into speech, so that he never reveals in public what is displeasing." Yet even with this friend, Aelred says, "We give in to each other so that sometimes he yields to me, but I generally yield to him."[34] This is an example of the way a fluid hierarchy might work within a friendship. The person who is the superior, as Aelred was in terms of his position at the monastery, might yield to the one generally considered the inferior, because it is necessary for the continuance of the friendship and the shaping of both people in virtue.

My grandfather spent years as a counselor in Florida's prison system, during which he befriended one of the states more notorious serial killers. This man who had taken the lives of so many others confided in my grandfather that he had felt like people ignored him and treated him as worthless. Therefore, as he began to think of himself as worthless, he concluded others must be as well, therefore it meant nothing to take a life.

However, in my grandfather he found someone who treated him with dignity and recognized his humanity, who befriended him. That had a profound impact on the man as he became a model citizen in the prison, sharing that dignity-recognizing behavior with others. It even got to the point where my grandfather told me that if this man was ever to be released from prison that he and my grandmother would even let him live with them. That is the power of friendship, of taking a risk to spend time with someone in order to speak goodness into their life. My grandfather was willing to give up his safety, allowing this man to once again have power, even the power over my grandfather and grandmother's life and death. This is precisely what Jesus

---

33. See Edgar, *God Is Friendship*, 143.

34. Aelred, *Spiritual Friendship*, 92.

has done for us, and we chose to send him to the cross when we betrayed him with the kiss of our friendship. Yet even now he extends that invitation of friendship, tearing down static hierarchies with his offer of new life in the Kingdom in which mutual deference defines the King's reign.

A Final Word on Friendship and Fluid Hierarchies

Mutually charitable, long-lasting, and risk-taking friendships set up fluid hierarchies that dignify self and others. They allow for the one in power to learn from and be changed by the one who is powerless. For God's people, however, there is ambiguity about who is truly the power-holder:

> If we see that care for persons in need is a response of love to Jesus (Matthew 25:31–46), a chance to walk on holy ground, then our entire understanding of mission and ministry shifts. It is not what "we" do for "them," but an opportunity for all of us to be enveloped by God's grace and mercy. In God's economy, it's less clear who is donor and who is recipient because all are blessed when needs are met and when individuals receive care.[35]

One of Christine's friends runs a ministry to people on the margins in Ohio. He says that their ministry operates on an "ethic of inefficiency." Within static hierarchies, it is easy to offer (and demand) efficiency because the boundary lines and the direction of the flow of power are apparent. In contrast, the fluid hierarchies formed in godly friendships are often inefficient because of the extra effort it takes to address ambiguity about who is in charge, about who is serving whom. The messiness of friendships and the ambiguity of fluid hierarchies will require us to set aside efficiency for the sake of relationship.

Friendships make this "godly ambiguity" regarding power possible, and thus the exchange regarding who is caring for whom fluid, as well. For example, the Bible recounts the relationship of Nathan and David, in which the prophet was able to point out the sin of the king's adultery with Bathsheba and the murder of Uriah.[36] This rebuke was possible because of their friendship grounded in their love for God, which disrupted the power structure, allowing the lesser one to be the authority and to care for the one responsible for caring for a whole kingdom.

35. Heuertz and Pohl, *Friendship at the Margins*, 77.

36. Aelred, *Spiritual Friendship*, 121. Aelred's point here is a bit different than the one I make, in that he focused on the way in which Nathan approached David. The point still remains, though that it was because of their friendship that Nathan's rebuke was truly possible. This story is found in 2 Samuel 12.

Edgar writes about the ancient concept of the "friend of the king," which was a title given to some able to speak truth into a king's life. Abraham and Moses were friends of the King of kings, and their friendship with God even allowed them to argue with the Almighty. Edgar writes, "A servant does not tell the master what to do, nor does a subject instruct the king, and so bargaining with God and reminding the Lord of what should be done is scandalous, but this is the right, even the duty, of the friends of the king."[37] Because of their friendship, God condescended and deferred to Moses, so much so that "the Lord changed his mind" (Exod 32:14). Even in friendship with the Almighty, we see that friendship can cause the one with power to defer to the one without, thus preventing violence.

Ultimately, the way that Christian friendships "critique unjust and inequitable power structures, and reimagine them in ways that are just and equitable" is by growing the circle of friendship outward to create an alternative community that recognizes the *imago Dei* in each member.[38] Thus, the Christian practice of evangelism is "an offer of friendship by both the community and Christ to those who [have] not yet come to faith . . . The principle is that Christian community is created through the offer of friendship."[39] Edgar continues by arguing that the gospel has long been spread among friends and then lived out by those friends in communities around the world. Even to this day, it is the best way to grow the church and share the good news of Jesus.[40]

Finally, it is essential to remember that neither this alternative community, nor the friendships of which it is comprised, exists for itself. It exists to make the world a more just and equitable place to live. As Edgar notes,

> In the first and twenty-first centuries, friendship, social equality and community well-being are closely and inextricably linked. Research shows that friendships are protective of good health and well-being, while inequality and status differences are harmful . . . less equal societies are less healthy in every respect. Consequently, friendship, which is either indicative of a less stratified society or which actually bridges the gaps in stratified societies, creates a healthier society for everyone.[41]

37. Edgar, *God Is Friendship*, 45.

38. This is a portion of the abstract for Edgar, "Embodiment, Encounter, and Power."

39. Edgar, *God Is Friendship*, 143.

40. Edgar, *God Is Friendship*, 144. This is true, negatively put because "It's hard to imagine why we would think people would want a relationship with Jesus if they sensed no interest on our part in a relationship with them" (Heuertz and Pohl, *Friendship at the Margins*, 42).

41. Edgar, *God Is Friendship*, 156. Edgar goes on to write, "In the developed world,

Furthermore, Edgar argues that "Friendship is also vital in countering social division; it only needs a couple of people to establish a friendship across a social divide to create a healthier relationship that influences many people."[42] Often though, to the chagrin of many people, the residual effects of these sorts of friendship simply do not change society fast enough.

However, this does not mean that it cannot or does not change society. For instance, we see in Paul's Letter to Philemon a radical example of the power of friendship when Paul writes to Philemon and encourages him to forgive his slave Onesimus and receive him back into his household.

> [Paul] could have required Philemon to release Onesimus on the basis of Paul's authority and Christian responsibility, but instead he appealed to him out of friendship . . . It began with the friendship between Paul and Onesimus that led Paul to appeal to Philemon as a friend and to consider the implications of friendship in Christ that there was between Philemon and Onesimus. This friendship in Christ overrode all other roles and relationships and called for equality rather than slavery.[43]

Furthermore, acting from within Christian friendship is a "more radical and fundamentally subversive approach" than compelling someone by force—or even than working to enact new laws.[44] It is possible to do acts of mercy and justice without them shaping us in righteousness, but in building friendships across boundaries, we do these acts in such a way in which we ourselves are challenged to grow, and as people grow in Christ they become more just, thus having a residual effect where the justice of Jesus' Kingdom spreads across all parts of society.

Rather than attempting to write my own clever conclusion, I instead return to Aelred, using the words with which he concludes his own dialogue with his friends.

> How advantageous is it then to grieve for one another, to toil for one another, and to bear one another's burdens, while each considers it sweet to forget himself for the sake of the other, to prefer the will of the other to his own, to minister to the other's needs rather than one's own, to oppose and expose one's self

---

the level of equity within a society is a more important determinant of well-being than the overall level of wealth . . . And what is really important to note is that greater levels of equity benefit everybody, not just the poor" (157).

42. Edgar, *God Is Friendship*, 196.

43. Edgar, *God Is Friendship*, 210.

44. Edgar, *God Is Friendship*, 210. Edgar's discussion on what he calls "Public Friendship" hashes out some of the details that I am not able to explicate here.

to misfortune! Meanwhile, how delightful friends find it to converse with one another, mutually to reveal their interests, to examine all things together, and to agree on all of them! . . . Ascending from that holy love with which he embraces a friend to that with which he embraces Christ, he will joyfully partake in abundance of the spiritual fruit of friendship, awaiting the fullness of all things in the life to come. Then . . . we shall rejoice in the eternal possession of Supreme Goodness; and this friendship, to which here we admit but a few, will be outpoured upon all and by all outpoured upon God, and God shall be all in all.[45]

Bibliography

Aelred of Rievaulx. *Spiritual Friendship.* Edited by Marsha L. Dutton. Translated by Lawrence C. Braceland. Trappist: Cistercian, 2010.

Blodgett, Barbara J. *Lives Entrusted: An Ethic of Trust for Ministry.* Minneapolis: Fortress, 2008.

Edgar, Brian. "Embodiment, Encounter, and Power: Theological and Mystical Frames for Subverting and Reimagining Power Structures." Paper presented at Christian Scholars' Conference, Lipscomb University, Summer 2015.

———. *God Is Friendship: A Theology of Spirituality, Community, and Society.* Wilmore: Seedbed, 2013.

Heuertz, Christopher L., and Christine D. Pohl. *Friendship at the Margins: Discovering Mutuality in Service and Mission.* Grand Rapids: InterVarsity, 2010.

45. Aelred, *Spiritual Friendship*, 128–29.

Part Four

Practicing in Context
New Alliances and Good News

Forming Disciples,
Extending Mission

The Role of Practices in Evangelicalism

Wyndy Corbin Reuschling

Introduction

In this chapter, I will explore Dr. Pohl's contributions to evangelical ethics based on her work on Christian practices.[1] I will start with a historical approach, probing how the social location and circumstances in three broad periods shaped the social engagement and ethical priorities of American evangelicals.[2] First, I will explore the social ethical commitments and engagements of evangelicals of the mid-nineteenth century as discussed in

1. This chapter is written in honor of Dr. Christine Pohl. Given the respect due her, I want to acknowledge her academic status as such. Yet she is more than a colleague. She is a dear friend, so it seems appropriate to acknowledge this as I refer to her as Christine in the remainder of the chapter. I hope nobody is offended by this decision, especially Dr. Pohl.

2. I realize broad, sweeping descriptions of historical periods are problematic in many ways, particularly so when written by a person who is not a historian. I will use the historical descriptions as "types," something we see in H. Richard Niebuhr's *Christ and Culture*. For a good example of how types are contested, in particular Niebuhr's five types in *Christ and Culture*, see Stassen, Yeager, and Yoder, *Authentic Transformation*. "Types" are helpful for organizing ideas as long as we acknowledge their limitations and the dangers of painting historical periods and perspectives with such big brushes. There are always exceptions to rules and danger in omitting important stories, counter-narratives, and different viewpoints when telling history from any one perspective. I acknowledge this without trying to solve it in order to keep this chapter focused on salient aspects of evangelical social commitments as I understand them and the particular bearings they have on strategies of social change.

Donald Dayton's *Discovering an Evangelical Heritage*.[3] Second, I will utilize George Marsden's *Understanding Fundamentalism and Evangelicalism* that highlights the ethical commitments of evangelicals that emerged from and within the modernist and fundamentalist controversies of the late-nineteenth and early twentieth centuries (and which shaped evangelical social ethics well into the late-twentieth century). Finally, I will examine the resurged involvement of evangelicals in the public sphere in the 1970s and 1980s, prompted by what is commonly referred to as the "culture wars," as described by James Davison Hunter in his book, *Culture Wars: The Struggle to Control the Family, Art, Education, Law, and Politics in America*.

The final section of this chapter will offer very general descriptions of the current "historical moment" in evangelicalism in the United States, noting the welcomed expansion of evangelical moral concerns beyond its traditional (and very limited) focus upon sexuality and abortion to encompass such things as the environment, peacemaking, war and violence, racial reconciliation, human rights, and economic justice. To this is added Christine's work on hospitality, which has expanded the moral horizons of evangelicals "in this historical moment" by reminding us that we are called to open our lives and spaces to others as a form of welcome, just as God welcomes us in Christ. The necessity of her work in evangelical ethics is obvious as we encounter displaced persons, refugees, and those shunned by their own communities because of difference. In many ways, our evangelical moral commitments rely on hospitality as openness to an Other with whom we are in relationship and who we come to know. Our commitments to human rights, economic justice, welcoming yet-to-be-born children, care for the elderly, and reconciliation between enemies assumes hospitality as a prerequisite, of sorts.

After my brief historical foray, I will focus in the second part of this chapter on the significance of Christine's work on Christian practices. I will suggest two important contributions of her work, coherent with commitments which evangelicals tend to hold dear. First, practices can become an important means by which Christian disciples are formed. Second, practices are also a means of witness, a form of sharing the gospel in service and deed, an embodiment of God's goodness and grace in the world—thus fulfilling the missional impulse which has defined much of evangelicalism.

Before moving forward, a few caveats are in order to qualify how I will represent "evangelicalism" in my reflections on Christine's work. I realize "evangelicalism" and "evangelicals" are both contested terms, defined

---

3. See also the recently released second edition by Dayton and Strong, *Rediscovering an Evangelical Heritage*.

differently according to the theological tradition and various social locations of evangelical groups. There is no time in this chapter to enter into these ongoing debates, so I will offer my own perspective on commitments that seem central to a broad evangelical identity. "Evangelical," from the Greek *euangelion,* means a heralding of "good news." For most evangelicals, this good news carries with it a missional impulse toward witness, evangelism, and service—impulses shared by a variety of Christian traditions. Evangelicals believe this faith in Christ must be shared with others verbally, and personally accepted and appropriated as an entrance into new life in Christ. We have received good news, that salvation has come to us in and through Jesus Christ, and we must share this good news with others. Evangelicals may also be characterized by their attention to and emphasis on discipleship and spiritual growth as ongoing life processes, important for growing into Christ-likeness. Evangelicals also tend to be known by their commitment to the authority of the Bible. While this authority may be expressed and practiced in a variety of ways, the role which Scripture plays as an authoritative and normative source for Christian belief and practice remains central. Robert Johnston provides a helpful summary of the evangelical spirit and ethos:

> For all their variety and particularity, descriptions of contemporary American evangelicalism have a commonality centered on a threefold commitment: a dedication to the gospel that is expressed in a personal faith in Christ as Lord, an understanding of the gospel as defined authoritatively by Scripture, and a desire to communicate the gospel both in evangelism and social reform.[4]

Moral commitments for evangelicals emerge notably from the place which Scripture holds in evangelicalism.[5] While various hermeneutical approaches may be utilized, and as interpretive issues remain contested, evangelicals rely on Scripture as a primary source for ethics. Evangelicals tend to use Scripture for moral formation and ethical discernment in a variety of ways: for ascertaining duties and responsibilities, for understanding God's moral vision for human life and creation, for growth in virtues and becoming a certain kind of person, for personal devotion, for understanding the demands of Christian community, and as a source of wisdom and guidance on a variety of issues. This is not to say that theological claims, tradition,

---

4. Johnston, "American Evangelicalism," 261. For additional insights on definitions of evangelicalism see also Dorrien, *The Remaking of Evangelical Theology* and Corbin Reuschling, *Reviving Evangelical Ethics.*

5. See Reuschling, "Evangelical Ethics."

social analysis, and experience are unnecessary sources in Christian ethics. They are crucial and have an important role in conversation with Scripture. One can see how these sources function in Christine's work as she brings scriptural insights, theological frameworks, historical insights, and social analysis together in her work on Christian practices.

The Nineteenth Century: Evangelical Social Reform

Evangelicals of the nineteenth century were deeply involved in addressing the social issues of their day. I see two main reasons for this. First was the strong Wesleyan streak that informed much of the revivalistic and transforming spirit of evangelicals during this period. As John Wesley was known for saying, "There is no holiness but social holiness." Evangelicals were active in addressing a variety of social problems, viewed as their own responses to love of God and love of neighbor. The kind of holiness that informed this involvement extended beyond notions of mere personal piety, in that active love for neighbor was evidence and an expression of one's love for God.[6] As noted by Dayton in *Discovering an Evangelical Heritage*, the work of evangelicals during this period was extensive. From the founding of venerable institutions such as Wheaton and Oberlin Colleges, to confronting racial injustice, working to abolish slavery, championing women's rights, and advocating for just business and employment practices—evangelicals in the nineteenth century were actively involved in ameliorating social ills as well as attempting to confront and transform the conditions which brought about these ills in the first place.

Evangelicals worked to transform their society out of their own sense of social holiness and based on certain theological convictions that informed their ethical practices. During the nineteenth century—at the height of Protestantism's influence in the United States   many evangelicals operated with a sense that it was their responsibility to bring the Kingdom of God to concrete reality in society. This postmillennial view suggested that the Kingdom of God is an already present reality and is the means by which societies would improve. A commitment to justice, the equality and dignity of all persons, naming the evils of slavery and exploitation, and establishing institutions that attempted to embody these commitments—these moral actions reflected the deep theological commitments which many evangelicals held, and reflected the gospel imperative that we are called to live out what we believe since we have been "saved by grace through faith" and "created in

---

6. For a sustained exploration of holiness, see Brown et al., *Becoming Whole and Holy*.

Christ Jesus for good works" (Eph 2:8–10). While assumptions of a "Christian" nation and an association of any one nation as *the* Kingdom of God should be rightly contested, this neither negates nor delegitimizes the admirable contributions of evangelical social ethics in the nineteenth century.

In the final chapter of his book, Dayton poses the question, "Whatever happened to evangelicalism?"[7] He identifies a number of insightful reasons for the declining social involvement of evangelicals and shifts in emphases, particularly in ethics. Notable for this discussion and for understanding the transition into the late-nineteenth and twentieth centuries are the following considerations. According to Dayton, the horrors of the Civil War shattered the optimistic notions of a "Christian America" which redirected evangelical practice to a focus on inward acts of piety and spiritual devotion.[8] Massive social changes, such as immigration, industrialization, and urbanization reminded evangelicals of the complex nature of social issues.[9] With these changes came shifts in theological views, whereby evangelicals, based on their dislocating experiences of this social change, moved toward a more premillennial position on historical and social events. In other words, things were not becoming better, and not everyone shared the kind of evangelical Christianity which held such dominance in the eighteenth century. Dayton notes one of the effects of this shift.

> But more characteristic was the tendency to abandon long-range social amelioration for a massive effort to preach the gospel to as many as possible before the return of Christ. The vision was now one of rescue from a fallen world. Just as Jesus was expected momentarily on the clouds to rapture his saints, so the slum worker established missions to rescue sinners out of the world to be among those to meet the Lord in the air. Evangelical effort that had once provided the impulse and troops for reform rallies was rechanneled into exegetical speculation about the timing of Christ's return and into maintenance of the expanding prophecy conferences.[10]

Finally, Dayton also attributes declining evangelical social involvement to the rising influence of "Princeton Theology" which held vastly different views on the implications of the gospel, the interpretation of Scripture, and the mission of the church.[11] This growing influence would change the shape

---

7. Dayton, *Discovering an Evangelical Heritage*, 121.

8. Dayton, *Discovering an Evangelical Heritage*, 124–25.

9. Dayton, *Discovering an Evangelical Heritage*, 125.

10. Dayton, *Discovering an Evangelical Heritage*, 127.

11. Dayton, *Discovering an Evangelical Heritage*, 128–34. See also Noll, *The*

of evangelical social involvement and redirect its moral energies in the late-nineteenth and early twentieth centuries.

Late-Nineteenth and Early Twentieth Centuries: Evangelical Social Retreat

Certain segments of evangelicalism were shaped by the dynamics of the modernist and fundamentalist controversies of the late-nineteenth and early twentieth centuries. According to Marsden, fundamentalism (and its later offspring, evangelicalism) emerged as a response to three predominant challenges to American Protestantism from 1870 to 1930.[12] First, there were the intellectual challenges of Darwinism, the rise of the social sciences, and the historical criticism of the Bible, which leveled epistemological challenges to its status as the sole arbiter of truth. Second, rapid urbanization and immigration exposed the plurality of religious belief, which had always existed but was previously masked because of the influence of white Protestantism in many areas of culture. Third was the general secularization of modern culture, which was perceived as a threat to the status of white Protestantism.[13]

Christian denominations responded in different ways to these challenges. "Modernists" appropriated new epistemological insights, particularly those related to biblical interpretation, which led to the charge that "they" developed a lower view of the Bible's unique authority.[14] "Fundamentalists" responded by battling for the Bible as a way to combat the waywardness of American culture. As it was appearing that fundamentalists were losing the battle, in that the influence of white Protestantism seemed to be waning, they retreated from larger social engagements by developing fundamentalist and evangelical enclaves—havens in a troubling society. It is important to note that out of fundamentalism emerged what historians and sociologists describe as "neo-evangelicalism." While sharing the fundamentalist commitment to the inerrancy of Scripture and other doctrinal positions,

---

Princeton Theology, and Worthen, *Apostles of Reason.*

12. Marsden, *Understanding Fundamentalism and Evangelicalism;* in particular, see ch. 1 for Marsden's historical overview.

13. See Lincoln and Mamiya, *The Black Church in the African American Experience,* for an analysis of the strengths of the black church during this similar time frame that reflects the ways in which responses to cultural power and dislocation are influenced by race and social location.

14. I am putting modernists and fundamentalists in quotation marks simply to acknowledge how broad these terms are without further explication of them, which I cannot do in light of the limits and purpose of this chapter.

neo-evangelicals rejected the separatist spirit of their fundamentalist brethren in favor an "engaged orthodoxy" that was "fully committed to maintaining and promoting confidently traditional, orthodox Protestant theology belief, *while at the same time* becoming more confidently and proactively engaged in the intellectual, cultural, social and political life of the nation."[15] The neo-evangelicals did not spurn more active social and political engagement—as we will soon see in the culture wars of the mid-to-late twentieth century.

How did this impact evangelical social engagement? I suggest that while there remained a strong social ethic (in that fundamentalists and evangelicals retained particular moral visions about how society should operate), their theological commitments shifted, their strategies of engagement became individualized, and their social concerns narrowed. In light of the secularizing influences in American society, fundamentalists and evangelicals shifted from a postmillennial to a premillennial view. Premillennialism held that social conditions would deteriorate—which fundamentalists believed they had—until the time of Jesus' physical return to earth for a reign of a thousand years and a time of judgment. This position, which became a characteristic theological marker (and often a doctrinal litmus test), decidedly shifted their strategy of social engagement. The commitment to change society by bringing the Kingdom to God to bear was replaced by a focus on personal evangelism and cross-cultural missions to save as many as possible before the return of Christ. In this way, changed individuals will change society, but never completely until the consummation of the age. Personal holiness became more important than social holiness, which now seemed nary impossible. In *Divided by Faith: Evangelical Religion and the Problem of Race in America*, Michael Emerson and Christian Smith describe this as the personal influence strategy: the tools of freewill individualism, relationalism, and antistructuralism now undergird how evangelicals respond to social issues.[16] Social issues were, therefore, merely extensions of bad personal morality and cannot be solved by addressing systemic injustice; hence antistructuralism. Racism is addressed by becoming friends with persons of a different racial and ethnic background; hence a commitment to relationalism, freewill individualism, and antistructuralism.[17]

At the same time a retreat from society was occurring, so was a narrowing of ethical concerns. Gone were concerns about structural racism

15. Smith, *American Evangelicalism*, 10. See also Carpenter, *Revive Us Again*, ch. 11.

16. Emerson and Smith, *Divided by Faith*, 76.

17. This was a focus in my doctoral dissertation, *The Relationship between Personal and Social Ethics in Protestant Evangelicalism: Toward an Integrative Ethic for a Postmodern World*.

and social equality, and diminished were concerns for economic justice. The roles of women in church and society were also contested among fundamentalists and evangelicals and became a particular target as blame was sought for the fraying of American society and perceived social disorder. Betty DeBerg notes that the loss of control felt by fundamentalists was parallel to recent gains made by white women in voting rights and political equality. Therefore, in response to greater freedom for white women in the larger society, fundamentalists emphasized the need for order—particularly in gender relations—to stem the tide of growing confusion and chaos.[18] Gender roles became a specific locus of social critique as their shifts were seen as one of the causes of moral disorder. This period of retreat and narrowing set the stage for what later emerged as the "culture wars," as evangelical social commitments became solidified in the arenas of the family, education, the media, law, and politics.[19]

Twentieth Century: Evangelical Re-Engagement

In the mid-to-late twentieth century, these dividing lines solidified into what James Davison Hunter refers to as the "culture wars." There were two sides at war—the orthodox on one side, the progressivists on the other—both armed with competing ideals and values.[20] The orthodox vision, according to Hunter, was informed by a transcendent understanding of authority, which was believed to be the necessary source for the moral ordering of society codified in revelatory sources of religion, such as the Torah or the Bible. This appeal to objective sources of authority was believed to stabilize the moral ordering of American society. The progressivists, on the other hand, recognized the historical nature of religious expressions along with a loosening grip of one particular religious source of authority, such as Christianity, in a pluralistic culture. The locus of authority in a progressivist vision came from personal experience and pragmatism. Hunter notes the results of the culture wars' divide between orthodox and progressivists:

> The central dynamic of the cultural realignment is not merely that different public philosophies created diverse public

---

18. DeBerg, *Ungodly Women.* See also Bendroth, *Fundamentalism and Gender.*

19. Hunter, *Culture Wars*; see also Miller, *The Age of Evangelicalism.* Miller provides an overview of the historical and cultural emergence of evangelicals since the 1970s. He recognizes the depictions of evangelicals are not always reflective of the actual realities in such a broad and diverse movement. He leaves us with a more complicated and nuanced picture about evangelical social engagement during these years, and even today.

20. Hunter, *Culture Wars*, 108–16.

opinions. These alliances, rather, reflect the *institutionalization and politicization of two fundamentally different cultural systems*. Each side operates from within its own constellation of values, interests, and assumptions. At the center of each are two distinct conceptions of moral authority—two different ways of apprehending reality, of ordering experience, of making moral judgments. Each side of the cultural divide, then, speaks with a different moral vocabulary. Each side operates out of a different mode of debate and persuasion. Each side represents the tendencies of a separate and competing moral galaxy. They are, indeed, "worlds apart."[21]

The arenas of battle in this culture war were over the family, media and the arts, education, law, and politics. Hunter places American evangelicals on the orthodox side of the war, given their appeal to the authority of Scripture and notions which many white evangelicals had about the religious foundations of the nation. This period did see a strong movement of evangelicals into public arenas. With the passage of *Roe vs. Wade* in 1973, abortion became a particular focus for social action among evangelicals. Evangelicals waged battle in courtrooms over such issues as abortion rights and prayer in schools. We witnessed the rise and growing influence of the Moral Majority, which focused attention on local issues such as school boards and curriculum; it also addressed the larger issues of endorsing candidates for public office who shared the assumptions of the orthodox. Conservatives focused much attention on reinforcing traditional notions of women's places in church and home as a way to stem the tide of perceived moral decline. This led to the growing evangelical alarm about sexual ethics, as rights for gays and lesbians entered into public discourse. Christians founded media stations as a source of news to combat the perceived liberal slant of mainstream media.[22] The strategy of evangelical social action was often focused on changing (or blocking) legislation on such issues as abortion, and electing Christian public officials who would carry their own moral commitments to their elected seats and legislative practices. The concerns which drove evangelical social involvement were similar to those which created the divide among earlier fundamentalists and modernists. A significant difference in the "culture wars" was that evangelicals seemed to have the political clout and "manpower" to bring their moral vision to the public arena.[23]

21. Hunter, *Culture Wars*, 128.

22. For example, the Christian Broadcasting Network was founded in 1977.

23. See Hunter's recent book, *To Change the World*. Hunter provides his own sociological, theological, and historical critique to evangelical strategies of social

However, this kind of social conservatism was not characteristic of all who claimed an evangelical identity. Also emerging were such groups as Sojourners, Evangelicals for Social Action, the Evangelical Women's Caucus, and Daughters of Sarah. Disagreements *within* evangelicalism became apparent; differences emerged about how Scripture was to be interpreted and how Christian faith should be expressed in the public square. One could claim to take the Bible seriously as an evangelical and embrace more progressive social policies for addressing poverty, for protesting war, and other forms of political and social engagement.[24] These differences remain today as evangelicals continue to divide along conservative and progressive lines which appear quite stark, especially during election cycles, taking different positions on a variety of issues.

Where Does This Leave Us Today?

The historical and social contexts of American evangelicalism in these three broad periods have left particular legacies that have shaped evangelical social ethics. Evangelical ethics has tended to be issue oriented, particularly focused on abortion and expressions of human sexuality. Personal integrity and character formation have always been important for evangelicals, yet not always clearly connected to social ethics. Because of the focus on issues, evangelical ethical critique has tended to focus outward on the views and behaviors of others, without necessarily providing an internal critique of our own practices, affections, dispositions, and loyalties. Gaining access to social, cultural, and political power has been a strategy that evangelicals have employed, believing this kind of access will be a means for bringing about the changes in society important for evangelicals. This has created a troubling reliance on political processes and parties to affect change, seeking the legislative victories that some evangelicals believe will win the day. Much energy in evangelicalism has gone toward changing laws, whether through electing like-minded politicians, becoming more engaged in the legislative process, or creating evangelically minded political action committees to lobby Congress. Ethics in evangelicalism has also tended to be conflated

---

engagement, particularly in the desire to access and use political power to secure religious ends. He suggests we opt for "faithful presence" based on the Incarnation, and God's faithful presence to us so that we can be faithful in time wherever we happen to be (Hunter, "Toward a Theology of Faithful Presence," 238–54).

24. The examples are myriad. For a start, see Sider, *Rich Christians in an Age of Hunger*; Scanzoni and Hardesty, *All We're Meant to Be*; and Wallis, *Call to Conversion*.

with apologetics.[25] Apologetics is a branch of Christian philosophy that attempts to establish and defend the credibility of the Christian faith based on arguments of reason. The ethical task for an apologist is establishing the credibility of one's position against an opposing position. For evangelicals who see themselves in an ongoing battle with culture, defending the right position on an issue is the right thing to do.

However, in what many call this post-Christian context, the assumptions and effectiveness of these strategies have been called into question on both pragmatic and theological grounds. One reason, I believe, is recognition of the diverse perspectives *within* evangelicalism that have provided helpful correctives to these legacies.[26] Wesleyan evangelicals remind us that the means and ends of social engagement are an expression of loving what God loves and responding to humans with grace. Anabaptist evangelicals provide an important voice for peace and the church's primary witness to Jesus' non-violent response to evil and wrongdoing. Liberationist evangelicals suggest that the church's greatest impact might come at the margins of society, reminiscent of the early church's position in society. Pentecostal evangelicals take the lead in recognizing the "powers and principalities" at play, both on a cosmic scale and their earthly manifestations. Anglican evangelicals offer us ways of understanding how the Christian moral life is formed by the church's liturgical practices.

Evangelicals have also expanded moral concern for a variety of issues such as combatting human trafficking, care for creation, peacemaking, economic justice, and torture.[27] There is a growing appreciation in evangelical ethics for the larger scriptural and theological narrative that orients and grounds our moral sensibilities; in so doing, it expands the arena of our concerns and actions beyond isolated issues to broader social concerns.[28] While there are a variety of reasons for this shift, two seem important to note. One is a crumbling of the walls between disciplines, such as biblical studies and ethics, and a growing appreciation for the rich depth that can be added in this integration. Biblical scholars are in greater conversation with ethicists; ethicists and theologians discover they share common ground; and church historians remind us of central pastoral practices focused on the formation of persons and Christian communities.[29] This has been coupled with a re-

25. See the Introduction in Reuschling, *Reviving Evangelical Ethics*.

26. See Gushee and Sharp, *Evangelical Social Ethics*.

27. For just a few examples, see Brunner et al., *Introducing Evangelical Ecotheology*; and Gushee, *A New Evangelical Manifesto*.

28. See Stackhouse, *Making the Best of It*.

29. The following sources are representative of this trend: Hays, *The Moral Vision of the New Testament*; Verhey, *Remembering Jesus*; and Wright, *Old Testament Ethics for*

newed interest in the role of the church as an "alternative community" and virtue ethics in Christian life.[30] There has been a recovery of sorts of the role which virtue plays in the Christian moral life. While ascertaining duties remains important, Christian ethics has benefitted from a richer conception of the moral life and the role of community as a site for formation. This has been an important reminder that ethics is about who we are, how we live, and how we embody our fundamental commitments about the goodness of God and what fosters goodness for other human beings.

It is here where I find the role of practices a welcome and significant move in evangelical ethics. A robust understanding of practices brings together necessary aspects of Christian ethics. Practices rely on a moral vision of God's desires and goods for the world that we derive from Scripture and a wise use of the church's reflection across time and space. This vision needs persons and communities who are willing to embody it, with obedience and loyalty, as a vision that is true for the world. Both as persons and as communities, we are formed for our task through practices that mold and shape us. Practices enable us to stay true to our fundamental commitments to make disciples and to embody and extend God's mission in the world God loves and still works to redeem.

A Way Forward: Participation in Practices

Craig Dykstra and Dorothy Bass offer this definition of practices: Christian practices are "things Christian people do together over time to address fundamental human needs in response to and in light of God's active presence for the life of the world."[31] This definition signals the formative and missional dimensions of Christian practices that are important in Christine's work. Practices such as hospitality, community, and friendship extend the good news of God's love, grace, and welcome to all persons, recognizing first that we have been the recipients of God's hospitable love and grace in Christ. This becomes an important motivation in service and witness. Practices are not ungrounded or random; they contain a reason why we do what we do. They are connected to what we understand the gospel to be, and flow from

---

the People of God and *The Mission of God.*

30. Alasdair MacIntyre's work in *After Virtue,* while written from a philosophical perspective, has been influential in the renewal of interest in virtue in Christian ethics. See the following: Hauerwas, *A Community of Character*; Hauerwas and Pinches, *Christians Among the Virtues*; Kotva, *The Christian Case for Virtue Ethics*; and Murphy, Kallenberg and Nation, *Virtues and Practices in the Christian Traditions.*

31. Dykstra and Bass, "A Theological Understanding of Christian Practices," 18.

what we have hopefully experienced ourselves. Practices "preach" the gospel in what we do and in how we live. Practices help to foster formation crucial for our continual growth as disciples of Christ. Christian formation is not a given, nor is it automatic. It takes time, attention, help, perseverance, and experimentation. Practices can be a means by which formation happens as we learn to live out the gospel in particular ways.

Christine identifies hospitality as such a practice that Christians do together, one that has extended over time and has met human needs in various ways and in various places.[32] It is an expression and extension of the gospel, one that "encompasses physical, social, and spiritual dimensions of human existence and relationships."[33] Hospitality is offered in the name of Christ, particularly to the sick, the poor, strangers, and sojourners:

> Hospitality is central to the gospel . . . A fuller awareness of the richness of the hospitality tradition and the extraordinary experiences associated with hospitality enriches Christian faith and brings Christian practice into closer alignment with the basic values of the Kingdom. Hospitality is a lens through which we can read and understand much of the gospel, and a practice by which we can welcome Jesus himself.[34]

As Christine notes, practices can be deeply awkward, risky, demanding, and uncomfortable for us.[35] She sees this particularly as we learn to relate to strangers, welcoming others into our space, relationships, and routines, adjusting as needed. Practices, therefore, take practice; in other words, "people learned hospitality by doing it."[36] It requires others willing to take on the risks which practices imply. The risky nature of practices causes us to rely on God and others, to reflect more deeply on our fears and prejudices. These are good things if we are serious about growth in our lives. In her book *Living into Community,* Christine explores the complications of certain practices, offering important reminders that practices are not automatic or simple— much like Christian formation. Practices need to be cultivated, learned, explored, talked about, and thought about. Even as practices extend God's goodness to the world, they work on us in deeply formative ways. Practices form disciples while simultaneously extending and embodying God's reconciling mission in the world.

32. Pohl, *Making Room*, 6.
33. Pohl, *Making Room*, 6.
34. Pohl, *Making Room*, 8.
35. Pohl, *Making Room*, 11.
36. Pohl, *Making Room*, 11.

Practices are also necessary parts of our own formation. If a goal of our Christian lives is union with God, and the means by which this happens is growth in Christ-likeness, then we must be willing to participate in practices that help to facilitate this process.[37] Practices train and shape us in particular ways. Even as they extend God's goodness and grace to others, practices work on us in significant ways. They help us to think about and reflect on what we believe and explore various ways for living this out.[38] Learning how to read Scripture and do prayer are practices that foster our relationship with God, and require that we develop habits and dispositions relating to priorities and taking time for important matters. Engaging in active service heightens our proximity to others, which reminds us of our interdependence and mutual moral obligations. Participating in worship and attending church are essential to our growth, especially when such involvements can be difficult. When the tensions and conflicts in our communities get the best of us, or when our church doesn't meet our particular needs, we are tempted to find the perfect or ideal church.

Engaging in practices reminds us that we learn by doing. While this may be good pedagogical theory, it is also reflective of Jesus' own engagement with his disciples. We know, as readers of the Scriptures, that the disciples did not understand the larger purpose of Jesus' ministry. Yet while Jesus was ministering, he was inviting his disciples to *do* the same: feeding the multitudes, healing the sick, casting out demons, teaching, and preaching good news (Matt 10:5–15, 14:13–21, 15:32–39; Mark 6:7–13). This performative aspect of practices may have been an important means by which the disciples learned, early on, to follow Jesus; they provided the necessary context to more fully understand the significance of Jesus' life and death when they witnessed the resurrected Christ and received his commands to go and make disciples in Jerusalem, Judea, Samaria, and the ends of the earth (Matt 28:16–20; Acts 1:6–8).

I suggest this is so for persons in our churches. Those of us who "grew up" in the church, in many ways, were "practiced" into belief.[39] Before we had a well-developed Christology, a high view of the sacraments, a robust ecclesiology, or a nuanced view of God's providence and sovereignty, we were already participating in the story of God which practices tell and embody. We were learning the story through practices, just as the early disciples. Practices assist us in learning about our faith while we are practicing it and growing in our desires and dispositions to live out the story as

---

37. See Reuschling, "The Means and End in 2 Peter 1:3–11."

38. See Reuschling, *Desire for God and the Things of God*, ch. 3.

39. See Dykstra and Bass, "Times of Yearning, Practices of Faith."

followers of Christ. Practices, therefore, offer us fresh ways to think about our educational and disciple-making strategies in churches.

Practices are a means by which we concretize our faith. Christian discipleship captures a key notion of "following" Christ which reminds us that becoming a disciple involves entrance into learning a particular way of life patterned after Christ, beyond just "head knowledge." Christian practices are means by which the cognitive and experiential dimensions of our faith can be brought together for a more coherent understanding of Christian discipleship. This is an important corrective to the legacy of the fundamentalist/modernist controversies discussed earlier in certain segments of American evangelicalism. Stress on getting the facts about the faith right tended to see the locus of change in the mind, while casting suspicion on the experiential dimensions of Christian faith. I suggest that strategies of Christian discipleship in evangelicalism have tended to be highly cognitive, with a focus on memorizing Bible verses and filling in the blanks in various workbooks. I do not mean to discount the important cognitive and intellectual components of our faith while holding a privileged place for "experience" with all of its contestation and complications. Perhaps today we have ignored the cognitive dimensions of our faith in favor of the experiential. Practices place experience and mind in a necessary synergistic relationship; one supports the other, and both are necessary. We see this again in the life of Jesus' early disciples. While they were still and always learning,

> . . . they were still asked to go and practice what Jesus valued: healing, preaching, compassion, and feeding the hungry. In spite of what the disciples actually knew and believed, they performed concrete actions, and in doing so, fostered degrees of good and help for those they served. They practiced what Jesus preached, and one hopes, grew in their understanding of Jesus' mission and identity.[40]

"They practiced what Jesus preached." Practices "preach" to various degrees, and in doing so, they extend and embody God's mission of reconciling love and grace in the world.[41] Evangelical faith has been shaped by its sense of mission to share the good news of salvation and reconciliation offered to us through Jesus Christ. Evangelical commitment to this witness is expressed in word and deed. Building on Dykstra and Bass's definition, Christine reminds us that "practices can also be understood as responses to the grace we have already experienced in Christ, in light of the word and work of God,

---

40. Reuschling, *Desire for God,* 57.
41. Reuschling, *Desire for God,* 49.

and for the sake of one another and the world."[42] Evangelicals have grown in their appreciation for the importance of practices as a means of witness in the world. For too long, in my view, evangelicalism's primary form has been verbal, one that created the strange dichotomy between evangelism and social justice that many evangelicals accept as normative. While still a hugely important scriptural mandate, our post-Christian context has enabled evangelicals to think more deeply about the various forms of witness which the gospel of Christ takes. Building on St. Francis' famous saying, "Preach the Gospel at all times; use words if necessary," evangelicals have paid more attention to practices as ways of living out their faith as a form of witness to a watching world. From experimenting with communal living, to making commitments to live simply, to challenging the social policies for their impact on the poor, to involvement with combatting human trafficking—evangelical social practices have been in response to the grace we have received in Christ, and for the sake and healing of broken persons, communities, and creation. Practices are concrete expressions of God's extending grace and love, an important means of reaching out to the world in mission and service. And in doing so, we are changed.

Conclusion

Christine Pohl's contribution to the field of Christian ethics cannot be overstated. As one of the first social ethicists to explore the importance of Christian practices, her concern to speak about and into her own faith tradition has offered us important gifts. She has helped us to recognize the important connections between who we are and how we live. She has graciously reminded us of the importance of our Christian communities without succumbing to a false idealization. She understands that as recipients of God's hospitable love, we are both privileged and obligated to share this love with others. She offers no illusions about easy paths of Christian discipleship and witness; rather, she gives us challenging, creative, and faithful ones. For those of us privileged to know her as friend, professor, colleague, or family member, we see Christine practice what she preaches. And we, therefore, become the recipients of God's hospitable love and grace.

42. Pohl, *Living into Community*, 5.

Bibliography

Bendroth, Margaret Lamberts. *Fundamentalism and Gender: 1875 to the Present*. New Haven: Yale University Press, 1996.

Brown, Jeannine K., Carla H. Dahl, and Wyndy Corbin Reuschling. *Becoming Whole and Holy: An Integrative Conversation about Christian Formation*. Grand Rapids: Baker Academic, 2011.

Brunner, Daniel L., Jennifer L. Butler, and A. J. Swoboda. *Introducing Evangelical Ecotheology: Foundations in Scripture, Theology, History, and Praxis*. Grand Rapids: Baker Academic, 2014.

Carpenter, Joel A. *Revive Us Again: The Reawakening of American Fundamentalism*. Oxford: Oxford University Press, 1999.

Dayton, Donald W. *Discovering an Evangelical Heritage*. Grand Rapids: Baker Academic, 1976.

DeBerg, Betty A. *Ungodly Women: Gender and the First Wave of American Fundamentalism*. Macon: Mercer University Press, 2000.

Dorrien, Gary. *The Remaking of Evangelical Theology*. Louisville: Westminster John Knox, 1998.

Dykstra, Craig, and Dorothy C. Bass, "A Theological Understanding of Christian Practices." In *Practicing Theology: Beliefs and Practices in Christian Life*, edited by Miroslav Volf and Dorothy C. Bass, 13–32. Grand Rapids: Eerdmans, 2001.

Emerson, Michael O., and Christian Smith. *Divided by Faith: Evangelical Religion and the Problem of Race in America*. Oxford: Oxford University Press, 2000.

Gushee, David P., ed. *A New Evangelical Manifesto: A Kingdom Vision for the Common Good*. Danvers: Chalice, 2012.

Gushee, David P., and Isaac B. Sharp, eds. *Evangelical Ethics: A Reader*. Louisville: Westminster John Knox, 2015.

Hunter, James Davidson. *Culture Wars: The Struggle to Define America*. New York: Basic Books, 1991.

———. *To Change the World: The Irony, Tragedy, and Possibility of Christianity in the Late Modern World*. New York: Oxford University Press, 2010.

Johnston, Robert K. "American Evangelicalism." In *The Variety of American Evangelicalism*, edited by Donald W. Dayton and Robert K. Johnston, 252–72. Eugene, OR: Wipf and Stock Publishers, 1997.

Lincoln, C. Eric, and Lawrence H. Mamiya. *The Black Church in the African American Experience*. Durham: Duke University Press, 1990.

Marsden, George. *Understanding Fundamentalism and Evangelicalism*. Grand Rapids: Eerdmans, 1990.

Miller, Stephen P. *The Age of Evangelicalism: America's Born-Again Years*. Oxford: Oxford University Press, 2014.

Noll, Mark. *The Princeton Theology 1812–1921: Scripture, Science, and Theological Method from Archibald Alexander to Benjamin Warfield*. Grand Rapids: Baker Academic, 1983.

Pohl, Christine D. *Living into Community: Cultivating Practices That Sustain Us*. Grand Rapids: Eerdmans, 2012.

———. *Making Room: Recovering Hospitality as a Christian Tradition*. Grand Rapids: Eerdmans, 1999.

Reuschling, Wyndy Corbin. *Desire for God and the Things of God: The Relationships Between Christian Spirituality and Morality*. Eugene, OR: Wipf and Stock, 2012.

————."Evangelical Ethics." In *Dictionary of Scripture and Ethics*, edited by Joel B. Green, 284–87. Grand Rapids: Baker Academic, 2011.

————. "The Means and End in 2 Peter 1:3–11: The Theological and Moral Significance of 'theōsis'." *Journal of Theological Interpretation* 8, no. 2 (Fall 2014) 275–86.

————. *Reviving Evangelical Ethics: The Promises and Pitfalls of Classic Models of Morality*. Grand Rapids: Brazos, 2008.

Scanzoni, Letha Dawson, and Nancy A. Hardesty. *All We're Meant to Be: Biblical Feminism for Today*. Grand Rapids: Eerdmans, 1992.

Sider, Ron. *Rich Christians in an Age of Hunger: Moving from Affluence to Generosity*. Nashville: Thomas Nelson, 2015.

Smith, Christian. *American Evangelicalism: Embattled and Thriving*. Chicago: University of Chicago Press, 1998.

Stackhouse, John G. *Making the Best of It: Following Christ in the Real World*. Oxford: Oxford University Press, 2008.

Stassen, Glen, D. M. Yeager, and John Howard Yoder. *Authentic Transformation: A New Vision of Christ and Culture*. Nashville: Abingdon, 1992.

Wallis, Jim. *The Call to Conversion: Why Faith Is Always Personal but Never Private*. New York: HarperOne, 2005.

Worthen, Molly. *Apostles of Reason: The Crisis of Authority in American Evangelicalism*. Oxford: Oxford University Press, 2016.

Holy Alliances

New Vessels for Contemporary Feminism

Nicola Hoggard Creegan

An Example: My Own Context

I write this short piece on feminism from the extreme margins of the world. I have lived for the last fifteen years in New Zealand, my country of origin—a place that is not only small and remote, but with very unusual social parameters. On many Indices of Social Progress, New Zealand scores near the top with the Scandinavian countries (although we also have astoundingly high levels of child abuse and associated mortality).[1] Alongside Denmark, New Zealand routinely scores the lowest in the world on scales of political corruption. In 1893, the young New Zealand Parliament became the first nation-state to give women the vote. We have had three women Prime Ministers and three women Anglican bishops; and we are home to Marilyn Waring, author of one of the finest works of feminist economics.[2] Somewhat surprisingly, then, feminism is not high on the radar in New Zealand society or churches. While the public media tend to be sensitized to racial issues, and even to some aspects of the quickly changing gender-politics, it remains oblivious to feminism. Moreover, our ethnic profile is changing rapidly, as New Zealand is now as Asian and Polynesian as it is *pakeha* (white). This creates a complex situation for a country whose founding document is the Treaty of Waitangi—made between English settlers and indigenous Maori, but not people of other races and ethnicities.

---

1. See socialprogressimperative.org.
2. Waring, *Counting for Nothing.*

All these developments complicate enormously both the assumptions and the challenges of white academic feminism. One has to ask how we might disentangle the issues of immigration, alienation, and imported religions from the expectations surrounding gender in a myriad of new ethnicities. The mainline churches in New Zealand, like many others that long ago "solved" the problem of women's ordination, now struggle with homosexuality, transgender, and intersex identities in terms of marriage blessing and ordination. Many churches have taken the first steps toward an ecological consciousness, often also associated with a more feminist outlook. All the while, the larger non-denominational evangelical world is still often embracing "headship," ignoring or rejecting the arguments and biblical scholarship of the last half century. For all these reasons, feminism has become a complicated and obscured place within the churches in New Zealand, as it has for different reasons in other parts of the Western world.[3] This paper, then, asks two related questions: Where has feminist theology gone? And how do the new faces of feminism relate to Christine's ongoing work on the practices of community and the recovery of hospitality?

Feminism and Patriarchy

Within both the church and the larger society, the setbacks for feminists—and women more generally—are typical of most human societies where gender bias (among others) is probably deeply culturally and also biologically embedded. Christianity struggles, I believe, because there appears to be a justification for patriarchy in the text (both the sections on headship and the existing male practice of the first centuries). Thus, the conservative churches' emphasis upon headship as a Christian distinctive may only be the rationalizing of deep human proclivities. Given these deep proclivities, resisting patriarchy may well be a slow and ongoing task, both outside and inside the church.[4] However, feminist theology does more than merely resist oppressive theologies; it is also the creative and constructive reimagining of Christian doctrine from an alternative perspective—women's experience, the liminal person, or the "other." Both these aspects of Christian feminism are alive in different forms; and both, I will show, are highly synergetic with Christine's work in hospitality and practices.

3. There is some evidence of an emerging popular feminism; see Bates, *Everyday Sexism Project*.

4. Equality has been achieved to some extent in Western countries by the adoption of Enlightenment legalization around equality. This does not erase—though it does modify—the deep texture beneath the surface.

Permanent gains and final recognition will always be hard to achieve, and cannot be the work of one or two generations. Feminist theology of previous generations (typified by the likes of Elizabeth Schüssler Fiorenza) is no longer game-changing for theological conversation.[5] While popular works of feminism are increasingly available for niche audiences, deeply scholarly feminism is now less visible because it has, in some sense, gone underground. In keeping with the third-wave critiques of second-wave feminism, feminist theology made significant shifts; moving away from universal arguments that might hope to transform the church at large, it is now resident in and within other transforming movements and theologies.[6] Feminism itself has also gone deeper. While second-wave feminism was still concerned with matters of justice that were accessible on the surface and open to popular movements, third-wave and post-feminist theology have dug deep into theoretical corners that do not have an obvious activist parallel.

Third-wave feminism and post-feminism is, therefore, more of a conversation. The voices do not all agree or read from the same text. Discussion and debate exist around issues of biblical interpretation, ecology and domination, and the use of the male pronoun for God.[7] There is a genuine exploration going on that is long past the point of feminist theology's heyday. Rather than engage almost endlessly with the debates around post-structuralism and gender, feminist theology has claimed the salvific countercurrents of the biblical text and has entered into natural partnerships with ecotheology, post-colonial theology, and new strategies for dogmatics.

Granted, some of feminism's well-tried methodologies are still in use—the deconstructive voice; the hermeneutics of suspicion; the need for praxis;

---

5. Fiorenza, *In Memory of Her*.

6. First-wave feminism is generally conceded to refer to the nineteenth- and early twentieth-century movements for women's right to vote and enter the work place. Second-wave feminism is a post-War phenomenon, digging deeper into overcoming the structures of a patriarchal society. Second-wave feminism was concerned with justice in the church and workplace; second-wave feminism worked to include women in worship and the leadership of the church, advocating for inclusive language and the ordination of women. Third-wave feminism since the nineties has recognized difference, and that privileged white feminism was often oppressive of and imperialistic towards women in other circumstances. Third-wave feminism speaks in many different voices, and from many different cultures and contexts. These voices do not always agree, nor expect to agree, though the fulfilment of women, the unmasking of patriarchy, and equality with men in all areas of society are often persisting themes.

7. As an example, Daphne Hampson and Sarah Coakley have had sharp exchanges; see Hampson, *Swallowing a Fishbone?* See also the disagreements over dominion in Trible, "The Dilemma of Dominion," and those over the Syro-Phonecian woman in Kinukawa, "The Journey of a Girl Who Talks Back."

and the reconstruction and reimagining of biblical and historical narratives. Yet even these are developing across and within new categories. For example, while feminist theology's use of "experience" is an often critiqued method, experience is now being used in unusual ways—phenomenologically in an attention to desire, in empathic criticism in biblical studies, and in attending to the effects of silent prayer.[8] But consider also praxis. Feminism has shared with other liberation theologies in insisting that the discussion not take place outside the visible tangible community in which faith is practiced. Praxis insists that an honest reflection take place of the ways in which ideas and theologies manifest themselves in people's lives, and especially in the lives of women. While the concept of "flourishing" may be difficult to assess cross-culturally, it is nevertheless possible to ask: Does this particular incarnation of faith lead to human flourishing in this context? And who is flourishing and who might be marginalized? Similarly, the "hermeneutics of suspicion," especially as applied to the Bible, can be translated to other more particular contexts and places. What have we missed in our hermeneutics? Who or what is being marginalized? What are the new methods by which we can bring to life the Scriptures in ways that are surprising and that give wisdom and conviction to the Body of Christ?

Moreover, if feminism showed anything, it is that language is powerful and its effects almost invisible. Any number of sophisticated biblical-hermeneutical methods dig deeper into these ancient texts than has previously been done. It is true that early feminisms were somewhat imperialistic in their application; it is equally true that we live in a radically relativized world. Yet feminist theological methods continue to resonate with a biblical world that is surprising—a world that overturns hidden hierarchies, pays attention to language, speaks of "eyes" that do not see and "ears" that do not hear, and expects grace for marginalized and unexpected people from hidden and counter-intuitive sources. While we may have trouble grounding these insights philosophically or universally, they carry their own momentum. Feminism now continues, albeit under the radar.

Feminism and Hospitality

These old methods and new alliances, I would argue, both complement and typify Christine's ongoing work in hospitality and community. She has taken as her point of reference the least, the alien, the stranger—amongst whom women are disproportionality represented—and has argued for Christian

---

8. See Farley, *The Wounding and Healing of Desire,* and Coakley, *God, Sexuality, and the Self.*

hospitality as the first of the practices that might exemplify the Christian life and coherent Christian community.[9] She advocates, therefore, that attention be paid to those who are often invisible and overlooked; that is, the Christian practice of hospitality should go beyond theory (the theory that women are invisible, for instance) to making these people feel at home, to befriending them. Salvation is not a private matter of the heart; it is also a duty and a task and a different way of living. Indeed, Christine's emphasis on the outsider, the marginal, and the alien is itself a mark of resistance to evil and oppression of all kinds. She has shown that it is in action that words of hospitality become powerful, that hierarchies are overturned, that the host is changed and made holy, and that even angels might be welcomed. Christine has returned to old texts and has reclaimed a tradition that has always been powerful but has also been overlooked. She has placed the outsider at the center of Christian practice and reflection and salvation. Grace is to be found, not only in sacraments and prayer, but in making oneself vulnerable to the stranger.

Although Christine and I together wrote a book on feminist theology and practice, Christine has never been a "full-time" feminist.[10] Her feminism has, nevertheless, informed her work and life. She has imagined and lived out a moral world in which everyone is included. Her work is not abstract and theoretical, nor is it simplistic and idealized. Rather, she takes as her first sources the messy world of human interactions across cultural, racial, gender, and class boundaries—whether these occur in the Bible, in texts, or in her own or others' experience.[11] This is feminist work, even if not full-time. She has used traditional feminist methodologies as well as ones that are fit for the more contemporary alliances. As with feminist theology, her texts of hospitality are reclaimed texts, previously forgotten by the church. Christine has always been attentive to language as an indicator of power. And her work resonates with experience. One cannot just write theoretical books about hospitality; it has to be a part of one's life in order to have any integrity. Thus both experience and the empowerment of those who are silent and the least are part of the arsenal of hospitality, and these have been predominant feminist themes through second- and third-wave feminism.

Christine has also worked for a quarter of a century within a Wesleyan institution. Wesleyanism has a history of women's leadership as part of its

---

9. See Pohl, *Making Room,* and *Living into Community*, ch. 11.

10. Hoggard Creegan and Pohl, *Living on the Boundaries*. Regarding the term "full-time feminist," see McKinnell and Kidd, *Science and Self,* 87.

11. Pohl, *Making Room.*

founding narrative (although it has been somewhat forgotten). As one of the first women hired at Asbury, she has had to make her way—and this way was always generous, open to the best in those who surrounded her, convinced that prayer and gratitude would in the end cover sins of omission and commission. Yet Christine has never been afraid of naming power and its hidden effrontery. At the same time, she has remained faithful to the Wesleyan tradition, reframing it, developing it, and speaking truth to its leaders and bishops. Although we may have hoped, when we wrote *Living on the Boundaries* a decade ago, that real progress in feminism might take place in more conservative churches, the reality is much more patchy and ambiguous than we anticipated. In Methodist and Wesleyan circles, however, there already existed a feminist "DNA" that has opened doors, enabling Christine's life and work to be an example and inspiration to a whole generation of men and women at Asbury.

These shared themes in both feminism and hospitality—hermeneutics, language, experience, embodiment, and attention to power dynamics and oppression—reoccur as dominant themes in many of the new feminist alliances. Of particular import to this essay are the fields of post-colonialism, eco-theology, and a renewed focus upon pneumatology within systematic theology.

The Ongoing Work of Feminist Theology: Post-Colonialism

Post-colonialism is a movement sensitive above all to the representations of philosophy and religion as they have been shaped and influenced by the colonial experience. It shares with continental philosophy a generally critical stance towards Western dualities and thought forms. Like feminist theology, post-colonialism is often biblically based, examining biblical interpretation through new lenses and imaginations.[12] In post-colonial readings, patriarchy and imperialism are seen as intertwined; and post-colonial theology shares with older feminisms its attention to cultures and power. Symbols are multi-faceted and excessive, often both liberating and oppressive in their effect.

A recent, very vivid example of post-colonialism from close to the New Zealand heart is that of Angeline M. G. Song. A student of the post-colonial scholar Judith McCinley, Song is a New Zealand immigrant of Malay-Chinese (Peranakan) ancestry. She was adopted at birth and thus narrowly

---

12. In the North American context see Pui-Lan, *Postcolonial Imagination,* and Dube, *Postcolonial Feminist Interpretation of the Bible.*

avoided being sold into prostitution. Her thesis, *A Postcolonial Woman Encounters Moses and Miriam* uses empathic studies and postcolonial methods to interrogate the Exodus story and the Mosaic birth narratives.[13] Song has used feminist methods to understand her own boundary crossing within Singapore—itself an Asian ex-colonial power—across classes, the experience of being saved from slavery, and the experience of being an immigrant who doesn't fit the established categories in yet another ex-colonial state. She then incorporates the discovery that the Bible has stories that resonate with these boundaries—resonances which may have been obscure to the colonizer. Song has brought the whole of her history and education to bear on the task of biblical interpretation, interrogating not only the culture and circumstances of her birth but the difficult, and at times highly charged, culture of her adopted country.

Post-colonialism thus reveals newer, stronger outworkings of original feminist thinking, but the subject is not the isolated apolitical woman sometimes found in second-wave feminism. Rather, women's experience is placed within the greater story of political subjugation and imperialism. In post-colonial readings of the Bible, the reader discovers, unsurprisingly, that these same dynamics are to be found in sacred Scripture also. The Bible was given by the colonizer but has been read and interpreted by the colonized at a new and deeper level. What was often hidden to the colonizer is uncovered by the colonized. As Kwok Pui-Lan, the quintessential postcolonial scholar, has said,

> Feminist theology in the twenty-first century must have a broader vision to develop a new theoretical discourse to analyze how economic domination intersects with cultural and religious production, and to articulate ways women can participate in shaping their future in the age of globalization.[14]

While these readings can certainly lead to antagonism, they can also be used to heal. The colonized open up the Scriptures for the colonizer and welcome them into the world they have given us. In this case, hospitality and grace abound. The dynamic whereby the host is blessed by the stranger in acts of hospitality is similarly present in the post-colonial biblical reading.

---

13. Song, *A Postcolonial Woman*. Empathy as a method relies on a deep identification of the reader with the circumstances of the biblical character, to the extent that unspoken particulars can be guessed or apprehended. The reader maintains a sense of her own self, while nevertheless entering into a profound relationship with a biblical character. Empathy draws its legitimacy from scientific studies of motor neurons in humans and other mammals (2.8).

14. Pui-Lan, "Feminist Theology at the Dawn of the Millennium," 11.

Post-colonial readings also show the dynamics of power and of collective sin and its effects. They deconstruct the view of sin as something done by the lone individual with full consciousness and intent. Post-colonial feminism should make all of us more humble as we see the extent of our participation in silent oppression.

Something similar happens when we befriend the outcast and the stranger. They let us into their story and the multiple oppressions that have resulted in their alien status. Friendship and befriending have been of enormous importance in Christine's life and work, as most of us will testify. She states: "Because we are unaware of the significance of our friendship and fellowship, our best resources often remain inaccessible to strangers. But it is also the case that building friendships across significant social differences can be challenging."[15]

Contemporary feminism has critiqued the polar nuclear family as being too inadequate and too isolated to carry the heavy moral lifting of community and church. In Christine's world, while families are of immense importance, friendship is, if anything, equally important.[16] Hospitality is all about be-friending; it is not just the provision of food and drink and medicine, but rather the practice of making someone feel at home, becoming their friend, caring about their lives and hardships, overcoming cultural and linguistic barriers to the extent that that is possible. Christine says, "Shared meals break down social boundaries."[17] Befriending is an active way of doing resistance to the much-named "powers" of contemporary society, including those of colonialism and domination.

The Ongoing Work of Feminist Theology: Eco-Theology

Living within a time characterized as the *anthropocene,* in which human activity is now understood by many scientists as *the* major impact on life on earth, the second feminist theological partnership is eco-theology. Feminist women and men have formed natural alliances with those who seek to further an ecological and sustainable life style, and with those who would wish to read the Scriptures—and thus to do theology—through the lenses of the earth and its delicate ecosystems.[18] Anne Elvey says:

15. Heuertz and Pohl, *Friendship at the Margins,* 160.

16. Heuertz and Pohl, *Friendship at the Margins,* 160.

17. Heuertz and Pohl, *Friendship at the Margins,* 81.

18. See Habel, *The Earth Bible in Genesis,* and Deane-Drummond, *Christ and Evolution.*

> Feminist theology is, in my view, no longer an "endpoint," if it
> ever was, for theological engagement. Rather feminist theology
> has opened up ways of being toward the world that enable us to
> see and imagine ourselves and our world otherwise, to affirm
> our being one species among many with particular gifts and
> challenges.[19]

Women have long been categorized as lower on the hierarchy of consciousness and rationality than men, and in eco-theology this association has been
turned on its head. Where once women were labelled as closer to nature
and therefore inferior, it is now more commonly recognized that being in
touch with our embodiedness makes us more truly human and spiritually
aware. Thus women and men are able to recognize that the deep connections between human and all other life are almost endless and that we live in
a delicate interconnected biological and spiritual world.

Eco-theology is also a counter-balance to the post-structuralist claim
that all power dynamics are linguistic ones. The earth pushes back—the
climate changes whether we pay attention or we don't, whether or not we
even have a word for it. Both the rape of the earth and violence against
women happen in hidden, unnoticed, unspoken places. Thus, the earth and
women's bodies claim a natural alliance. Together with men, women are
claiming a new association with the life-empowering forces of the earth,
leading to new readings, new imaginative strategies, new "social imaginar-
ies" for life in the twenty-first century, and new hope for earth and humanity
of the healing promised by the Gospels. Both the hermeneutics of suspicion
and the power of deconstruction can be brought to bear on narrow, fixed
anthropomorphic readings of biblical texts. Norm Habel, resident in one
of the driest and most arid of countries, Australia, has spearheaded the im-
mensely influential Earth Bible project.[20] One of the writers for that project
is Elaine Wainwright, Emeritus Professor of Theology at Auckland University, and a Sister of Mercy. Interrogating Matthew 13 from the perspective
of the earth, she states:

> Pervasive anthropocentrism and a domination and/or erasure
> of women, the colonized and the more-than-human [all life
> forms] other have characterized the ideology of/in author, text
> and reader from the genesis of the biblical text through its long
> history of interpretation to the present. It is essential, therefore,
> that a suspicion attentive to these interlocking processes of

19. Elvey, "Matter, Freedom and the Future," 200.

20. Habel, *The Earth Bible.*

erasure and mastery characterize every phase of the ecological reading process.[21]

The exercise of eco-theology, however, is not just about earth-liberation or saving ourselves as we face climate change. It is also about transformation and salvation at the deepest levels. It is about the turn that sees that the hand of God's glory is in nature, a fact that has been partially forgotten in the twentieth century. Eco-theology critiques our distanced (left-brained) approach to both Scripture and the earth. As philosopher Bruce Folz argues, an attention to the depth of nature resonates with the world of the Psalms.[22]

Yet a theological appreciation of climate change goes far beyond our being busy with sustainability. It is also about healing and revealing hidden glory in the depth of nature, a nature that reflects our inner subjectivities—and turns us from anthropomorphic observers of nature to participants who recognize its bio-centric depth. As Christine has looked for angels in the welcoming of strangers, we might also expect transcendence when we open ourselves to the creation so embedded in the old stories we know so well. Eco-theology requires a recognition and understanding of the deep interconnections and solidarities that exist between species. The parable of the feeding of the five thousand shows how interconnected hospitality is done with eco-theological sensitivities. Hospitality has only ever been thought to be possible because God will provide. We can be generous because God is generous. But this generosity flows out of the heart of nature; it is not abstractions that are served up, but rather grains and fish.

Like those working in traditional "full-time" feminism and ecology, Christine has emphasized the needs and moral demands of the body—the need for shelter, love, bread, and companionship, and above all sharing a meal. "Meals," says Christine, "are at the heart of the Christian story."[23] Words alone are not of any use. Humans and the ecological systems in which we live are interdependent. Hospitality is our way of recognizing this in human society. Care of creation is a way of acknowledging our dependence on the earth. Whatever equality women hope for and desire, it is not one that is separated from this embodied nature.

---

21. Wainwright, "Hear Then the Parable of the Seed," 127.

22. Folz, "Nature's Other Side," 330.

23. Heuertz and Pohl, *Friendship at the Margins,* 81.

The Ongoing Work of Feminist Theology: New Pneumatology

Feminism in the early twenty-first century is in some ways becoming more theological. Feminism went through a long period of deconstruction and wariness about God-language that had been often used in gender oppressive ways. Who is this God who has been so closely associated with women's oppression? But there has also been a slowly growing strand of feminism that has reclaimed and reinterpreted the tradition to speak in new ways about God, ourselves, and the church. Elizabeth Johnson, Catharine LaCugna, Kathryn Tanner, Serene Jones, and Wendy Farley have transformed and reinterpreted their traditions in feminist directions.[24]

Perhaps more than any other, Sarah Coakley has taken theology into the heart of God, marrying theory (often eschewed by feminism) and deep, prayerful, reflective experience of the divine. Her theology is closely aligned to a movement within theology that can only be understood as a new focus on trinity and pneumatology. In her systematic work, there is a distinct sensitivity to gender issues as central to theology—along with other modalities like race. She insists that theology is a submissive task and that vulnerability before God is important. The only way to overcome the alterities and dualities of social and gender existence is by prayer. For Coakley, theology emerges out of the crucible of prayer, and this includes feminist theology. Here dualities and "natural" alliances are deconstructed.

Coakley, for instance, acknowledges the dangers and critiques of systematic theology, especially for women. "The first resistance to systematic theology," she states, "resides in the philosophical critique of so-called 'onto-theology': it claims that systematic theology falsely, and idolatrously, turns God into an object of human knowledge."[25] The second critique

> . . . arises from the moral or political critique of so-called "hegemony": it sees systematic theology as inappropriately totalizing, and thereby necessarily suppressive of the voices and perspectives of marginalized people . . . The third resistance is a feminist critique, arising from a particular brand of French, post-Freudian psychoanalytic thought. It accuses systematic thinking (of any sort) of being "phallocentric," that is, ordered according to the "symbolic," "male" mode of thinking which seeks to clarify, control, and master.[26]

24. See Tanner, "Social Theory"; Jones, *Feminist Theory*; Farley, *The Wounding and Healing of Desire*.

25. Coakley, *God, Sexuality, and the Self*, 42.

26. Coakley, *God, Sexuality, and the Self*, 42.

In response to these critiques, Coakley takes an unusual route—she recommends prayer, especially silent prayer. The "unmastery" of silent prayer is relatively protective of these challenges, she claims, because it is chastening and purifying. The pray-er is also forced to encounter God, and God's tri-unity, including Golgotha, including sacrifice—thus forcing the pray-er to relinquish their own agenda, their own projected images of God. The work of the Spirit is also, she says, an interruption of any hard dualistic alterity, of which gender is the most prevalent. The Holy Spirit interrupts and forces the habit of listening, allowing the possibility of that which is marginal.

> In the incorporative model . . . the Holy Spirit is construed not simply as extending the revelation of Christ, nor even merely as enabling Christ's recognition, but as actually catching up the created realm into the life of God (making it "conformed to the likeness of his Son").[27]

For Coakley then, in some sense it is the Holy Spirit who is first experienced by the Christian; then we are taken up into the nexus of trinitarian life; we sense the desire of God for us, and simultaneously the love of God for the Son. Neither God the Father in the Father's otherness nor the Son in the Son's particularity can be accessed directly by the Christian. The Spirit, however, moves freely—drawing the whole of the created order, and in particular the praying person, up into the inner dynamics of God. That this has not always been the case can be seen in the virtual absence of the Spirit in many artistic depictions of the Trinity, to which "spot the vanishing dove" might be an appropriate reaction.[28]

From the experience of the praying Christian, however, this means that the Spirit comes first, not ontologically but experientially. After this something even more amazing happens. The pray-er senses and experiences that their desire is derivative, that God is desiring them—is desiring *us*. This mixing of desires is a clue to God because all of this happens *in* prayer. Thus Coakley enters the holy grail of systematic theology, but she does it in disarming and surprising ways. Here lies the future of feminist theology, participating fully and certainly in praxis and experience of the divine while not eschewing theory.

For Christine, a similar and parallel vulnerability is involved in opening ourselves to the stranger. This is both Christian practice and a way of being vulnerable before the divine. We practice hospitality, Christine claims, not only as a duty, but as a means of living out the compassion and holiness

---

27. Coakley, *God, Sexuality, and the Self*, 111–12.

28. Coakley, *God, Sexuality, and the Self*, ch. 5.

of God, accessing the Spirit in actions and in prayer. Drawing on Wesley, she argues that although we think of prayer, Scripture, and fasting as the primary means of grace, "[w]orks of mercy . . . are equally important as conduits of God's grace."[29]

Conclusion: Back to the Beginning

As I reflect on Christine's work and new directions in feminist theologies, what of my own context in one of the "borderlands" of the world?[30] I am in a place where there is decreasing institutional support for theology, especially of a feminist kind. Theology departments and schools are under strain. In the borderlands and at the margins, we in Aotearoa (New Zealand) will increasingly depend upon a larger and wider community at the geographic centers of the world. Yet important work has always been done from outside the center, even if it is not institutionally supported. New Zealanders have always been known for "making do," a postmodern attribute and skill. At the boundaries of theology, we will continue, with God's help, to spin our tales and work our resistance into the fabric of reflection upon God and all that is known as theology in its greatest and widest expressions. We will gain strength from the work of theologians like Christine who have always welcomed the stranger and the alien (and even Antipodeans) in anticipation of the feast of heaven.

Christine's work will serve always as a reminder that welcome is the first act of God, and ours also to continue, whatever our context. She reminds us that the great acts of biblical hospitality were done in places of hardship and confusion—when Abraham and Sarah were old and aliens, and must have been despairing of this God of theirs, for instance. Similarly, these new feminist alliances also speak to a world in which feminist theology is hard to do full time, and is unpopular in its pure form. We are reminded that feminist theology is as necessary as ever, but can be done in subversive partnerships with eco-theology, systematic theology and ethics, or post-colonial theology. It is done as we pay attention to the needs of others and welcome them into friendship and home. At the borderlands of the world, we have had to make hard choices about species and about welcoming the stranger. We can be satisfied that working to stem the effects of climate change, becoming reacquainted with the earth, critiquing colonial aspirations and prerogatives, and even entering into mystical theologies, are

---

29. Heuertz and Pohl, *Friendship at the Margins*, 77.

30. "Borderlands" is a term used in Anzaldua.

all ways of doing feminism under the radar, and they are all better if inspired by Christine's egalitarian and welcoming vision.

Bibliography

Anzaldua, Gloria. *Borderlands*. San Francisco: Aunt Lute, 1987.

Coakley, Sarah. *God, Sexuality and the Self: An Essay on the Trinity*. Cambridge: Cambridge University Press, 2013.

Deane-Drummond, Celia. *Christ and Evolution: Wonder and Wisdom*. London: SCM, 2009.

Dube, Musa W. *Postcolonial Feminist Interpretation of the Bible*. St. Louis: Chalice, 2000.

Elvey, Anne. "Matter, Freedom and the Future: Reframing Feminist Theologies through an Ecological Materialist Lens." *Feminist Theology* 23, no. 2 (2015) 186–204.

Farley, Wendy. *The Wounding and Healing of Desire: Weaving Heaven and Earth*. Louisville: Westminster John Knox, 2005.

Foltz, B. V. "Nature's Other Side: The Demise of Nature and the Phenomenology of Givenness." In *Rethinking Nature*, edited by B. V. Foltz and R. Frodeman, 330–42. Bloomington: Indiana University Press, 2004.

Habel, Norman C., and Shirley Wurst, eds. *The Earth Bible in Genesis*. Sheffield: Sheffield Academic Press, 2000.

Habel, Norman C. "Geophany: The Earth Story in Genesis 1." In *The Earth Story in Genesis*, edited by Norman C. Habel and Shirley Wurst, 34–38. Sheffield: Sheffield University Press, 2000.

Hampson, Daphne Margaret. *Swallowing a Fishbone?: Feminist Theologians Debate Christianity*. London: SPCK, 1996.

Heuertz, Christopher L., and Christine Pohl. *Friendship at the Margins: Discovering Mutuality in Service and Mission*. Grand Rapids: InterVarsity, 2010.

Hoggard Creegan, Nicola, and Christine Pohl. *Living on the Boundaries: Evangelical Women, Feminism and the Theological Academy*. Grand Rapids: InterVarsity, 2005.

Jones, Serene. *Feminist Theory and Christian Theology: Cartographies of Grace*. Minneapolis: Fortress, 2000.

Kinukawa, Hisako. "The Journey of a Girl Who Talks Back: Mark's Syrophoenician Woman," In *Faith and Feminism: Ecumenical Essays*, edited by Phyllis Trible, 69–84. Louisville: Westminster John Knox, 2014.

McKinnell, Liz, and Ian James Kidd, eds. *Science and Self: Animals, Evolution and Ethics: Essays in Honour of Mary Midgley*. London: Routledge, 2016.

Pauw, Amy Plantinga, and Serene Jones, eds. *Feminist and Womanist Essays in Reformed Dogmatics*. Louisville: Westminster John Knox, 2006.

Pohl, Christine D. *Making Room: Recovering Hospitality as a Christian Tradition*. Grand Rapids: Eerdmans, 1999.

———. *Living into Community: Cultivating Practices that Sustain Us*. Grand Rapids: Eerdmans, 2006.

Pui-Lan, Kwok. "Feminist Theology at the Dawn of the Millennium: Remembering the Past, Dreaming the Future." *Feminist Theology* 27 (2001) 6–20.

———. *Postcolonial Imagination and Feminist Theology*. Louisville: Westminster John Knox, 2005.

Schüssler Fiorenza, Elisabeth. *In Memory of Her: A Feminist Theological Reconstruction of Christian Origins*. New York: Crossroads, 1994.

Song, Angeline M. G. *A Postcolonial Woman's Encounter with Moses and Miriam*. London: Palgrave MacMillan, 2015.

Tanner, Kathryn. "Social Theory Concerning the New Social Movements and the Practice of Feminist Theology." In *Horizons in Feminist Theology*, edited by Rebecca S. Chopp and Sheila Greeve Devaney, 179–97. Minneapolis: Fortress, 1997.

Wainwright, Elaine M. "Hear Then the Parable of the Seed: Reading the Agrarian Parables of Matt 13 Ecologically." In *One Who Reads May Run: Essays in Honour of Edgar W. Conrad*, edited by R. Boer, M. Carden, and J. Kelso, 125–41. London: T&T Clark, 2012.

Waring, Marilyn. *Counting for Nothing: What Men Value and What Women Are Worth*. 2nd ed. Toronto: University of Toronto Press, 1999.

A Religion of Love

Miroslav Volf

Christianity is a religion of love.[1] That's what most Christians believe. Some, like the great Protestant theologian of the last century, Karl Barth, in his commentary on Paul's Epistle to the Romans, might object to the idea that Christianity is a "religion."[2] But still, most Christians would insist that, religion or not, Christian faith is all about love.

According to a study by the Fetzer Institute, between 90 and 95 percent of human beings want "meaningful love," and they want it more than they want anything else, more than riches, health, great food, or passionate sex.[3] We seem to have a happy situation: there is at least one religion—a way of life, a spirituality—which offers what people want most.

If you haven't detected a distancing chuckle in this suggestion, you may be inclined to remind me, perhaps with understatement, that things are more complicated than I make them out to be. I grant that: there is both a match and a mismatch between Christianity as a religion of love and the desires of humanity for love. I will keep returning to this issue throughout the essay. But first, I need to explore precisely what kind of love the Christian faith is and isn't about and whether, as many secularists and adherents of other religions claim, the Sacred Scripture and history of Christianity are at odds with the claim that the Christian faith is all about love. In the

---

1. This essay is a re-worked version of a lecture presented at the open symposium on "Love in Three Abrahamic Religions" at Regent's Park College, University of Oxford, celebrating the fifth year of the issuing of A Common Word, on October 12–13, 2012. Without the help of Justin Crisp, a first-rate research assistant, this text could not have been written.

2. Karl Barth, *The Epistle to the Romans*.

3. See Fetzer Institute, *Survey on Love and Forgiveness in American Society*.

second part of the essay I will sketch the character of the Christian faith as a religion of love of a particular sort, rooting my sketch in the texts of the Sacred Scripture, and particularly in the writings of St. John.

Like some "men of wealth," "love" is a word too rich for its own good; it's full of diverse and unruly meanings. We say, for instance, both that we love chocolate and therefore devour it and that we love our children and therefore sacrifice ourselves for them (though sometimes when we are particularly fond of them we say to them "You are so sweet that I could eat you up!"). When two people say that they want "love," they may want two very different things. The match between what most people want and what the Christian faith is all about may, then, only be verbal and, in any case, less perfect than it may seem. Theologians are aware of this. That's partly why many note that Christian faith doesn't satisfy human desires without first transforming them—and that includes the desire for love and love as a form of desire.

"Meaningful love," the supreme desire of most people, generally refers to deep and close connection with another human being—a lover, a child, a friend, a parent, or a sibling. We contrast it with work, especially in business and politics. "Love," we think, belongs to the domain of tender feelings, generosity, and care; "work" belongs to the domain of hard-knocks, self-interest, and disregard for others. The contrast is too sharp, of course, for we recognize that there is love in all good work and that there is work in all good love. Still, it captures the popular sense of the characteristic features of the two domains.

As a religion of love, is the Christian faith all about such intimate ties of mutual belonging? That's part of it, but not the whole or even the most of it. For the Christian faith is not a "mystical" religion, concerned mainly with the unity of the soul with God in a small community of the intimates; it is a "prophetic" religion oriented toward the vision of the kingdoms of the world with all their spheres, from the most intimate to the very public, being transformed into the Kingdom of the one God.[4] Can the Christian faith, then, still be a religion of love?

The contrast between "love" and "work" isn't just too sharp; it's seriously misleading. The sphere of work, including business and politics, is also about love—about desire for, attachment to, and care for something, whether the interests of the self, the well-being of the company or nation, or the global common good. In a sermon, St. Augustine famously said, "There is no one of course who doesn't love, but the question is, what do they love?

---

4. For more on the distinction between "mystical" and "prophetic," see Volf, *A Public Faith*, 6–8.

So we are not urged not to love, but to choose what we love."[5] Augustine is making two crucial points. First, all people love, and they love in all their activities. St. Francis's enterprising merchant father dressed in finery no less than his Christ-obsessed son was married to the Lady Poverty.[6] Second, though people cannot choose whether to love, they can choose what to love (merely themselves or also God and others) and how to love (with the mere feeling of attraction or with commitment to beneficence, for instance).

The Christian faith is about love in this broad sense, love without which we wouldn't be able to act at all and the entire enterprise of the world would grind to a halt—and, more fundamentally, it is about Love that makes both us and all our ordinary loves possible. The key question with regard to love is this: which varieties of such love are worthy of us as human beings and make for our individual and global flourishing, and which are not because by engaging in them, we betray our humanity and ruin our world? Which loves should we love and which should we hate?

Critics object that Christians delude themselves and mislead others by claiming that the Christian faith is all about love. Christian talk about love—or Christian talk about the Christian kind of love—only serves to mask and legitimize the violent nature of Christianity, they argue. For the most radical and intelligent of such critics, Friedrich Nietzsche, the Christian faith is more about hatred than about love, or it is about hatred by being about love. At bottom, he argued that Christian love is inverted hatred. To put Nietzsche's point in St. Augustine's terms, Christian faith is about the perfidious love of a weakling self, a self which, resentful on account of its frustrating inability to achieve its overambitious dreams for itself, invents self-giving love so that those who stand in its way can be roped into its service. For Nietzsche, Christian love doesn't merely mask and legitimize violence, but is itself violence, is hatred.

Christianity, a religion of hatred! This is the most serious charge against the Christian faith—more serious than the charge of "irrationality"—for it calls into question its central content rather than merely its plausibility. People want meaningful love, and the Christian faith, on this account, gives them the poison of hatred wrapped in white cellophane with red hearts. The critics believe that both Christian convictions and Christian practices warrant the charge (though Nietzsche himself, perhaps wisely, was more interested in Christian convictions). Are they right?

5. Augustine, *Sermon* 34, 167.

6. For Augustine, love is, as John Burnaby puts it, "the directive energy of the will in its most general aspect" (Burnaby, *Amor Dei*, 94).

Let's take up first, and very briefly, the matter of practices. I will not strictly respond to the criticism but merely try to blunt its edge by making one additional clarification about the kind of love the Christian faith is about. I agree with the critics on two important matters. First, there is a disturbing trail of blood and tears in the wake of Christianity's march through history (though many Christians console themselves—falsely, I suspect—with the claim that Christianity has a comparative advantage over other religious and secular groups in this regard). Second, that trail stands, obviously, in deep tension with the claim that the Christian faith is a religion of love. The critical question is whether that trail contradicts the claim that the Christian faith is a religion of love. My sense is that it doesn't, for two main reasons. The first one is easy to state: it can be plausibly argued that the violence is due to the illicit and unequal marriage of the faith to political power, a marriage in which faith becomes the servant of worldly power.[7] The second reason is more complicated and has to do with the precise way in which Christianity is a religion of love.

Contrary to the opinion of many, the Christian faith doesn't have at its heart the commandment "you shall love your neighbor as yourself," nor even the commandment "you shall love the Lord your God with all your heart." These two commandments—inseparable and, in a sense, one, as we shall see later—are an indispensable component of the Christian faith, but they are not its heart. If they were its heart—in fact, if any commandments were the heart of the Christian faith—the Christian faith would be more a religion of law than a religion of love. In fact, in obliging people to love God with their whole hearts and neighbors as themselves, the Christian faith would then be a religion of an impossible law. As a religion of love, however, the Christian faith is not primarily about what human beings are obliged to do, about human beings' concrete relations to one another, their various neighbors and fellow creatures, and God. Instead, the Christian faith is primarily about God's relation to human beings and the world. Love here is not first of all human love, but God's love; in relation to humans, it is primarily love received, not love practiced—or rather, it is love practiced as love received.[8] The Christian faith is a religion of love because it teaches that the God of love has, paradoxically perhaps, embraced humanity in love before the foundation of the world, before there was anything to embrace,

---

7. See Volf, *Flourishing*, 183–90. See also Toft et al., *God's Century*.

8. The insight that the Christian faith isn't a religion of love because the command to love God and neighbor sums up the law and the prophets, but because God is love and loves human beings unconditionally lies at the heart of Martin Luther's reformation discovery. For a simple statement of this insight, see Martin Luther, *Freedom of the Christian*.

so that the embrace of love is the reason for creating. Consequently, human love—the push and the pull of all human longing, desiring, and willing—is truly love when it is an echo of that divine love, when God's gift-giving love courses through them to both their own and their neighbors' good.

Critics may grant that the Christian faith so understood is a religion of love but may still object that love so understood issues in spoiled children.[9] Christians see themselves as God's favorites without them having done much to deserve God's favor. They smugly let God love them, and scream bloody murder when they are not pampered. Or they lazily let God do all the loving through them, which ends up not then being very much. Such a religion of love seems complaisantly otherworldly, especially in secular cultures permeated by a deep conviction—mostly unthematized but, for just this reason, very powerful—that human beings alone act in the world. And it seems self-servingly and morally irresponsible, especially in cultures shaped by religions concerned primarily with salutary human practices, as, for instance Judaism and Islam are.

If "meaningful love," which human beings desire above all things, is love to be given, received, and passed on without conditions, then Christian faith offers the kind of love most people, all happy to be God's favorite children, desire. But is that kind of love also what human beings need? Is this non-moralizing account of love true to the moral fabric of our lives, a pattern of life for responsible adults rather than bratty little princes and princesses? That is the fundamental question about the character of the Christian faith as a religion of love. The Christian contention is that the Christian account of love is true to both our highest moral aspirations and our inescapable moral failures and that, far from being otherworldly, it is the key to the flourishing of persons, communities, and our whole world.

But how exactly does this love unconditionally given and received look, and how does God figure in it? And how does it, or should it, shape Christian practices? To answer, we need to remind ourselves of some basic Christian convictions.

What follows is a brief sketch of the Christian faith as a religion of love, a Christian "credo" of sorts, organized around love.

---

9. Immanuel Kant expressed a similar idea, though not in rejection of the Christian faith as such, with the image of an "undisciplined servant" who appeals exclusively to God's grace: "It is arduous to be a good servant (here one always hears only talk of duties); hence the human being would rather be a favorite, for much is then forgiven him, or, where duty has been too grossly offended against, everything is again made good through the intercession of someone else who is favored in the highest degree, while he still remains the undisciplined servant he always was" (Kant, *Religion within the Boundaries of Mere Reason*, 190).

Before all beginnings there was God, existing eternally as Love, the one and undivided divine reality internally differentiated in three "persons," a field of perfect love given and received. Then—though not really "after" God had existed for a while as such a field of perfect love—then God created the world out of the overabundance of divine love. As the crown of creation, God created human beings so that they would recognize themselves and the world as gifts of God's eternal love and would be channels of God's love to each other and the world—so that they themselves would be a creaturely field of love.

But human beings failed to recognize the world and themselves as fruits of God's love and to pass on the always-already-received love of God to each other. In that very failure, they severed themselves from the paradise of the Field of Love for which they were created. Yet, the God of love did not abandon them—and, in a sense, could not abandon them—to their own misguidedly chosen fate. Though they wronged God and one another by failing to recognize their own and the world's existence as a gift and by claiming it as their own possession apart from God, God sought to return them to themselves—and did so just because God is love and therefore always loves, irrespective of the behavior or the state of the creatures to whom God is relating.

In the life, death, and resurrection of Jesus Christ, the unique self-expression of God in human life, God undertook to justify and restore the humanity marred by the deficiency of love. This, too, was a gift of God, utterly gratuitous and therefore not to be "earned" in any way. Instead, as a gift of love it was to be received "in faith," faith being the only proper posture for receiving love: the empty hands stretched out to God with an open heart to honor God's love in receiving God's gifts, gifts which are all summed up in the gift of God's own loving self. More, through the power of the Spirit, God dwells in human beings who have embraced God and themselves in faith and seeks to be the force of love in them. After their earthly pilgrimage, whose goal is for them to learn to love God and those outside the community of faith no less than those inside it, God promised to glorify them, to give them eternal life in the fullness of unfailing love in God's everlasting loving embrace.

According to this sketch, the Christian faith is not primarily about the ordinary or heroically self-sacrificial love of human beings, but about God, the original and originating Lover, bringing about a world of love out of the inexplicably crooked timber of a both tragically and culpably self-centered humanity.[10] The time and the space of human history are the stage for turn-

10. The "crooked timber of humanity" is Kant's phrase in "Idee zu einer allgemeinen

ing of these self-centered and self-indulgent creatures—spoiled children, as are most of us—into true lovers.

But does the Bible, the holy book of the Christian faith, support this rendering of the love that God is and that God intends to bring about? Or have I, perhaps nudged by the criticism that Christian faith is a religion of violence and hatred masquerading as a religion of love, offered here a velvety version of a jaggedly steely original, unyielding in its insistence on the single God and single truth of human existence, implacably judgmental and bent on imposing itself on all, irrespective of their wishes? To put the question differently: Is John Winthrop of the would-be "city on the hill," who executed blasphemers and adulterers and imposed fines on religious slackers, a better representative of the Christian faith than St. Francis of Assisi, who sought not so much "to be loved as to love," because he believed that "it is in giving that we receive"? To find the answer to these questions, we need to return to the biblical sources of the Christian faith.

If the Christian faith is a religion of love and the Bible is its holy book, then the Bible must be a book of love. But is it? To many non-Christians, the claim that Bible is a book of love seems self-delusionally and dangerously false. In their view, the Bible is "one long celebration of violence,"[11] which, to apply the phrase Christopher Hitchens used to describe religions more generally, "poisons everything."[12] How could a book which on its first pages endorses God's destruction of the whole humanity in a global flood (Genesis 6), which contains a long narrative of a people acting on God's command to wipe out entire populations, women, children, livestock, and all (Joshua), and which at its end tells of a fearsome rider on a white horse executing the fury of God's wrath upon the world's inhabitants (Revelation 19)—how could such a book be a book of love? And if it is a book of love, isn't it as much a book of festering resentment and fierce revenge, because it is a book of unrequited and disappointed love?[13]

In the reminder of this essay, I will make one small step toward showing that the Bible is indeed a book of love and therefore that the Christian faith is originally, and not just in some of its modern versions, a religion of

---

Geschichte in weltbürgerlicher Absicht": "*aus so krummem Holze, als woraus der Mensch gemacht ist, kann nichts ganz Gerades gezimmert warden*" ("Out of the crooked timber of humanity no straight thing was ever made."). (Quoted in Hardy, *The Crooked Timber of Humanity*, xxiii).

11. Pinker, *The Better Angels of Our Nature*, 6. For a literary presentation of the same point, see Saramago, *Cain*, and Saramago, *The Gospel according to Jesus Christ*.

12. Hitchens, *God Is Not Great*.

13. For a literary account of God as disappointed lover, see Rakow, *This Is Why I Came*.

love. I will make this task easier for myself by limiting myself to the writings of St. John, namely his Gospel and epistles. This biblical writer was known early on as a "theologian of love," not just because, as the tradition would have it, he was the "disciple whom Jesus loved" and who reclined next to Jesus at the Last Supper (John 13:23), but because more than anyone else in the Bible, he writes about love. Elsewhere, I have undertaken the slightly more difficult but still relatively easy task of interpreting St. Paul as a theologian of love—a theologian of God's utterly gratuitous gift of creation and, above all, of salvation, whose entire theology can be expressed in a rhetorical question: "What do you have that you did not receive?" (1 Cor 4:7).[14] The ease of reading John and Paul as theologians of love is revealing, however. For of all biblical writers, John and Paul together have arguably shaped the Christian faith more than anyone or anything else.[15] If the two of them are theologians of love, then the Christian faith is a religion of love.

Let's assume for a moment that my argument about John and Paul is sound. Though the texts of these two writers are substantively central to the Christian Bible, they comprise a relatively small portion of it. If the rest of the Bible cannot also be read as a book of love, then the claim that Christianity is a religion of love will rest on a foundation that's firm in two of its central pillars but wobbly elsewhere. So before taking up John's texts, a few comments on the Christian interpretation of the Bible as a whole are needed. They will amount to the claim that hermeneutically, too, and not just substantively, Paul and John, or rather, what Paul and John are all about, is central to the Christian faith.

Consider the precise way in which Bible is the holy book of the Christian faith. Though properly counted among "religions of the book," in one sense Christianity is not a religion of the book. It is the religion of the divine Word-become-flesh. Jesus Christ, the embodied and enacted self-revelation of God, is at the center of the Christian faith; the Christian faith is most properly the "religion of Jesus Christ"; he is the source and the content of the Christian faith, and therefore his kind of life ought to the goal of each Christian's life.

---

14. Volf, *Free of Charge*.

15. St. Luke the Evangelist, with his Gospel and Acts, rivals John and Paul in influence on the course of Christianity when all three are considered individually, though not if John and Paul are taken together. It would not be difficult to show that Luke, too, slightly differently than either Paul or John, is a theologian of love. Between the three of them, they cover most of the formative scriptural influence on the development of Christianity, as they provide lenses though which Christians have read the rest of the Bible. To the three of them, one could also add St. Peter. Though not as influential as the writings of Luke, Paul, and John, his First Epistle pulls together various strands from the whole New Testament and can easily be read as a text governed by the idea of love.

The Bible is related to Jesus Christ in a two-fold way. On the one hand, since his ascension and the death of the apostles, the Bible has been the main source of knowledge about Christ and, therefore, the criterion for everything that claims to be Christian. On the other hand, the main purpose of the Bible is to "bear Christ"; its "holiness" as a book derives from its "Christ-bearing" function, more precisely, from its Spirit-inspired Christ-bearing function. Martin Luther, the great Protestant reformer, famously stated that the content of the Bible—a book written over a millennium and a half of God's engagement with the people of Israel, the church, and humanity more broadly—must be assessed by whether it *was Christum treibet* ("inculcates Christ").[16] So the Bible gives and norms access to Christ, but Christ is the purpose and the measure of the Bible.[17]

When we ask whether the Bible, as the holy book of Christians, is a book of love, we ask first of all whether Christ—on whom the whole Bible, read as the Christian Scripture, pivots—is a person of love. For Christians, the answer is plain:[18] Christ is love; he is the self-revelation of God as love.

---

16. See Luther, *Word and Sacrament 1*.

17. To see the idea of Christ as the measure of the entire Bible at work in the Bible itself, consider the Evangelist Matthew's report of Christ's teaching about his relationship to the Law, a key component of the Hebrew Bible (Matt 5:1–48). In the passage, Christ (1) radicalizes the commands against murder and adultery (turning them into commands against anger and lust) and provisions for divorce (turning them into a prohibition against divorce with one exception only), and he (2) overturns the law of retaliation (replacing the urge to hit back with the requirement of letting oneself be hit one more time) and the command to love one's neighbor but hate the enemy (replacing it with the command to love one's enemies). Now, as good a proof as any that the Bible is not a book of love can be found in the book of Joshua, as I indicated earlier. Most relevant for how Christians ought to interpret the passages about violence in Joshua is that Jesus grounds the teaching about the love of enemies in the character of God, who makes the sun shine on the evil and the good and sends rain on the just and on the unjust (Matt 5:45). This generosity of God towards all—this *love* of God—is God's perfection, and Christ insists that the children of God ought to imitate it, ought to be perfect as their "heavenly Father" is perfect (Matt 5:48). In line with Christ's teaching, early Christian theologian Origen interpreted the violence against enemies in the Old Testament allegorically as violence against vices in the soul (see, for example, *Hom. Josh.* 15.1: "Unless those physical wars bore the figure of spiritual wars, I do not think the books of Jewish history would ever have been handed down by the apostles to the disciples of Christ, who came to teach peace, so that they could be read in the churches. For what good was that description of wars to those to whom Jesus says, 'My peace I give to you; my peace I leave to you,' and to whom it is commanded and said through the Apostle, 'Not avenging your own selves,' and, 'Rather, you receive injury,' and, 'You suffer offense'?"). Similarly, in their daily recitation of Psalms, monks have interpreted the often-mentioned enemies as the internal enemies of the soul (see Smith, *War and the Making of Medieval Monastic Culture*, 9–38, especially 23–28).

18. This may not be so plain to non-Christians, partly because they may have a different notion of love. If any dimension of culture is generically human, it seems that

It follows that the extermination of whole peoples in Joshua, the laws demanding the death penalty for adultery in Leviticus, the fury of God's wrath in Revelation and the like must all be measured by the yardstick of Christ and fitted to his pattern. And that takes us back to the evangelists and the apostles and their account of Christ, the one who on the cross embraced the whole of humanity irrespective of their deeds and misdeeds—or as John, to whom I now turn, puts it: the one who is the Lamb of God and bears the sin of the world.

The last words of Jesus' last prayer are the culmination and summary of the entire Gospel of John. The prayer marks the end of his private instruction to the disciples (John 13:1–17:26), and the private instruction follows the end of his public ministry (John 1:19—12:50). After the prayer, Jesus is arrested and crucified, and upon rising from the dead and appearing to his disciples, he returns to where he, the Word-become-flesh, had originally come. "Righteous Father," Jesus says at the very end of his prayer, "the world does not know you, but I know you; . . . I made your name known to them [the disciples], and I will make it known, so that the love with which you have loved me may be in them, and I in them" (John 17:25–26). What these words mean and imply tells much about a Christian understanding of love.

(1) Love in Eternity and in Time. Before all beginnings and across all times, there was love, eternal love. This is the love with which the "Speaker" (or the "Father") has loved the "Word" (or the "Son") before the foundation of the world and therefore apart from any of the world's beginnings and endings. The Son is eternally the only begotten of the Father and therefore utterly loved by the Father (John 1:18). Radically set apart from everything created, these two, along with the Spirit, dwell in each other in indivisible unity, giving to and receiving from each the single and singular divine glory. This one God, in principle indivisible and yet internally differentiated, "is love" (1 John 4:8). Love is what God is. The Alpha and the Omega of everything that is not God is love.

But God is invisible, inaccessible to human senses. How, then, do we, bodily beings dependent for knowledge on our senses, know God's love, its character and extent? The first time the word "love" shows up in John's

---

love should be. And yet, this is not the case. We love in culturally and religiously specific ways—for the most part recognizable to others as modalities of love, but sometimes very alien. Christians, of course, have to answer probing and sometimes uncomfortable question about their claim that Christ is the embodiment of love, such as why would he, according to the Gospels, curse the fig for not bearing fruit when it was not its season (Matt 21:18–20), send demons into a heard of pigs who, as a result, ended up drowning (Mark 5:1–13), or why God would save from Herod's rage Joseph, Mary, and Jesus, but not other innocent children (Matt 2:13–23).

writings is three chapters into his Gospel, in the most famous verse of the entire Bible, John 3:16: "For God so loved the world that he gave . . ." What did God give? The verse goes on to describe the gift as God's own Son. In his First Epistle, John describes the gift incarnate as "the Word of Life," the one we can hear with our ears, see with our eyes, touch with our hands. We know that God is love, that "God's love is revealed among us," in that "God sent his only Son into the world so that we might live through him" (1 John 4:9). God loves, and therefore God gives. To love is to give—or to love is at least to do that much.

With regard to God's own reality, the Holy Three, who dwell in each other and are indissolubly One, give divine glory to each other (John 17:4–5) and in this way constitute the divine reality. With regard to the world, God gives existence to all creatures as "all things came into being through him" (John 1:3); the Word, which enlightens everyone, is the Son who gives the Father's "name" to be known, makes God accessible to human beings (John 17:25); and, as the Word-become-flesh, Jesus Christ bears the sin of the tragically and culpably wayward world (John 1:29) and grants them communion with the triune God. In sum, God's love is creatively and empathetically giving love, generating realities, intensifying joys ("glory"), identifying with and bearing away the troubles ("sin") of others, generating a life of love in them ("love in them"), and opening the circle of its communion to all ("I in them").

(2) Love, Pain, and Dance. At the most extreme edge of gift-giving love is the readiness to give one's life for another person. "No one has greater love than this, to lay down one's life for one's friends," says Jesus to his disciples (John 15:13). "We know love by this," writes John to his community, "that he [Jesus] laid down his life for us—and we ought to lay down our lives for one another" (1 John 3:16). The full measure of love is the sacrifice of life.

Sacrifice for whom? For friends alone? At one level, it is on account of their friendship and attachment to Christ that Christ gives his life for disciples and therefore that the disciples should be ready to lay down their lives for one another. But in a crucial sense, it is the other way around: Christ's giving of his life for them elicits (or deepens) their friendship and attachment to him and constitutes them as his friends and followers. He has chosen them; they have not chosen him (John 15:16). More precisely: they have chosen him because he has chosen them. As John puts it in his First Epistle, "In this is love, not that we loved God but that he loved us and sent his Son to be the atoning sacrifice for our sins" (1 John 4:10). God loves the whole world, not just God's friends, and therefore Christ dies for the whole world—for those who sin, for those who don't love God and indulge the "desire of the flesh, the desire of eyes, the pride of riches" (1 John 2:16), and even for those who seek to kill Jesus because he doesn't conform to their religious convictions and practices because he speaks what they deem to be blasphemy and transgression of law (John 5:18). God's love manifest in Jesus' death on the cross isn't just utterly self-giving but is also universal and unconditional. Self-sacrificial in measure, this love is utterly gratuitous in character.

Is self-sacrifice an eternal aspect of divine love in the same way that utter gratuity is?[19] From the claim that God is love (as distinct from the claim that God loves), follows the utter gratuity of divine love. Just as there is "no darkness at all" in the God who is light (1 John 1:5), so there is absolutely no absence of love in the God who is love; God loves all the time and, therefore, every human being at any point in his or her life. In addition to gratuity, is self-sacrifice implied in the claim that God is love, as well? It is not. Notice how John links God's love to Christ's self-sacrificial death: "We know love by this, that he laid down his life for us" (1 John 3:16); "God's love was revealed among us in this way: God sent his only Son" (1 John 4:9). Christ's self-sacrifice manifests God's eternal love, but it is not identical with it. It is the form God's love takes when faced with human sin and enmity.

Before all beginnings—prior to the world with its sin and pain—God's love was gratuitous but non-sacrificial, pure delight in the glory of each and in the mutual glorification of all. After sin's ending, both divine and human love will be just that: pure delight in the glory of each and the mutual glorification of all—a love without suffering or loss.

(3) **All Love is God's Love.** Why do Christians love (when they do, which is not nearly as often as they should, of course)? "Beloved, since God loved us so much [so that God sent his Son as an atoning sacrifice for us] we also ought to love one another" (1 John 4:12). We learn that God loved us completely, we are moved, and we love. How should Christians love? "This

---

19. Famous Catholic theologian Hans Urs von Balthasar argues as much: "In giving himself, the Father does not give something (or even everything) that he has but all that he is—for in God there is only being, not having. So the Father's being passes over, without remainder, to the begotten Son." So far so good. But then comes an illicit projection of the fate of love in a sinful world onto God: "This total self-giving, to which the Son and the Spirit respond by an equal self-giving, is a kind of 'death', a first, radical 'kenosis', as one might say. It is a kind of 'super-death' that is a component of all love and that forms the basis in creation for all instances of 'the good death', from self-forgetfulness in favor of the beloved right up to that highest love by which a man 'gives his life for his friends'" (von Balthasar, *Theo-Drama*, V:84). On this aspect of von Balthasar's account of trinitarian love, see also Tonstad, "Sexual Difference and Trinitarian Death."

is my commandment, that you love one another as I have loved you," says Jesus to his disciples (John 15:12). We hear or read that Jesus gave his life for the life of the world, we recognize the greatness of that love, and we try to emulate it in our own limited way.

Many people—even some of those who are serious about the life of love—think that to understand love (and to actually love) you need only to know the answer to two questions: "Why should I love?" which takes care of the motivation, and "How should I love?" which gives you a model. For John, the motivation for love and the model of love are clearly impor- tant; he elaborates on them repeatedly. The heart of his theology of love lies elsewhere, however. The purpose of the Word's becoming flesh, indeed the purpose of the Word's creating the world, consists in this: "so that the love with which you have loved me may be in them, and I in them" (John 17:26). From John's angle, we understand love properly only when we realize that all love is God's love because "love is from God" (1 John 4:7). All human love is participation in the divine love. The eternal love of the Holy Three that are uniquely and indivisibly One, the love out of which the Word cre- ated the world, the love out of which God, in Jesus Christ, redeemed the world, that very love (and not merely a love like it) is to be in the followers of Christ. How is that possible? Only if Christ's followers dwell in God and if God dwells in them. That's why the four last words of the last prayer of Jesus for his disciples are "and I in them": "so that the love with which you have loved me may be in them, and I in them" (John 17:25–26). When God gives love, God doesn't give merely something God has but something God actively is. We love when Christ is in us, when Christ loves through us. And when we love, we are "Christs" to others.[20]

The idea that human love isn't just motivated by divine love and mod- eled on it but is, in fact, a modality of divine love helps us understand two things: why we are to love both God and our neighbors and why these two loves are inextricably united. First, if human love is God's love, then just as God's love is the love of the Holy Three for each other and for the world, so also proper human love is love for God and for the world. Second, if human love is God's love, then if we don't love God—and we would have to explore what love for God means here and how explicit it must be—we won't truly love either ourselves or our neighbors, for without abiding in the Word-become-flesh, we are unable to bear the fruit of love, like a branch cut off from the vine (John 15:1–10).[21] Inversely, if we don't love our neighbors,

20. See Luther, *Freedom of the Christian*, 368. On the idea, see also Volf, *Free of Charge*, 49–52.

21. Most Christians believe, at least upon reflection, that a person cannot truly love without the reality of the God of love as revealed in Jesus Christ. After all, it is this God

then God's love is not in us and we therefore don't truly love God either, which is why John insists that those who say that they love God but "hate their brothers and sisters, are liars" (1 John 4:20). By loving our neighbor—by keeping God's commandments—we love God; in loving God—in abiding in Jesus' love—we love the neighbor. If we love, we love both God and neighbor because we love with God's love, love among the Holy Three and love of the Holy One for the world.

Perhaps surprisingly for "religious" texts, in John's writings the test of whether we love at all is not whether we show extraordinary devotion to God but whether we help neighbors "in need" and, in extreme situations, are willing to lay down our lives for them (1 John 3:16–17). One might have expected John to say the exact opposite, namely that our devotion to God means that we are true lovers. After all, John insists that those who do not love God can do "nothing" when it comes to love (see John 15:5). Yet, John is clear that the only way we can tell whether someone loves God is by observing his or her love of neighbors. Since God is invisible, love for God is invisible, as well; unlike God, though, the neighbor is visible, and love for neighbor is visible, as well. Since the love for neighbor and for God is one, "those who do not love a brother or sister whom they have seen, cannot love God whom they have not seen" (1 John 4:20).

(4) Love, Judgment, and Hate. Love elicits love, we might think. If all people search for love, they must *love* love. And yet this isn't true, or at least, it isn't true in a straightforward way. Sometimes love elicits hatred. Of course, injustice and hatred elicit hatred, as well. That's what we expect: for hatred to be returned for hatred. Similarly, we expect love to be returned for love and are disheartened when we see hatred being returned for love. And yet, hatred is love's stubborn shadow—not just our hatred of the very people we love (when they disappoint our expectations) or hatred of us by people we love (when we don't meet their expectations), but hatred of true lovers by those unwilling or unable to love anyone but themselves and their own cliques (as when couples or adherents of a religion carve out spaces for themselves in tight-knit familial or religious communities and are hated for that).

"If the world hates you," says Jesus to his disciples in John's Gospel, "be aware that it hated me before it hated you. If you belonged to the world, the world would love you as its own. Because you do not belong to the world, but I have chosen you out of the world—therefore the world hates you"

---

that created human beings for love. But that is an entirely different matter from the claim that a person cannot love without faith in the God of love, for it roots the practice of love in God rather than in human faith in God.

(John 15:18–19). Often enough, of course, the world has perfectly good reasons for hating disciples of Jesus either because they lead despicable lives or because they are insufferably proud of their own presumed goodness. But sometimes the world hates those who love just because they love; people hate those who love those they hate.

The disciples shouldn't be surprised if the world hates them. What is this world, which God loves but which hates those who love God? The "world" consists of people governed by the principles of the "world," the domain that rejects love as God's character and the determining reality of creation. This rejection doesn't amount to the utter absence of love; it amounts to corrupt love, twisted and turned toward the lover and lover's community alone. John describes that love as "the desire of the flesh, the desire of the eyes, the pride in riches" (1 John 2:16). Put in more contemporary terminology, corrupt love is the internal self-centered cravings of the self, augmented by external attractions, and accompanied by boastfulness about the means of their satisfaction.

There are two kinds of love: a genuine, unconditional, generous, and self-forgetful love, and a corrupted, conditional, and self-seeking love. Those whose love is genuine love both themselves and others, God and all neighbors; the righteous Abel is their representative. Those whose love is corrupted love themselves alone but hate all others or are indifferent toward them; Cain, murderer of his righteous brother, is their representative (see 1 John 3:12). Each of us is never only either an Abel or a Cain but almost always both at the same time, the two brothers struggling in our souls, hopefully with Abel winning over Cain, with the struggle continuing until the day when God will transform this present world into the world of God's unadulterated love.

When our flesh trembles with desire, when our soul is made alive by the attractions around us, and we are brimming with pride on account of our ability to satisfy our desires—in other words, when in loving everything else we love ourselves—we may seem to ourselves extraordinarily alive, but in fact we may be in the realm of death. When we give ourselves to others, even when we, like seeds, fall to the ground and die, we are in the realm of life, God's life of love coursing through us. For "those who love their life lose it, and those who hate their life in this world will keep it for eternal life" (John 12:24–25; cf. 1 John 3:14). The choice between life and death is not a choice between love and non-love. It is the choice between loving only ourselves in all our loves and being voided thereby of God's love or loving God and neighbor and being filled with God's love and thereby flourishing.

All people are equal, but all loves aren't. The Christian faith is all about love—about mean and perfidious loves that eat away and, at times, devour both the beloved and the lover, about truthful and nourishing loves that make people flourish and bring genuine and lasting joy, about healing and purifying loves that turn devouring loves into ones that bring joy. Above all, the Christian faith is about divine love in which all our truthful, nourishing, healing, and purifying loves participate.

The great calling of human beings is to receive themselves, the world, and God as gifts of love and to become Love's instruments themselves. From the perspective of the Christian faith, this is the kind of love for which we are made, whether or not it is the kind of love we say that we want more than we want anything else.

Bibliography

Augustine of Hippo. *Sermon 34*. Vol. 6, Nicene and Post-Nicene Fathers. Edited by Philip Schaff. Translated by R. G. MacMullen. Buffalo: Christian Literature, 1888.

Balthasar, Hans Urs von. *Theo-Drama: Theological Dramatic Theory*. Vol. V, *The Last Act*. San Francisco: Ignatius, 2003.

Barth, Karl. *The Epistle to the Romans*. Translated by Edwyn C. Hoskyns. London: Oxford University Press, 1933.

Berlin, Isaiah, and Henry Hardy, eds., *The Crooked Timber of Humanity: Chapters in the History of Ideas*. Translated by Isaiah Berlin. Princeton: Princeton University Press, 2013.

Burnaby, John. *Amor Dei: The Religion of St. Augustine*. Norwich: Canterbury, 2012.

Hitchens, Christopher. *God Is Not Great: How Religion Poisons Everything*. New York: Twelve, 2009.

Kant, Immanuel. *Religion within the Boundaries of Mere Reason and other Writings*. Edited by Allen Wood and George di Giovanni. Cambridge: Cambridge University Press, 2018.

Luther, Martin. *Freedom of the Christian*. Translated by Mark D. Tranvik. Minneapolis: Fortress, 2008.

———. *Word and Sacrament I*. Vol. 35, *Luther's Works*. Edited by E. Theodore Bachmann. St. Louis: Concordia, 1960.

Origen of Alexandria. *Homilies on Joshua*. Vol. 105, *The Fathers of the Church*. Edited by Cynthia White. Translates by Barbara J. Bruce. Washington, DC: Catholic University of America Press, 2002.

Pinker, Steven. *The Better Angels of Our Nature: Why Violence Has Declined*. New York: Penguin, 2012.

Rakow, Mary. *This Is Why I Came*. Berkeley: Counterpoint, 2015.

Saramago, José. *Cain*. New York: Houghton Mifflin Harcourt, 2011.

———. *The Gospel According to Jesus Christ*. New York: Houghton Mifflin Harcourt, 1994.

Smith, Katherine Allen. *War and the Making of Medieval Monastic Culture*. Rochester: Boydell, 2011.

Toft, Martha Duffy, Daniel Philpott, and Timothy Samuel Shah. *God's Century: Resurgent Religion and Global Politics*. New York: W. W. Norton and Co., 2011.

Tonstad, Linn Marie. "Sexual Difference and Trinitarian Death: Cross, Kenosis, and Hierarchy in the Theo-Drama." *Modern Theology* 26, no. 4 (October 2010) 603–31.

Volf, Miroslav. *Flourishing: Why We Need Religion in a Globalized World.* New Haven: Yale University Prsss, 2017.

———. *Free of Charge: Giving and Forgiving in a Culture Stripped of Grace.* Grand Rapids: Zondervan, 2005.

———. *A Public Faith: How Followers of Christ Should See the Common Good.* Grand Rapids: Brazos, 2011.

Conclusion

Practicing the Kingdom of God

Christine Pohl once remarked that ethicists, perhaps more than colleagues in other disciplines, often find themselves working in the liminal places between categories, within the tensions that arise from ambiguity. Indeed, this is often what draws ethicists to their vocation—a fascination with the fruitful nature of these tensions. These essays are examples of this fruitful liminality, engaging her work through expansion, clarification, and dialogue. As noted in the section on hospitality, this volume starts with thoughts on our openness to the ideas of others. This is an appropriate beginning, as a posture of humility and hospitality is essential to the academic enterprise. However, it is equally essential to the human enterprise, as each person is, in some ways, fundamentally an outsider to ourselves, an "other." The tensions that exist between ideals also exist between individuals; the ambiguities that perplex categories also perplex communities. A posture of welcome engagement is essential for both conversations and communities to persevere and flourish.

This work is intentionally broad in scope, moving from market exchange relations to love as the basis of the Christian life. In a sense, this content reflects the content of Christine's academic contributions. She does not deny the significance of such realities as marketplace economics; an acknowledgement of costs, boundaries, and limits is an integral part of her own work. Christian ethicists are tasked with continually fine-tuning the balance between practicality and perfection, between present reality and promised eschaton. Yet Christine recognizes the scriptural truth that these considerations must begin and end in love, as revealed in the reality of the incarnated Christ. During the discussions that inspired *Living into Community*, Christine would remind the group: "We are not approaching these issues managerially or therapeutically. We are considering them *scripturally*; we are working *theologically*." She would later conclude the book with this observation: "The goal in all of this is not to try harder to build community or to get the practices right. It is about living and loving well in response to Christ."[1] While it is possible to value hospitality and community for their own sakes, for the Christian their ultimate purpose is helping us practice the Kingdom of God.

Christine's work has helped many people to live and love well, both individually and corporately. One example is Good Works, Inc., a ministry to people experiencing homelessness in Athens, Ohio. Keith Wasserman, its founder and director, reflects on the impact Christine's work and friendship have made on the shape and understanding of their vocation.

> No one has had a greater influence on the paradigm of our ministry with strangers than Christine Pohl. I am indebted to her for the wisdom, insight, and perspective she has shared with us for more than a quarter of a century. From the day in 1989 when I sat in on her first class at Asbury Theological Seminary to this very day, the ministry God has trusted us with at Good Works has been profoundly influenced, impacted, and re-directed by the insights God has given to Christine.
>
> Soon after I started Good Works, God gave me the gift of naiveté. This was illustrated in the first paragraph of *Making Room* as she reflects on her interview with me; although I was welcoming people in need, I did not associate it with what I considered "hospitality."[2]
>
> What we have received from her teaching is an *infrastructure*, a *framework* for navigating the most important parts of the ministry. Years before *Living into Community* was published, Christine helped us "live into community" and establish practices that would later become essential for our sustainability. Indeed, I don't think I considered the matter of sustainability for our Christian community until the hard work of Christine revealed it.
>
> I have also had the privilege of listening to Christine teach on hospitality in many different settings over the years. Her voice is both strong and unique. She calls the body of Christ to be our "best self" by laying out practical aspects of love for the stranger. Christine has helped so many of us see hospitality as doable with people who feel excluded. More importantly, the way she addresses the hard subjects of inclusion not only invites people listening to her to feel comfortable sharing from their vulnerability without feeling judged; it "makes room" for the

---

1. Pohl, *Living into Community*, 175.

2. Pohl, *Making Room*, 3.

Holy Spirit to breathe new life into the thoughts and comments of those who are listening.

We have continued to feel guided with wisdom and courage over these many years to grow deeper and deeper in our vision of "welcome." Much of what we have become in our Community of Hope has resulted from the mentoring of Christine Pohl. I continue to be guided by what I have learned from her long obedience in the same direction.

Keith's sentiments are by no means isolated. Countless individuals and ministries have been impacted by her "long obedience in the same direction." Christine's work on hospitality has literally reshaped the understanding of Christian welcome in our day, and her reflections on community, friendship, feminism, and evangelicalism have provided an important strand in the ethical discussions of the past thirty years.

Christine often states that she is not truly a practitioner, that this designation rightfully belongs to persons such as Keith. But Christine has never cloistered herself behind abstractions, as we who know her will confirm. Nicola Hoggard Creegan, whose friendship with Christine began when they were roommates at Gordon-Conwell, affirms this in the clearest language.

She has imagined and lived out a moral world in which everyone is included. Her work is not abstract and theoretical, nor is it simplistic and idealized . . . And her work resonates with experience. One cannot just write theoretical books about hospitality; it has to be a part of one's life in order to have any integrity.

This integrity is present across the breadth of Christine's work. For Christine, all theology is practical theology; all theology is *lived* theology. Her life is replete with examples of practicing the very things she explores academically—friendship, community, hospitality. She has done these things in both large and small venues, in both "official" and "unofficial" capacities. Within her church communities, she has resettled hundreds of refugees, pursued an explicit committment to racial reconciliation, and served in neighborhood outreach. Whether launching a Christian bookstore in her native New York City, hosting dinners for her students, or caring for ailing friends and family—Christine Pohl embodies her commitments. She practices what she preaches. And through her life and her work, we too are guided and strengthened in our lifelong vocation of practicing the Kingdom of God.

Printed in Great Britain
by Amazon